THE
PRENATAL
SHADOW

"In this book, Cherionna gives a knowledgeable overview about the history, insights, and therapeutic application of prenatal psychology. Her book realizes a convincing connection between the Jungian concept of shadow with the observation and insights of the consequences of early traumatization before, during, and after birth. It brings insights that were not available in the time of Jung and opens up new insights of prenatal psychology to public awareness."

LUDWIG JANUS, M.D., PSYCHOANALYST, RESEARCHER
IN PRENATAL PSYCHOLOGY, AND AUTHOR OF
THE ENDURING EFFECTS OF PRENATAL EXPERIENCE

"This is a monumental contribution to medicine, psychology, and counseling. Menzam-Sills brings to light a forgotten dimension of human development that holds the key to maximizing potential. This is not just the stunning insight of identifying the shadow components of prenatal and perinatal experience. It is the entire field of prenatal and perinatal psychology that is upgraded by her clear and straightforward writing. Such a revelatory awakening is profoundly needed now for people to actualize their power to act on behalf of future life and the Earth."

STEPHANIE MINES, PH.D., AUTHOR OF *THE SECRET OF RESILIENCE*
AND FOUNDER OF THE TARA APPROACH

"In *The Prenatal Shadow*, Cherionna meticulously and compassionately peels back and sheds light on the many layers of the shadow that influence our earliest moments of life and then further influence us throughout our lives. No aspect of the prenatal shadow escapes her expert gaze as she expands our horizons and deepens our understanding of it, from the individual to the cultural and the collective. *The Prenatal Shadow* is a must-read for every therapist, parent, and educator."

NIR ESTERMAN, THERAPIST, TEACHER,
AND DEVELOPER OF SHADOW CONSTELLATIONS

"Cherionna's book is a well-researched antidote to the cultural blind spot of not recognizing the lifelong consequences of our birth and prenatal experience. One of the greatest wounds many of us carry is that we have to hold our birth and womb trauma on our own, usually without even knowing where the trauma came from. In shadow, these traumas have powerful influences on our behaviors and perceptions. This is knowledge that we need to disseminate if we are going to live as more conscious beings."

"A thorough, gentle, necessary text about prenatal and perinatal somatics that presents the many difficult layers of experience for humans starting at preconception. She shines the light on elements often overlooked in modern maternity care and supports the reader with explanations and reflections about their prenatal and birth journey for their awareness and growth. *The Prenatal Shadow* is a welcome contribution to the field of birth psychology and a must-have for healing enthusiasts."

"Cherionna tenderly holds us in a field of both shadow and light. Rooted in years of research, story, and observation, *The Prenatal Shadow* not only affirms our ability to feel into our innate wisdom and be met with awareness and compassion, but also deftly illuminates the profound harm caused by our entrenched cultural refusal to acknowledge that living organisms possess direct perception and conscious knowledge. This is an essential book for everyone."

"An abundance of cutting-edge, proven knowledge—most of it little known and all of it important—whether you're a health professional, therapist, educator, parent, or parent-to-be. This book is so rich, so helpful, and full of hope."

"This complete guide makes prenatal psychology and emotional healing clear for anyone interested in understanding themselves, healing emotional trauma, and transforming limitations. An amazing contribution to planetary healing."

"Cherionna has written a kind, personable, and knowledgeable book that brings together a great deal of information and references from leaders in the field. At the same time, she is able to reassure concerned parents and others and help them understand the importance of this knowledge and how to use it to benefit, teach, and heal."

THE PRENATAL SHADOW

HEALING THE TRAUMAS EXPERIENCED BEFORE AND AT BIRTH

A Sacred Planet Book

Cherionna Menzam-Sills, Ph.D.

Park Street Press
Rochester, Vermont

Park Street Press
One Park Street
Rochester, Vermont 05767
www.ParkStPress.com

Park Street Press is a division of Inner Traditions International

Sacred Planet Books are curated by Richard Grossinger, Inner Traditions editorial
board member and cofounder and former publisher of North Atlantic Books. The
Sacred Planet collection, published under the umbrella of the Inner Traditions
family of imprints, includes works on the themes of consciousness, cosmology,
alternative medicine, dreams, climate, permaculture, alchemy, shamanic studies,
oracles, astrology, crystals, hyperobjects, locutions, and subtle bodies.

Note to the Reader: *The information provided in this book is not intended to serve
as therapeutic diagnosis or treatment. If you are interested in further addressing
pre- or perinatal issues, please consult with a therapist or other qualified professional.
The names of the clients described in this book have been changed, and some
characteristics or events changed or combined from several clients with similar situations
to protect their identities.*

Cataloging-in-Publication Data for this title is available from the Library of Congress

ISBN 979-8-88850-114-6 (print)
ISBN 979-8-88850-115-3 (ebook)

Printed and bound in the United States by Lake Book Manufacturing, LLC

10 9 8 7 6 5 4 3 2 1

Text design and layout by Debbie Glogover
This book was typeset in Garamond Premier Pro with Gill Sans MT Pro, Gotham,
ITC Legacy Sans Std, and VC Garamond Condensed Trial used as display typefaces

Illustrations by Cherionna Menzam-Sills

To send correspondence to the author of this book, mail a first-class letter to the
author c/o Inner Traditions • Bear & Company, One Park Street, Rochester, VT
05767, and we will forward the communication, or contact the author directly at
BirthingYourLife.org.

This book is dedicated to the little ones within us all,
who long for recognition, acknowledgment, and healing.
May this book support them and the little ones arriving,
who also need to be heard, seen, and welcomed.

Contents

Foreword

by Antonella Sansone

As a psychologist, I have long wondered why the body and the embodiment processes of the mind have been overlooked in psychology and within psychotherapy settings, despite the abundant scientific evidence that our psyche runs not only in our brain, but in our cells, organs, and nervous system. This inseparable interweaving of mind and body starts at conception, and even beforehand, through a bio-sociopsychological (and even ecological) heritage that is passed down through generations—from parents, grandparents, and ancestors. Indigenous small-scale societies have intuitively known all of this from the beginning of humanity. So, how can a therapist understand and support a client or patient, ignoring such a source of valuable information that is the body and the prenatal and perinatal period of our life? How can we understand our own history, the origins of our trauma and suffering, and the path toward healing without this awareness?

What we arrogantly like to call our civilized culture is the result of a patriarchal denigration of feminine wisdom, materialization of the body, and male medical control and interventions at birth that induce trauma in mothers and infants. Both early trauma and original potential of prenatal experiences are not acknowledged individually and culturally, thus remaining beyond conscious awareness as shadows.

Likewise, this so-called civilized culture dominated by the intellect and technology (left brain) and seeing itself as superior in intelligence and accomplishment to our Indigenous cousins who are considered primitive, has violated our connection to Nature, our caregiving mammalian nature, emotional intelligence, and feminine holistic wisdom. I shared with my young daughters and husband the life of the Himba, an African Indigenous culture of Northern Namibia where I had the privilege to witness their wellbeing, compassion, self-regulation, confidence, and other healthy human qualities at play in every interaction with us and within their community. These qualities are served by the emotional dynamics generated by the cerebral circuits of the right hemisphere. This process only unfolds when there are the proper nurturing circumstances, that is, only if the child's development is supported by certain pre- and perinatal nurturing practices and the shared care from a connected community. In fact, in Indigenous cultures, these nurturing qualities are transmitted by default right from conception, through pre- and perinatal practices that are consistently passed down through generations, as they are meant to. The memories of early experiences are kept alive by collective acknowledgement, validation, and sharing through celebrations (dances, storytelling, connection with the ancestors). For instance, like other Indigenous women, a Himba woman conceives her child first in her mind. She goes into the bush or forest and calls the child's soul with a song. When she has heard the soul of the child, she goes into her hut to welcome the child in her body and will sing the same song throughout her pregnancy, birth and beyond, creating a familiar element of continuity from life before birth. This reveals an awareness of the union of mind and body, and the child's ability to remember prenatal experiences.

Cherionna Menzam-Sills's book teaches us how Nature, with whom our Indigenous cousins live in synchrony, has designed this continuum to be supported by collaboration, empathy, and communal love, and to be the necessary legacy for the optimal development of babies and children. A sensitive, compassionate welcome from the parents as well as the community is part of the original blueprint for human birth. How the baby experiences their first moments in the world outside the womb needs to meet their biologically based expectations derived from evolution. One would never know this from how couples conceive, gestate, birth, and raise their babies and children in our modern world. With the loss of the pre- and perinatal nurturing practices and a supported community maintaining the continuum in human development, we have alienated our children from their nurturing nature, and thus alienated ourselves. For example, we are the only species of mammals who separate newborn babies from their mothers at birth, allow newborn babies to sleep apart from us, to cry without responding to their distress (thinking this is teaching them to sleep), neglect them (as when we are entertained by phones and other electronic devices), and punish them, thus altering their brain development and jeopardizing their mental health.

Cherionna Menzam-Sills invites us to realize that we never ask ourselves what we remember about our birth and life in the womb. She teaches us that in a world where babies are believed to be unable to remember before they can speak, prenatal and birth experience easily becomes unconscious shadow. Shadow is never a labelling work, unlike many medical terms coined by the old psychiatric paradigm. Throughout her book, Menzam-Sills is remarkably mindful of not triggering feelings of guilt or judgment in the reader. And her compassionate approach to therapy and healing is coherently present, establishing an easy sense of personal communication to readers: parents-to-be, practitioners, and to anyone who has been born and is interested in understanding their human condition and suffering. Her graceful guidance in developing awareness of the role played by our body in trauma and any psychological process, including the recognition of memories stored in our body, gives us clues to connecting with our own needs and our prenatal and perinatal blueprints.

Trauma is held in shadow, or implicit/subconscious memory, until awareness is brought onto it and emotions can be expressed, reflected, and given a name. This process allows one to accept the trauma as part of the human condition and to dance with the shadow rather than fighting, resisting, or denying it and thus being led by repeated patterns jeopardizing one's mental health. As a mindfulness facilitator, I can see the value of befriending challenging emotions and trauma, as doing so leads to resolution beyond alleviation of symptoms and toward establishing wholeness and harmony. The acknowledgement and meeting of our shadows hold the immense potential we long for. This is a core tenet of mindfulness. There is a sense of lightness, enlightenment, and grace while reading this book, which makes the way toward transformation.

This gem of a book, rich in insights, scientific observations, and ancient wisdom, will leave the reader in a state of wonder and gratitude and on the awareness path toward healing. Menzam-Sills's book elegantly presents the complexity of human condition with simplicity and clarity and a flowing narrative style, and illustrates with examples from her own life and her own and others' clinical practices. It provides a profound understanding of what our core needs are, right from conception and even before, of what we can learn from our ancestral human and Mother Earth ways, and from the mutual bidirectional dialogue between humans and Nature and between humans and the Cosmos. This is a new ecology that can drive historical change. This is a clear, concise, informative, and engaging book, telling the reader about a very innovative way to heal as an individual as well as a community and society by positively influencing the new generation of infants and ultimately healing the collective cultural mindsets and attitudes resulting from early trauma, including prenatal and birth trauma.

Those early experiences that we call trauma become embedded in the child's nervous system, emotions, cells, body, during the preverbal phase of development, including conception and the prenatal period, forming the implicit memory, and unconsciously manifesting themselves later in life as a shadow in all layers of human life: in relationship with ourselves, with each other, with pregnancy, birth, and babies, with Mother Earth. This coping mechanism is passed on through generations—from parents, grandparents, and previous ancestors—and is embedded in the social and cultural tissue generating an epidemic of ill health, mental disturbances, aggression, racism, discrimination, political conflicts, and war. Among these plagues that affect modern societies, there are medical control and interventions at birth that violate the mother's and baby's basic mammalian needs, a predominance of the intellect and technology (left brain) over emotional intelligence and feminine holistic wisdom (right brain), ecological neglect and disrespect for nature.

The Prenatal Shadow takes the reader hand in hand to discover the potential and resilience of babies before, during, and after birth, as sentient beings capable of healing their own trauma and the world if their voices are heard and implicit story telling is valued, observed, and listened to. It is only through this relational, meaningful engagement between babies and caregivers and community, beginning during conception and pregnancy, that implicit memories are integrated into individual and collective consciousness rather than becoming unconscious shadow acting out in relationship with ourselves and the world.

By drawing on scientific evidence of prenatal sciences and how prenatal memory works as well as speaking from the baby's perspective, Menzam-Sills's book synchronically connects the intellectual way of knowing with a heart and wisdom-based knowledge, fostering in the reader the integration of these two paths toward awareness and healing, which in our culture have divorced.

The title, *The Prenatal Shadow*, beautifully condenses the richness and depth of the book. In this book, Menzam-Sills has been able to weave together, in an exceptionally readable style, diverse disciplines, including prenatal and perinatal psychology, epigenetics, mindfulness, spirituality, ancient wisdom, ecology, and modern trauma therapies. She brings experiences in the womb and at birth into the psychotherapy setting, documenting well the powerful influence of these early experiences on later life. This very important early period of our life is too often overlooked in psychotherapy, the psychotherapist missing essential cues to understand a client's trauma and symptomatology and promote the healing process. Menzam-Sills's book offers a comprehensive grounding of prenatal and perinatal psychology in the broader context of somatic and transpersonal psychology and the world of Jung, who coined the term *shadow*, referring it to unacceptable aspects of ourselves that we have pushed down into the unconscious mind. Although buried in our unconscious mind, they long to be loved and welcomed.

This book acknowledges our vital relationship with Nature and provides answers to the questions about our own human nature. I wholeheartedly recommend this excellent book to all psychotherapy and bodywork trainers—not just those in the pre- and perinatal field—who are interested in exploring their field in depth and develop an integrated psycho-somatic transdisciplinary perspective that is so important in this field. This book can also be essential reading for those parents who want to deepen their journey and understanding of their baby's experiences as well as for anyone who is interested in the prenatal and perinatal roots of human development and well-being from a "wholeness" perspective.

ANTONELLA SANSONE, PH.D.

ANTONELLA SANSONE, M.A., PH.D., is an integrative health and clinical psychologist, mindfulness facilitator, and author with a focus on pre- and perinatal health, psychology, and education, mind-body approaches, psychosomatics, Indigenous cultures, integration of primal wisdom and science, and early human and Earth connections. She developed the Prenatal Mindfulness Relationship-Based Program (PMRB), which was piloted in her Ph.D., and is registered with the Australian New Zealand Clinical Trials Registry-ANZCTR. She is the author of *Working with Parents and Infants: A Mind-Body Integration Approach; Mothers, Babies and their Body Language;* and *Cultivating Mindfulness to Raise Children Who Thrive: Why Human Connection from before Birth Matters.*

Acknowledgments

This book has been written from within a well of gratitude for layers of support I will attempt to name and appreciate here.

I feel a need to first acknowledge the ancestral, familial field I arrived into at conception. The extensive trauma and creativity surrounding me laid a foundation for my urge to become a therapist and then to learn about prenatal and birth psychology.

I thank my teachers in Somatic Psychotherapy at Naropa University, Christine Caldwell and Susan Aposhyan, for guiding me into this territory and developing the embodied presence I feel is necessary to meet it. Naropa also introduced me to Dr. William R. Emerson, a pioneer in the field of pre- and perinatal psychology. William mentored me in this work for years. Particularly relevant to this book, he introduced me to the concept of prenatal and birth shadow and how it could leak out into our lives and relationships.

My other primary mentor in prenatal and birth therapy was Ray Castellino, with whom I also studied for years. I am indebted to Ray for so many aspects of his work, particularly the importance of pacing, resourcing, and relational safety.

My intention to study with Ray led me to also take a training in Biodynamic Craniosacral therapy with John and Anna Chitty, who taught me so much about how to be present with traumatic memories together with what we call the original blueprint, represented by subtle energetic rhythms we orient to in Biodynamics. A blueprint is the plan an architect draws when designing a building. The construction crew then follows the blueprint as to create the building. We can look at our development the same way. Nature has its blueprint for how we transform from conception onward. This includes layers of support from the mother, her partner, and the larger community.

The Chittys introduced me to their teacher, Franklyn Sills, a pioneer in the field of Biodynamics. Franklyn has since become my dear husband and life partner. As well as gratitude for all that I learned from him through our teaching together for years, I thank Franklyn for his love and support, including his willingness to read or listen to paragraphs from this book that I needed witnessed as they were written.

I want to include here profound gratitude for the many clients, students, and supervisees who have taught me through our work together. While some are described within these pages, all of them infuse the text less directly through how they have touched and influenced my heart and my understanding.

Finally, I deeply thank Stephanie Mines for her endless support in having this book published and connecting me with Richard Grossinger who initiated the process of it being accepted by Inner Traditions for publication. I feel profoundly grateful to everyone at Inner Traditions for their support in the birth of this book, especially my project editor Lisa P. Allen and copy editor Dorona Zierler. Thank you. I hope the book generates a similar wave of gratitude to all it touches who can benefit from its message.

Emerging from the Shadow

What we have called "karma" or "shadow" may, today, be called "trauma," since the effects of trauma propagate as dissociated and denied energies, frozen in shadow, bound to repeat. Trauma creates incoherence, fracturing us from ourselves and separating us from others. Its broken memories resurface repeatedly through exterior eruptions that are not directed by free will but by that part of the self that is held in darkness.

THOMAS HÜBL,
HEALING COLLECTIVE TRAUMA (2020)

SELF-KINDNESS ON YOUR JOURNEY

Before proceeding to discuss the profound effects of trauma at a very young age, I want to pause for a moment. This book introduces potentially challenging material. It could be activating because it may touch memories that have been held in shadow and not previously named or processed. I encourage you to take your time, pause as you need to be with your feelings and bodily reactions, and seek support to process what arises. I suggest reviewing the end of the introduction to this book, entitled, "Tips for the Journey," to support you in your reading.

Here, I want to appreciate that you may be a parent reading this.

You may find yourself feeling judged or criticized, which is not at all the purpose of the discussion. Or you may experience feelings of guilt or regret for what you now realize your child was exposed to and experienced in their earliest days. It has never occurred to me that prenatal or birth trauma is the fault of parents. If I blamed anyone, it would be doctors (particularly obstetricians), but I have always been more interested in acknowledging the cultural denial that underlies insensitive relations with babies. That is no individual's fault. There is, however, culturally generated ignorance about how exquisitely sentient and intelligent little ones are, and how we can meet them with the respect and empathy they need and deserve. Please, please, don't blame yourself for whatever may have happened in the past, and please consider that while repair is most effective early on, healing is possible at any stage of life.

I also apologize to any readers who may find my references to *mother, her,* and *she* as offensive. I acknowledge that this may not resonate for those who prefer terms such as "birthing person," "they," or "them," but I have not been able to find a way to use alternative language that communicates the content as clearly. I'm still learning! Please know that hereafter when I use such language, I am referring to the person in the *mothering role*. This caregiving position can and is intended to be inclusive of a variety of experiences.

MEETING THE SHADOW

Many years ago, I had a dream where I was being chased by monsters. I was running down a hallway and came to a locked door at the end. I could not escape. Suddenly, I remembered the common advice to face your monsters. Heartened, I turned around, where I beheld the three ferocious cartoon character-type monsters who had been chasing me. Holding out my hands, I dared to ask, "Do you want to dance?" The monsters were delighted! We all joined hands and danced together.

The *shadow*, a term coined by Carl Jung, refers to unacceptable aspects of ourselves that we have pushed down into the unconscious mind. Although buried and out of our own sight, our shadow aspects never disappear. Like any rejected child, they long to be loved and welcomed. Inviting them to dance, as I did in my dream, enables them to come home. We return to wholeness.

Fortunately, at the time of this dream, I had already done a fair bit of therapeutic work on myself. I had some ability to face and welcome my monsters into the dance. As shadow expert Robert A. Johnson writes, "We are advised to love our enemies, but this is not possible when the inner enemy, our own shadow, is waiting to pounce and make the most of an incendiary situation. If we can learn to love the inner enemy, then there is a chance of loving—and redeeming—the outer one."[1] The monsters in my dream represented my inner enemy, but they were often reflected in my outer life. I felt chased by the demands of a family and culture apparently requiring perfection. I often feared the criticism or judgments of others, and these three monsters represented angry, aggressive, and even violent aspects of myself that would have been dangerous for me to own or express as a child. My critical and mentally ill father was too unstable to tolerate anyone's anger besides his own. I could easily point to this time as when my monsters went into hiding in the shadow.

Shadow work commonly addresses the roots of painful experiences within our childhood. As I immersed myself in learning about pre- and perinatal psychology in the 1990s, I began to understand that the origins of this trauma were even earlier than I realized. *Prenatal* refers to the time before birth, generally considered from conception to birth. *Perinatal* refers to around the time of birth (the prefix, *peri* means "around."), including the actual birth as well as the period just before it, usually involving labor, and the postpartum time that can be defined as hours, weeks, or even a year after birth. This field of study has been amassing evidence of our memory, learning, and intelligence from this very early time in our lives. As we sense and respond to the context in which we form the physical body, we are also forming the psyche.

As a little one in the womb, I marinated in the psychic field of my mother, who was stressed and often frozen in the presence of my father's irrational outbursts. Prenates are intelligently preparing for the world their mother perceives. I was clearly entering a dangerous world where it was best to be a good, quiet, possibly frozen, child. Along with forming arms, legs, organs, brain, and muscles, I was also forming an unconscious home for my monsters. Later childhood experiences served to bolster, rather than to create, my shadowy patterns.

Personal shadow, which I have referred to here, differs for each individual and nests within a larger collective shadow. Though some aspects of collective shadow are universal, each culture strongly influences and expresses it differently, relating to their unique social mores. Pre- and perinatal experience, which profoundly affects our personality, relational tendencies, and other behaviors throughout life, is almost by definition shadow material, at least in the modern Western world. Cultural denial of early consciousness has only recently begun to shift in response to advances in research, development of more age-appropriate research methods, and ample clinical evidence of the effectiveness of addressing this early time in therapy. As a result, attempts to express prenatal or birth memories are just beginning to be reinforced and integrated into consciousness. Within a field of denial, aspects of us associated with these memories tend to be judged, rejected, and relegated to the realm of shadow. Now, we can begin to meet and integrate them, returning to our original wholeness.

DENIAL, RESISTANCE, AND COLLECTIVE SHADOW

The purpose of shadow is to protect us. There can be fierce resistance to efforts to reveal these parts of us in hiding. New information tends to be met with emotional reactions, generated by defensive hormones as we sense our beliefs and as the identity founded on them is being threatened. Fueled by the stress hormone cortisol, we are likely to react emotionally, often with anger.

Within the field of psychology, Sigmund Freud and his student Otto Rank discussed the effects of birth experience, but these ideas were not popular and continue to be widely unknown a century later.

Otto Rank's *The Trauma of Birth* (1929) is a classic in the field of birth psychology, yet I recently spoke with a psychoanalytic therapist who was shocked to learn that Freud and Rank had met and acknowledged this material in their patients.

Collective shadow is responsible for this ignorance.

Several of Freud's students, including Frank Lake, Otto Rank, J. Sadger, and Donald Winnicott, saw Freud as unknowingly being on the verge of perinatal work, and built upon his theories.[2] Freud acknowledged birth as "the prototype" of anxiety in later life. He initially focused on the physiological trauma of loss of oxygen at birth, but later included the trauma of separation from the mother.[3] He recognized birth symbolism in dreams and saw sleep as like being in the womb.

Freud, however, lived and worked in Victorian Vienna. So, when his patients revealed sexual abuse, he eventually renamed these memories as fantasies due to their unacceptable nature in Victorian society.[4] If these memories were imagined, surely memories of even earlier, prenatal and birth experiences must also be fantasy.[5] Otto Rank's *The Trauma of Birth* (1929) was first published in German in 1924, and "initially celebrated by Freud as the greatest advance since the discovery of psychoanalysis,"[6] but within the context of Victorian society, Freud then rejected this work by one of his favorite students, delaying its publication in English until five years later. The birth theory in the book was officially laid to rest.

DEVELOPING AWARENESS

Prenatal and birth trauma present so ubiquitously and unrelentingly that it was natural that others, including Nandor Fodor, M. Lietaert Peerbolte, and Frank Lake to later address birth trauma and the idea of prenatal consciousness. These ideas are still not fully accepted within the field of psychology but are becoming increasingly appreciated as the field of pre- and perinatal psychology grows. I am inspired by the increasing number of psychotherapists and psychologists inquiring about this work and participating in my workshops and trainings.

In 1971, the forerunner of the International Society of Prenatal and Perinatal Psychology and Medicine (ISPPM) was formed in Vienna by European psychiatrists.[7] Its former president, Dr. Ludwig Janus, a German psychiatrist and psychotherapist, published a courageous book in 1997 called *The Enduring Effects of Prenatal Experiencing: Echoes From the Womb*. This book explicitly described the cultural denial of prenatal consciousness and its profound effects in our patriarchal world. Another professional organization, now called the Association for Pre- and Perinatal Psychology and Health (APPPAH),* was formed in North America in 1983. These associations, each with their own conferences and professional journals, provided a place for researchers and professionals from many disciplines to present their work, so often rejected by established professional associations. The field of pre- and perinatal psychology, which had been struggling down the birth canal for some years, was finally born.

The first popular book on the topic, *The Secret Life of the Unborn Child* by Thomas Verny published in 1982, was soon followed by *Babies Remember Birth* by David Chamberlain in 1988[†] These two founders of the American association paved the way for many of us also encountering prenatal and birth material in our work with clients. As awareness of very early sentience and its effects has spread, how birth and babies are treated has also changed. For example, as recently as 1985, parents discovered that their baby had received surgery with a paralytic drug but no anesthesia.[8] This was a common, although not publicly known, procedure, based on the erroneous belief that consciousness begins with speech around the age of two. That we have a reaction to this news today is evidence of our intuitive knowing that little ones, even before they can speak, are aware, sentient beings with feelings and experiences. As the heavy pressure of cultural shadow begins to lift, we can listen to and trust this knowing.

---

*APPPAH's Birth Psychology website provides excellent information and relevant resources.
†*Babies Remember Birth* was re-published ten years later as *The Mind of Your Newborn Baby*.

Intuition and our ability to trust it are associated with the right cerebral hemisphere, which excels at perceiving wholeness and connectedness between all things, in contrast to the divisive dynamics that create shadow. These feminine qualities have been squelched in the modern world in favor of more masculine linearity, analysis, and control. In this context, the feminine has been in the collective shadow. It has been feared, denigrated, and dominated by the overly educated "left-brained" patriarchy. Intuition, pregnancy, gestation, and birth all belong to the realm of the feminine, as does the womb and life within it. Birth has largely been taken over by Western doctors with a masculine approach focused on disease, replacing traditional female midwives, and ancient Indigenous practices familiar with supporting and trusting the inherent health in natural birth. Fortunately, natural birth (birth without routine medical interventions, such as pain medication), which honors and supports the natural and instinctive progression of the birth process, is celebrating a comeback. As a collective, we are beginning to remember and return to the feminine as an essential aspect of ourselves.

I have observed this awakening over the thirty years I have studied and worked in the field. At the same time, I see other cultural shadows coming to light. Recently, for example, the Me Too and Black Lives Matter movements have worked to shine the light on what has previously been unspeakable. White bodied people previously in denial are beginning to listen, with at least some making attempts to acknowledge their privilege and learn to perceive and interact differently with an intention to address and reduce racism. It could not be addressed when it was not acknowledged. Now, the existence and effects of rampant racism, as well as other forms of ethnic, religious, sexual, and gender discrimination, are being more readily named. Similarly, attempts in the 1990s to report incest or sexual abuse tended to be met with denial, judgment, and shaming. It is now much more accepted that these phenomena occur and are frequent. Children are encouraged to set boundaries and to tell a trusted adult if they have experienced abuse. With this attitude, the potential for change arises.

My passion is shining the light of awareness on pre- and perinatal experience, which has likewise been held in shadow for too long in the West. In other cultures, there exists more acceptance and integration of this important time of development. For instance, prenatal consciousness has always been acknowledged in the far east, where it has been detailed in religious texts, such as the Hindu Garbha Upanishad. Forerunners of modern psychology, such as Aristotle and Locke, also appreciated this influential period.[9]

Other cultures acknowledge and respect prenatal intelligence. For example, Malidoma Somé reports that among his people, the Dagara of West Africa, a ritual, called a "hearing," is held a few months before a child is born. The purpose of the ritual is to allow the soul of the unborn child to communicate with the people, so that they can prepare for the newcomer. The soul takes over the body of the mother and speaks through her, answering questions posed by the priest. The people are informed of the infant's life mission and gender, as well as objects that must be prepared to help them remember his or her true identity after birth. Based on this communication, a name is chosen which represents the child's "life program."[10] When the child is small, the grandfather, who attends the prenatal ritual and has an intimate relationship with the grandchild, reminds them of what was said during the ritual.

This is quite different from how fetal intelligence is met in modern Western culture. As science has begun to acknowledge prenatal brain functions, parents have been encouraged to begin educating their baby in the womb. This may be as simple as talking with their baby to support prenatal language development. More specific prenatal studies have shown that unborn children learn and respond to prenatal "lessons," and show signs of remembering what they have learned.* A 2013 study involved pregnant women listening regularly to a short recording of sounds on a CD not found in their mother's native language. After birth, the babies' brains responded to these sounds as familiar whereas

---

*For examples please refer to an article by David Spelt, "The Conditioning of the Human Fetus in Utero," and a book by Rene Van de Carr and Marc Lehrer, *While You are Expecting: Creating Your Own Prenatal Classroom.*

babies who had not heard them in utero responded to them as unfamiliar. It was not mentioned in the research article if the women listened to the CD via headphones or speakers, but I recently met someone whose doctoral research was in this exact area. She agreed with me that the fetus would experience the vibrations and the mother's response to the sounds, regardless of how the mother heard them.

Clearly, babies also begin learning their mother's language in the womb. Singing or playing music to babies in the womb may support language learning, and newborns recognize lullabies they have been exposed to before birth.[11] Such efforts may also foster prenatal bonding once the parents can sense the baby's presence.[12]

Before the quickening (feeling the baby's movements), or perhaps earlier, when seeing the baby on ultrasound, there is often negligible acknowledgment or understanding of the baby's receptivity to what is around them. Older siblings are often aware of and communicating with the fetus before the parents even consider this possibility. We know from client reports that they may feel rejected or unwelcome when their presence is not acknowledged.

∽ Prenatal Memories ∽

Maria was adopted at birth. When we first met, her speech was rapid without apparent pauses for breath. She wanted to be more in her body, but her efforts tended to be hijacked by her busy mind. Maria's first mother had already been a single mother with not much income and no support when Maria was conceived. She could not manage another child. Maria reports feeling a sense of being paralyzed by dread and anxiety in the womb, knowing that her mother did not want her. She wisely attributed her tendency to be dissociative (not fully inhabiting her body) to this early terror experienced as her body was forming. She felt she stayed quiet in the womb so as not to contribute any more to her mother's anxiety. To be so quiet, she had to disconnect from her natural impulses to sense and move. Throughout her life, Maria had never felt like she had enough food and carefully guarded what food she had.

We recognized together that, in the womb, the food coming to her was insufficient and tainted with her mother's stress hormones. For Maria, some of her memories were somatic, in how she related (or didn't relate) to her body, and some were behavioral, as in her rapid anxious speech and her relationship to food. These were implicit, nonverbal, unconscious memories that Maria and I worked together to integrate into her conscious understanding. As we did so, her speech became more relaxed, and she began to become more aware of sensation in her body. With conscious awareness, she no longer needed the behaviors to remind her of her early beginnings.

Even as the pregnancy nears the time of birth, the fetus is usually not included in interactions the mother has with others in her family or life in general. Babies are generally assumed to be relatively passive passengers through the birth canal, despite their ability and willingness to respond to communications from parents and birth practitioners. For example, if a baby is in a breech position, which tends to lead to caesarean section (C-section), they will usually turn if someone explains to them that they can do this and why it would be helpful. Similarly, if a mother explains lovingly to her baby that it is not yet time for them to come, the fetus often chooses to leave via miscarriage, rendering an abortion unnecessary.[13] A mother recently described to me how her baby cooperated when she explained during premature contractions how much easier it would be to wait for the due date. The contractions stopped until the evening of the due date.

Even if babies receive operations nowadays with anesthesia to protect them from the shock of the pain, their sentience is still not fully acknowledged. This responsiveness to context does not require a mature brain, or even a brain at all! Every cell responds to the conditions around it, withdrawing from threat and opening to receive nourishment. A young baby's nervous system goes into shock, just as we would as adults, if exposed to intense pain. Even as recently as 2015, a UK newspaper article stated that, "although these babies experience an average of 11 painful procedures per day, 60% do not receive any kind of pain medication.[14]

The same article reported research demonstrating that babies are probably more sensitive to pain than adults, not less. This is reminiscent of the horrors of babies being operated on without pain medication. There are many other procedures that can also be very painful, even more so for delicate babies than for us as adults. Babies in intensive care, for example, receive multiple heel pricks, as well as having tubes inserted, and numerous other invasive procedures.

How does this relate to shadow? How could it take so long to stop performing surgery without anesthesia and continue applying painful procedures without pain medication when it was already known that babies would feel the pain of an operation? Consider this comment from Terry Monell in her article, "Living Out the Past: Infant Surgery prior to 1987":

> Doctors trained in surgery and anesthesiology adhered to an entrenched protocol and dismissed the reality unfolding in front of their eyes, every day for 140 years. The continuance of unquestioned belief kept the medical community from accepting their own humanity by consistently denying the primary language of the human race.[15]

Do you recognize the collective resistance here, reminiscent of defending shadow? As well as that the shadow permits such cruel treatment of infants? Babies clearly sense and suffer from the pain of surgery and other interventions, with potentially lifelong changes to their neurological and behavioral development.[16] Monell goes on to say, "Since no parental consent was needed for a 'standard of practice' and the preverbal infant could not self-report, the barbaric experience was lost to implicit memory. Today there are generations of people left to endure posttraumatic symptoms from a cause they cannot identify." I am reminded here of a client who is still resentful forty years later that his mother had her appendix removed during pregnancy without anyone acknowledging that it naturally affected him in the womb.

This is a description of personal shadow. It is unspoken, in this case because babies are preverbal and the adults around them either didn't know or didn't acknowledge the painful trauma. To assume that the grimaces, screams, changes in heart rate, and other responses to pain in infants represent only inconsequential mechanical or reflexive reactions must require severe dissociation in the practitioners making these claims. They are most likely acting out of their own very early trauma history that has yet to be resolved.

More specifically, babies exposed to the painful experience of circumcision without analgesic relief, demonstrate increased aversion to pain.[17] The same is true of premature, low birth weight infants who endure countless painful, invasive procedures in the Neonatal Intensive Care Unit (NICU). Such early pain exposure can not only generate higher sensitivity to and experience of pain, but also lead to Post Traumatic Stress Disorder (PTSD), depression, anxiety, altered immune function and digestion, impaired bonding, and delays in healing, learning, and development.[18]

Denying that babies are suffering and being harmed interferes with helping them. We now know that premature babies manage and recover from painful procedures better when they have their mother nearby and can hear her voice. This also may affect cortisol levels related to the stress response and positively affect development. Music has also been found to be a simple, kind intervention that reduces pain reactions in newborn babies during painful procedures.[19] Infant pain level is easily recorded by observing their facial expressions, as well as measuring heartbeat and levels of oxygen.[20] Is this not common sense? How do *you* feel reading this? Without acknowledgment, babies needlessly suffer, and continue to be affected by this experience throughout their lives. Therapists like me continue to see them as clients 20, 30, 40, 50 or more years later!

Take a moment to consider the following:

♪ Emotional Responses ♪

Do you ever feel like emotions come at you, as if out of the blue? Do you feel powerless, at the mercy of life conditions or other people? Do you have allergies or food sensitivities? Do you have strong reactions to other people engaging in smoking, drinking, or drugs? Are you extremely careful about your diet? Are you sensitive to pollution, electronics, perfumes, or other chemicals? Do you tend to get depressed, anxious, or easily overwhelmed? Do you have a sense of unexplained grief, loss, or fear? Are you highly empathic? Do you feel compelled to help people? Do you tend to have low self-esteem, feel like you don't belong or aren't welcome, like there's something wrong with you?

These are just some of the impacts that one might experience as a result of pre- and perinatal trauma, which we will explore in more detail together. The shadow, though unseen, infiltrates life, body, and psyche, and will not relent until acknowledged and appreciated. My hope is that this book can enhance awareness of these early experiences, including specific events in development, that are held in shadow, both on a personal and collective level.

- Chapter 1 introduces the concept of prenatal and birth shadow and its profound significance in our lives and our world.
- Chapter 2 explores how little ones who don't even have a nervous system and may not yet have much of a physical body can have experiences that they learn from and remember, although usually the memory is not conscious or verbal.
- Chapter 3 invites the reader to consider that shadow is not necessarily all bad, that it may include what I call our original embryological potential, the potential demonstrated when a unicellular organism at conception develops into a complex human being.
- Chapter 4 delves into the challenges of the journey through the birth canal, including prenatal influences and potential trauma that may arise at this time, along with how unresolved birth trauma may manifest later in life.
- Chapter 5 considers common issues related to the postpartum period and bonding, with their potential shadow material.
- Chapter 6 concludes our journey by addressing how to heal our relationship with primal shadow material and return to our potential.

TIPS FOR THE JOURNEY

In reading this book and exploring your own prenatal and birth shadow material, I have found it vital to practice mindful presence. Briefly, this can be summed up as having an intention to be oriented to present time.

Resourcing

Take a moment to consider, are there supports or practices that help you to feel present, safe, and curious? Curiosity is a sign of mindful presence. It tends to disappear when we are sucked into the defensiveness of shadow. In trauma therapy, we talk about resources. A resource is anything that supports you in being present, feeling safe, being able to be with your experience or memory, rather than becoming it. Little ones are not able to access resources themselves. They need others to help them. Usually, their primary resource is mother, but she may also have been a source of threat, danger, or fear. As adults, we can choose to focus on what supports us. That may be something in your body, like your sense of breath or ground. It could also be an object you love, an activity, a place in nature or elsewhere that you enjoy and feel safe in, a safe relationship with a person, pet, ancestor, or even a spiritual or imaginary being. Consider what is resourcing for you. If this is new to you, you may wish to take a moment and make a list that you can refer to and add to over time. This may be useful to you to keep on hand as you consider the content of this book.

Reading about prenatal and birth events can be activating. It can stimulate prenatal and birth aspects of yourself, which can lead you to begin reacting as if you were a helpless little one, which you are not. Please consider that the little one that you were may still be within you. Usually, it is in shadow. Essential to healing early trauma is being able to be present with these aspects of yourself, rather than becoming them. Orienting to resources can help you to differentiate between the little one you were and the capable adult you are now. Even if you don't think of yourself as capable, I can assure you that, if you are reading this page or hearing these words, you have abilities you did not have as a little one!

Journaling Prompts and Guiding Questions

Throughout the book I have included occasional exercises and questions that break down the shadow work in more detail and outline practical steps. You may find it useful to keep a journal throughout the course of this journey. This way you can take notes and react to the reflections as you go. You can also include poetry or artwork in your journal or create artwork as a way of processing and integrating what you are reading and experiencing. This draws on the right, more intuitive, integrative side of your brain, which can help to balance the collective left-brain, analytical focus. You might also find it useful to record dreams such as the one I described earlier, or other memories and sensations that pop up.

Please take your time responding to and journaling about any questions that resonate for you. Feel free, as mentioned, to draw as part of your journaling. Be curious about what is happening in your body—your breath and your sensations—as you journal. Somatic responses can offer valuable information.

This guidance is designed to help you understand and integrate your early history. Please pause to consider your answers. You may find this process therapeutic or possibly challenging. If you are uncomfortable with any of the questions, feel free to leave them for later. It may be helpful to review these questions with a trusted friend, partner, or therapist, particularly someone trained and experienced with prenatal and birth psychology. Remember that it is always helpful to begin an exploration by orienting to your resources—ask yourself what supports you now, assuming your current age and strengths.

You have already survived any challenges from your early life. Trust your intuition and consider all your responses simply as information, to be potentially explored further. Take note of how your body responds to each question. For example, does your heart begin to beat faster? Do you feel faint or dizzy? (If so, please pause and take some time to ground and resource yourself.) Perhaps you have a response in a particular part of your body, like a pain in your head or hip, or a tingling in your shoulder or heat in your umbilicus. Take note of such responses and allow yourself to be curious about them. Similarly, remain curious if you have a strong emotional reaction or resistance to any of the questions, or this entire process. If you find this too difficult, I encourage you to seek professional support from a trauma-informed therapist. It may just take a few sessions to enable you to be able to work with this material more gently.

Equipped with your sense of resource, support, and your current age, you are prepared to begin to become acquainted with prenatal and birth-related shadow. May these pages enlighten you and shine the light on primal aspects of you that have been held in darkness.

1

What Is Prenatal and Birth Shadow and Why Does It Matter?

Trauma and Separation from Feminine Wisdom

It's impossible to separate personal trauma and collective trauma because the very physiology of our nervous system is created in interaction with the nervous system of other people from the moment that we're conceived. Even in utero, the emotional states of the mother have an impact on the developing nervous system of the child, including all kinds of neurochemicals, chemical messengers, synapses, and connections. These states affect how brain systems will evolve and to what degree, and this will have a lifelong impact.

GABOR MATÉ

Humans naturally fear the dark. The unknown lingers there, threatening danger. This unknown may include aspects of ourselves that we are not consciously familiar with. Prior to relatively recent technological developments permitting visualization of the pregnant womb and its occupant, prenatal development remained mysterious. This is perhaps appropriate for this powerful expression of the mystery of how life comes to be, but for modern humans, in the efforts to analyze and control all of nature, prenatal and birth processes have been transferred from the realm of reverence to one of unknown territory to be conquered.

This rise of masculine dominance over feminine wholeness and receptivity has contributed to prenatal and birth experiences often being traumatic and relegated to shadow. From this unconscious station, shadow infiltrates our beliefs, attitudes, behavior, relationships, health, and more. We are victims to the shadow's power until we shine the light on it, reclaiming these hidden, rejected aspects of ourselves. We then return to our essential wholeness and potential.

DEFINING SHADOW

The shadow contains qualities of ourselves that we have repressed and are not aware of, although others may see them clearly. These usually are negative feelings, but also may include feelings of so-called "good" qualities.

For example, a young girl may be very intelligent and easily succeed in school. Then she approaches adolescence. Her standards shift as the acceptance of her peers becomes higher priority than her own values or those of her parents. Being "cool" doesn't include being good in school. To win or keep her peers' acceptance, she begins rejecting her own aptitude. Initially she plays the game, concealing her brain power. Gradually, she begins to believe the façade. Her grades suffer, affecting her future success as she now sees herself as incapable. Her bright mind descends into shadow, forgotten and ignored.

Similarly, a young boy may learn to hide and protect his sensitive nature, because it is judged as too girly. He may be beaten by his father to make him tougher, or bullied in school by other boys who see him as a sissy. In self-defense, he may develop a harsh persona. He may even become homophobic or abusive to those he perceives as weaker than himself, considering them overly sensitive.

Shadow qualities tend to be seen as forming early in childhood through the influence of parents and others pressuring us to behave "properly." However, as stated previously, shadow material can, and often does, begin to form much earlier, even before and around the time of birth. Because prenatal and perinatal experiences and memory are not commonly acknowledged, they seek attention however they can. Like Maria (see pages 9–10), babies in the womb may learn to stay quiet and small to avoid being discovered by parents who don't want them. This preverbal, prebirth learning influences how they behave throughout life, as if the early experience is calling for recognition through these behaviors.

Seeing how shadow forms from childhood experiences can enhance our understanding of how it may even form much earlier. For example, as a child, we may learn that anger is dangerous or unacceptable. When this natural emotion arises, we learn to deny it and push it back down. This can become automatic and unconscious. It may eat away at our health and express itself in unexpected moments. Depression is often said to be anger turned inward toward oneself. Other common shadow aspects relate to being too sexy, sensitive, emotional, happy, exuberant, curious, or . . . The list goes on. Perhaps you resonate with some of these listed traits, or you may be aware of others not mentioned here. The shadow, by definition, is unconscious, but this can change with therapeutic or other support.

Often, we try to deny that we have shadow. We must see ourselves as perfect, flawless, capable of anything, pure, superhuman, and beyond criticism or attack. We may be so devoted to a spiritual practice or tradition that we "spiritually bypass" our own humanness. In this guise, spiritual leaders manipulate and sexually abuse their willing followers. The concealed shadow of sexual urges or aggression finds its expression. It can be challenging to accept that we are all human.

We tend to see our shadow in others, without realizing these qualities we find annoying, irritating, objectionable, or irresistibly attractive are our own. This is called "projection" in psychology. We project onto other people aspects of ourselves that we cannot accept or acknowledge, like the sensitive boy bullying others for being too sensitive. If someone accuses us of being angry, we are likely to object, perhaps with *anger*.

We might similarly avoid or reject people portraying other common shadow qualities, like greed, selfishness, fear, tenderness, or aggressiveness. We might perceive someone as obnoxiously sweet if we learned to push down our own sweetness early in life (or if their sweetness is disguising their own shadow quality). Or we may see them as incredibly beautiful, creative, sexy, and so on. I learned during years of training with prenatal and birth therapy pioneer William R. Emerson to attend to what he called "shadow leaks." These are glimpses of shadow that can be seen in a person's eyes. One can learn to see this in oneself through video reflection therapy. This involves mindfully regarding a video of oneself stopped at just those moments when the shadow presents. This process needs to be done with the gentle support of a therapist because it can be shocking to see your own shadow in this way. Usually, we also need support to be able to perceive this aspect of ourselves that we have hidden for so long. Encountering our own shadow qualities in others may be activating, annoying, or strongly attractive. Do you ever find yourself thinking, "If only I could be as pretty/creative/assertive/sexy/intelligent as that person is . . . "

✿ Qualities of Self ✿

I invite you as you read this to consider what reactions or responses you are aware of. It can be helpful to make a list of qualities you are particularly judgmental of or attracted to, as well as those you dislike about yourself or wish you had. What happens to you emotionally or in your body as you consider these qualities? For example, you may sense changes in your breath or heart rate, a sense of nausea or clenching, or feelings of fear or anger. These can all be echoes of a time when your shadow was created. As such, they can offer you information about that time.

COLLECTIVE SHADOW, TRAUMA, BIRTH, AND THE SACRED FEMININE

Shadow abounds in human life and culture. Conception, pregnancy, and birth most often occur within the culture in which the mother or parents live, including all its collective shadows. In some situations, like adoption or surrogacy, the cultural shadow the prenate was preparing to meet is different from that of their new parents after birth. This can add to confusion and interfere with bonding. In the modern Western world, shadowy behavior is nourished by our separation from the sacred feminine.

In ancient Goddess cultures, the female form and its fertility were revered symbols of the great mystery of life. The circle of life re-tells the universal story of creation. Conception parallels the beginning of the world. Birth is the opening of a portal from the Mystery, just as death returns us to that source in the beyond. The feminine, represented in our brains by the right hemisphere, embraces wholeness.

As words, verbal history, and the left side of the brain with its linear thinking began to predominate, the feminine was designated evil and inferior. The men who began to take over positions of power denied and feared their own feminine qualities, which we all have. The masculine rejected the feminine, like an evil twin. Women who dared to embody their feminine wisdom and "right-brained," body-based intuition were burned or hung as witches. The physical body became the home of sin. Consider that so-called witches hunted in the 1500s tended to be older women who owned cats, or those considered eccentric and therefore dangerous to God-fearing folk. Although some men were accused, most of those considered witches were women. Some were healers or midwives.[1] Birth has been taken over by men who have been trained to find problems and solve them by doing something. The original blueprint for pregnancy, birth, and creation have been repeatedly vilified, distrusted, and judged as inadequate by those who do not understand it.

This is the ugly work of shadow. When we shine a light on an object, what is behind can become hidden in the object's shadow. The modern world venerates the masculine, characterized by analysis, separation, and division. Masculine focus omits elements beyond its range and places the sacred feminine in shadow. The spiritual potency of birth has been largely forgotten as medicine and machines have been promoted to take their place.

Collective shadow, passed down through generations, becomes

the background for the personal shadow we all carry with us. We now know through the relatively new field of epigenetics* that experiences of our ancestors can affect our genetic expression. Epigenetics refers to how genes are turned "on and off," or expressed, in relation to context or environment.

MAKING SHADOW CONSCIOUS

What is not spoken becomes shadow.
What is not welcomed becomes shadow.
What is not seen waits in darkness.
CHERIONNA MENZAM-SILLS

With awareness we can begin to shine the light on the shadow and awaken to our original potential. According to Jung, "One does not become enlightened by imagining figures of light, but by making the darkness conscious. The latter procedure, however, is disagreeable and therefore not popular."[2] Facing our inner monsters can be frightening. Meeting our shadow challenges our sense of our own identity. We find ourselves needing to own previously rejected qualities, like selfishness, which may translate into self-care and appropriate boundaries. Or aggression, which may transmute into assertiveness and the ability to stand one's ground and express oneself with confidence.

When we are little prenates, our survival is precarious. Maternal stress from mother's history, relationships, or other aspects of the world around her, affect our well-being. If she is not able to fully welcome and protect us, our life is in danger. This generates a sense of a need to defend against life-threatening peril, which persists somatically and unconsciously long after we have survived the prenatal stage. Our autonomic (automatic) nervous system stands guard, interfering with our ability to resiliently perceive and respond to current conditions.

---

*"Epi" means "over" or "above." The shadow of ancestral trauma can literally play out in our genes, affecting our perceptions, behaviors, and relationships.

Events or conditions experienced as life threatening or overwhelming have previously been defined as trauma. We now understand that trauma is not the event itself but rather the effect of the event, how it is replayed in an individual's or collective's system. This can generate PTSD. Instead of consciously remembering what happened, survivors of trauma may have symptoms signaling the trauma.[3]

This is an expression of implicit memory, which is either preverbal, as in the case of pre- and perinatal memories, or non-verbal. Overwhelming trauma can shift an individual out of the prefrontal cortex in their brain, where they can make conscious, rational decisions. When they are in a trauma reaction, their nervous system is doing its best to meet the emergency it detects. This is an automatic, unconscious process, like when you remove your hand from a hot stove before you consciously note that you have been burned. Implicit memory, rather than being recalled in words or a logical story, is stored and expresses itself through the body and emotions. When it is triggered, it feels like it is happening now. The sense of danger feels real, and the

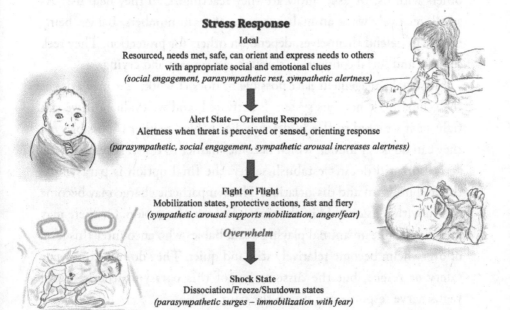

Stress Response

Ideal
Resourced, needs met, safe, can orient and express needs to others
with appropriate social and emotional clues
(social engagement, parasympathetic rest, sympathetic alertness)

Alert State—Orienting Response
Alertness when threat is perceived or sensed, orienting response
(parasympathetic, social engagement, sympathetic arousal increases alertness)

Fight or Flight
Mobilization states, protective actions, fast and fiery
(sympathetic arousal supports mobilization, anger/fear)

Overwhelm

Shock State
Dissociation/Freeze/Shutdown states
(parasympathetic surges – immobilization with fear)

Fig. 1.1. The Stress Response

nervous system reacts accordingly. In PTSD, this can present as sudden, intrusive flashbacks of the traumatic event, along with panic attacks, the urge to run away or fight, or other defensive reactions such as dissociation. This defensive reaction of the autonomic nervous system serves to protect us from intense pain by creating distance from it. A dissociated or numbed state also renders us less able to consciously record or remember a traumatic event. The word, *dissociation*, literally means disconnecting or separating. It may be for the conscious mind as if it never happened. The memory is held unconsciously as shadow.

This response occurs as a last resort when facing a threat. Our first response is to become alert and orient to the potential danger. This is not a fear response, but an automatic way to check if the stimulus, a sound for instance, is dangerous. If we assess it as threatening, we naturally check if there are other people around us. According to Dr. Stephen Porges, who developed polyvagal theory, we react to potential threat or safety in a hierarchical manner.[4] Our social engagement nervous system related to the ventral vagus nerve automatically seeks social support. If there are others with us, we ask, "How are they reacting? Can they help us?" As small, relatively weak animals, we seek safety in numbers. Babies, being unable to defend themselves, depend on others for protection. They seek support and social connection through eye contact and crying.

If social engagement isn't possible or doesn't work, fear may arise as the sympathetic nervous system is activated, and we evaluate if we can fight or if we need to flee in defense. For babies, neither is possible. All they can do is cry louder, which becomes harder to resist. If sympathetic activation still doesn't establish safety, the final option is parasympathetic shut down and dissociation. The sympathetic charge may become frozen with tension held in the tissues but without action. Or there may be collapse, like an animal playing dead. Babies who encounter this level of overwhelm become relatively still and quiet. They do not experience safety or rescue, but the dissociation of this parasympathetic dorsal vagus nerve response can numb the pain.

Trauma therapists also describe a fawn response, where the person tries to please and appease the source of danger. Although this often presents with ongoing abuse, we might consider that babies in the womb may try to soothe their mothers by becoming what we call a prenatal therapist, being sensitive to maternal needs and trying to meet them. Of course, babies are not very effective at meeting a mother's needs, but they may try. Many of us who become therapists feel that we began by trying to heal our parents, in an effort to create a safer, more nurturing layer of support for ourselves. This can begin in the womb.

In PTSD, these autonomic nervous system activations can be triggered by everyday life experiences. An unexpected loud sound may set off a sympathetically driven rapid heartbeat, a feeling of needing to do something, to run away, or to fight. For some people, particularly those with very early trauma, parasympathetic activation stimulates shut down, dissociation, and collapse. People with PTSD may alternate between these two kinds of activation, without much opportunity to rest in what Dan Siegel has named the "window of tolerance."[5] This is a relatively regulated state where social engagement system is online, and the person can socially interact and experience safety and support.

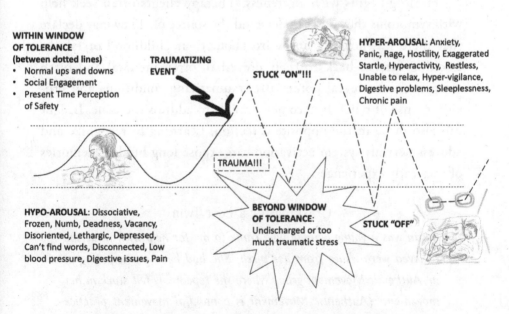

WITHIN WINDOW OF TOLERANCE (between dotted lines)
- Normal ups and downs
- Social Engagement
- Present Time Perception of Safety

TRAUMATIZING EVENT

STUCK "ON"!!!

HYPER-AROUSAL: Anxiety, Panic, Rage, Hostility, Exaggerated Startle, Hyperactivity, Restless, Unable to relax, Hyper-vigilance, Digestive problems, Sleeplessness, Chronic pain

TRAUMA!!!

HYPO-AROUSAL: Dissociative, Frozen, Numb, Deadness, Vacancy, Disoriented, Lethargic, Depressed, Can't find words, Disconnected, Low blood pressure, Digestive issues, Pain

BEYOND WINDOW OF TOLERANCE: Undischarged or too much traumatic stress

STUCK "OFF"

Fig. 1.2. Window of Tolerance is based on Lori Gill's Window of Tolerance from the Attachment and Trauma Treatment Centre for Healing website

With implicit traumatic memories, the window becomes smaller. The person is less able to tolerate emotional intensity. They relatively quickly become hyper-aroused with sympathetic activation or hypo-aroused with parasympathetic dissociative withdrawal. Pat Ogden, founder of sensorimotor therapy, refers to this window as the "zone of optimal arousal."[6] Just the right amount of nervous system arousal enables us to be present, alert, and simultaneously relaxed enough to socially engage, to listen to, communicate, and empathize with others. This is a state where we can perceive safety in present time and respond to conditions with resilience. It has also been called "the window of capacity," which I like because it emphasizes our ability rather than our disability.[7]

Where PTSD and other traumatic reactions present, the potential for creative resilience remains trapped as unconscious shadow, exerting its powerful influence. It begins to be accessed again as the traumatized physiology returns to a more regulated state. If the traumatizing events are held in shadow and denied, trauma resolution is less available.

Healing begins with awareness. Therapy clients often seek help with symptoms they don't understand the source of. They may declare that there was nothing untoward about their childhood or family. Looking further back to their preverbal, often prenatal and birth experience, can reveal potentially traumatizing conditions and provide a sense of relief. It becomes possible to address the issue. Insight can also move in the opposite direction. Learning to recognize and address nervous system activation can expose long hidden memories of very early experiences.

~ Grasping for a Lost Twin ~

Susan was a young woman who came to me for help with what she believed were issues from her birth. She had been participating in an Authentic Movement group where she repeatedly felt stuck in her movement. (Authentic Movement is a mindful movement practice where movers listen to inner impulses to move while being witnessed by a non-judgmental facilitator or group member, see page 60).

The group leader had recognized a birth theme and encouraged her to see me. Susan knew that her birth had been two weeks late. She tended to arrive late to therapy appointments, a common way to reenact a late birth. She reported that since piercing her navel five months ago, she had been waking up at night with an image that made her feel very sad and sometimes angry, although she didn't understand it. The image was of something pushing against something else. Then it was gone. As she told me about this, her eyes looked sad, as if she were on the verge of tears. She wondered if she had a twin. Her mother had always thought that she should or would have twins.

In our sessions, Susan moved spontaneously, as in Authentic Movement, with me assisting as needed. Her initial movement was birth-like, with her kneeling and pushing her head into her hands. To provide her with the potential for a more satisfying push, I put my hand in front of hers, so that her hand touched mine with her next push. She immediately responded by clutching onto my hand with her hand. She began to cry, pulling herself into my hand and pulling me toward her.

Although this had apparently started as a birth session, her response to my hand was not a typical birth response. A birth movement sequence would be more likely to involve her pushing into my hand and drawing the rest of her body forward to follow her head. The desperation with which she had clutched and pulled on my hand indicated that Susan may have experienced a traumatic or, at least threatening, event long before birth.

That she wondered if she had a twin suggested to me that she might be treating my hand as a lost twin, trying to make connection with it. When the movement was complete, Susan stated that it felt "right" and confirming, like when you go to the doctor thinking you have strep throat, and the doctor gives you that diagnosis. Further confirmation of her suspicion of having had a twin came the following week when her night image essentially disappeared. It was as if her twin psychology had been trying to get her attention.

Now that she had acknowledged it, she no longer needed to be awakened at night by this haunting image, which seemed to be a memory of her twin pushing against her before disappearing by dying. Instead, she began to be able to consciously mourn the loss of her twin, and to feel her anger about the conditions that led to her twin's death.

In our continuing work, Susan developed multiple insights related to having lost her twin. For Susan, being in the womb had meant being beware of toxicity that could kill her as it had her twin. Piercing her navel had triggered body memories of toxicity arriving umbilically, which tried to get her attention through dreams about her twin. She recognized her terror of letting go of relationships, which had represented her twin. She even tended to hold her breath, apparently afraid to let go of it.

Through our work she began to feel ready to move forward in life. Her eating disorder gradually healed, and she started eating healthily, no longer needing to "stuff" feelings with food. She became less hypervigilant and more relaxed in the therapy room, in her breathing, and in her life where she began cutting back excessive activities and started taking time to relax and just be. Being is the primary occupation of the fetus.

I recently listened to an inspiring webinar with Vincent J. Felitti, who coined the term, Adverse Childhood Experiences (ACEs).[8] This work demonstrates how childhood trauma is associated with later issues with mental health, addiction, and medical conditions. In the webinar, Felitti described his discovery that including questions about ACEs in a medical intake form resulted in a remarkable increase in success in a weight loss program for people with extreme obesity. He noted that "nice people" don't talk about certain things, like incest. This silence is an expression of cultural shadow.[9]

Some people in the obesity program left the program when they were successfully losing weight (in the range of hundreds of pounds!). Program participants who were asked questions from the ACE questionnaire about how these experiences had affected their lives more often stayed with the program. They also thanked the doctor for asking these questions. It wasn't therapy, yet simply asking the questions had this effect. The webinar host, Dr. Aimie Apigian, who is also a medical physician, underlined that not talking about traumas worsens the biological impact on a cellular level. Being invited to acknowledge what happened, and still be treated with respect, was a new, welcome, and healing experience. Most of the participants in the program had never had that opportunity.

Further illustrating cultural shadow at work is how Dr. Felitti's research on thousands of patients was rejected by medical practitioners, some of whom adamantly proclaimed that patients were fabricating their histories as an excuse for how their lives had failed! This echoes the sad effects of the False Memory Syndrome Foundation (FMSF) that was established in 1992 to protect so-called respectful people who had been accused of committing incest against their children. This movement arose in reaction to the current of awakening that supported women in acknowledging childhood sexual abuse, which had until then been unspeakable.

The rise of the FMSF and resistance to acknowledgment of childhood sexual abuse exemplifies cultural attempts to maintain traumatic shadow. Judith Herman, a pioneer in the field of modern trauma therapy writes,

> The study of psychological trauma must constantly contend with this tendency to discredit the victim or to render her invisible. Throughout the history of the field, dispute has raged over whether patients with post-traumatic conditions are entitled to care and respect or deserving of contempt, whether they are genuinely suffering or malingering, whether their histories are true or false and, if false, whether imagined or maliciously fabricated. In spite of a vast literature documenting the phenomena of psychological trauma, debate still centers on the basic question of whether these phenomena are credible and real.[10]

Those who have encountered PTSD, including by its war-oriented former names—shell shock, combat fatigue, or war neurosis—are aware that those diagnosed bear the burden of the unspeakable. Veterans often cannot talk about the horrors they have witnessed or committed; it is too painful. Terrifying memories held unconsciously arise in nightmares and flashbacks. The individual re-lives the experience as if it were happening in present time.

Modern trauma therapy acknowledges that such trauma memories are held in the body, as exemplified through the book *The Body Keeps the Score* by Bessel A. van der Kolk, 2014. Tissues tighten, freeze, or become numb, protecting us from what we cannot talk about. Supporting clients in developing mindful presence and body awareness facilitates integrating their traumatic experience. In contrast, cognitively diving into the details of the story behind the trauma can be overwhelming as it was when it happened, reinforcing trauma-related neural patterns without integration. Remember that integration involves a return to wholeness. This is a function the feminine right brain excels at. The left brain is better at describing and analyzing the experience, which is easier once the nervous system has returned to a regulated state and implicit emotional and body memories have been acknowledged. Unnamed or unacknowledged trauma remains stored in shadow, consuming life energy and persistently calling for attention. This effect can continue for generations.

Since moving to the UK where World War II had much more direct effects than in my home country of Canada, I have repeatedly encountered the intergenerational effects of wartime trauma on children, or even grandchildren, of those who fought or survived the bombing of the Nazis. These now adult children describe a father who rarely spoke or stayed quietly in a dark room throughout their childhood. Others raged or beat their innocent children, reenacting the violence they experienced at war. The autonomic nervous system of such adult children remains in defensive modes of fight-flight hyper-vigilance and/or dissociative freeze, or collapse triggered by the trauma of being raised by such a parent.

～ The Ghost of War Trauma ～

Jo described many levels of trauma to me in our work together, but one haunting one was her violent father who had spent three years in a German prisoner of war camp. He never spoke of his experience, but Jo could feel his anger and dissociation, and the tension in his face and body. She felt he was unavailable to her. He even forgot to pick her up after school one day when she was a young girl. After waiting in vain for a long time, she found her way home on foot. To deal with his violent outbursts, Jo learned to dissociate like her father. After years of trying to calm her raging father, she developed a tendency to appease others.

In our work together, Jo had a strong need to be heard. I listened to her reports of how others victimized her, and supported her in finding her inner knowing and her inner "no." Jo had been born a few years after her father returned from the Nazi camp. She had marinated in the womb of a very stressed mother who was afraid of the man who had returned from war in place of her beloved husband. Jo's nervous system had never developed a way to regulate itself, having missed the experience of a settled maternal system to co-regulate with. She grew up feeling unseen and unprotected. We realized that even the discovery of her conception had not been celebrated because of the field of fear and uncertainty of her parents.

Through our work together, Jo began to experience being seen and received within a safe relational field. She felt her body begin to relax. Her digestion improved. She began to feel hopeful about relationships. The ghost of her father's war trauma needed to move into the background for Jo to come into focus. This couldn't happen as long as Jo and her family could not mention the unmentionable. Being able to talk about the unmentionable and feel the feelings associated with it within our safe relational field of therapy provided for Jo what wasn't available in her family.

The same is true for survivors of childhood abuse. There has been so much shame associated with this all-too-common phenomenon that children have learned, and often been warned, to not tell anyone. These children may become doormats vulnerable to more abuse or, alternatively, become bullies to other children or to pets or younger siblings, reenacting what cannot be spoken. As adults, they may pass on the abuse to their children. It may be the only way they can respond when their child is loud, disagreeing with them, or having a tantrum.

I remember being shocked when as a dance/movement psychotherapy student in the 1990s, I visited a special psychiatric ward for sexually abused children. The staff explained to us students that these children required constant supervision because children as young as five tended to sexually abuse those younger or smaller than them. As part of that training, I also did an internship with an occupational therapist working with developmentally delayed children. I was strongly impacted by her account of one of our young patients, a toddler diagnosed with tactile defensiveness (a condition involving hypersensitivity to touch), who had been sexually abused. The therapist had noticed that children with tactile defensiveness frequently had similar sexual abuse history.

I compare this experience to my training as an occupational therapist in the 1970s where there was never any mention of incest or sexual abuse in any of our courses, including those on mental health and pediatrics. The topic was still taboo in the 1970s. It was just starting to come into view in the 1990s as popular books on the topic began to circulate.* The years of silence echoed Freud's renaming his patients' incest memories as fantasies to maintain his reputation in Victorian Vienna, which safely protected the shadow status of incest, sexual abuse, and other early trauma, as well as preverbal memory, until something began to shift.

⌒ Feeling Her Mother's Trauma ⌒

Claudia lived much of her life frozen and unable to feel her body. After many years of recovering her relationship with her body through

---

*Examples are *Father-Daughter Incest* by Judith Herman first published in 1982 and *The Sexual Healing Journey* by Wendy Maltz published initially in 1992.

yoga and therapy, she was surprised to find herself getting angry, her suppressed reaction to abuse. Within the safety and support of our therapeutic relationship, memories began to emerge. Claudia told me that she had once heard her mother telling her aunt how their brother's sexual touch when she was pregnant had terrified and angered her. We realized that Claudia had felt these emotions with her mother in the womb. Later on an interaction with her cousin had reinforced these prenatal feelings when he sexually abused her, which her family collectively denied.

Our work together included using the gentle breaths and sounding of Continuum (a practice of somatic inquiry, see page 90) to support melting of her tense fascia and muscles, particularly in her lower back. She began to recognize that she had legitimate grief, as well as anger. As Claudia's armor began to melt, she began to feel freer and stronger. Her lifelong depression began to lift. This involved feeling not only the repressed anger but also the tears she had held back all her life through holding her breath. She was now able to move beyond her deep fear and develop a romantic relationship. When her boyfriend was disrespectful, she now could feel her true reaction and demand respect. She had never been able to do this before.

The Canadian physician and addiction expert Dr. Gabor Maté writes of this kind of development and the effects of this kind of cultural shadow.

> As cultural traumas occur and accrue, distortions in societal perceptions are amplified. The resulting misapprehensions and misperceptions become cultural agreements: limiting or harmful stereotypes, a belief that "this is just the way things are," or other unconscious codes, values, and language built into a society as a result of collective distortions.[11]

Fortunately, some of our cultural agreements are loosening. It is becoming more acceptable to speak of having been abused. There are therapeutic programs to support veterans in effectively working through traumatic memories. The Me Too movement indicates a lightening of shadow, accompanied by the usual resistance. Another example is the acknowledgment of abuse of Indigenous peoples which is trying to gain a foothold.

In Canada, for instance, a Truth and Reconciliation Commission between 2008 and 2015 promised to document and rectify the historical situation. Full resolution was probably not possible for generations traumatized by intentional separating, relocating, and abuse of Indigenous families, but repair could at least begin. International coverage in 2021 of the discovery of hundreds of unmarked graves of children who died in residential schools, that they were forced to attend, shone additional light on this horrendous shadow. This revelation stirred the populace, awakening non-Indigenous people from a shadowy dream of equality. Still, denial continues.

Even as I write this, Pope Francis has visited central Alberta in Western Canada to address a gathering of survivors of these residential schools and their descendants to apologize. Typical of those entrenched in cultural shadow, the Pope apologized for "the ways in which many members of the Church and religious communities cooperated" in the residential school system, without acknowledging that the Catholic Church endorsed the assimilation policy that included genocide and abuse of all kinds.[12] The colonial attitude toward First Nations peoples continues as exemplified by thousands of missing and murdered Indigenous women in Canada, as well as in the USA and South America. Police bias has been blamed for lack of proper investigation into such cases in Canada, reminiscent of the racist brutality of American police toward people of color.

The Black Lives Matter movement is another attempt to shine the light on colonialist, racist shadow. Typical of attempts to protect and preserve shadow, centuries of racism and all its abuses continue to thrive even as it becomes more permissible and popular to speak about this cultural projection of colonialist fears and weaknesses onto people of color.

RACISM, BIRTH, SHADOW, AND BRAIN HEMISPHERES

Relevant to prenatal and birth experience is the neglect and abuse of birthing women of color. Infant mortality rates for Indigenous, Hispanic, and Black babies in the US are much higher than for white babies.[13] Facing double discrimination for race and gender, as well as racially imposed stresses of high rates of unemployment, poverty, incarceration and crime in their families and neighborhoods, increases prenatal stress levels for these women. Resultant raised cortisol levels can reduce blood flow to the placenta, contributing to common problems, such as low birth weight and prematurity. Babies exposed to chronic or very high levels of prenatal maternal stress tend to develop altered cortisol sensitivity, rendering them more reactive to stress throughout their lives.[14]

Racial bias also leads to much higher mortality rates for birthing Black women in places like the UK and USA, as well as for other BIPOC (Black, Indigenous, and people of color) people. Women likely to have chronic conditions due to culturally imposed stress require careful prenatal and birth support. Instead, systemic racism impedes quality healthcare and engenders a tendency for staff to ignore or judge these women as less cooperative or overreacting when they complain of pain.[15]

The shadow of racism and misogyny in healthcare is still in its early stages of coming to the light of cultural awareness. In the year 2000, an article in *The Journal of Perinatal Education* notes the disparity in rates between Black, non-white, and white women,[16] but the explanations for them fail to mention racism as a cause. Instead, lifestyle factors, lack of seeking medical care, and unintended pregnancies are suggested. There is no understanding of how these might relate to ubiquitous racism affecting these women, their health and lifestyle. It gives me hope to see that racism can now be spoken about in this context. It pains me that it has taken so long for it to enter the conversation or realm of research. This is typical of shadow that protests any attempt to reveal its presence and effects. Perhaps the double shadow of race and gender augments this tendency.

If we examine history, we can see that dividing people into "good" and "bad" according to their race or sex developed as the left brain began to dominate. Dale Allen eloquently describes this process in her book, *In Our Right Minds*.* She notes that, in her research into paleolithic, neolithic, and chalcolithic cultures, as well as in modern matriarchal cultures, she could find no evidence of racism or dehumanization of others through the use of abstract concepts. She notes that the left hemisphere of the brain, the hunter-gatherer side, excels at focusing in on its target. It can dissect and separate but doesn't see the whole picture. In contrast, the right hemisphere perceives wholeness and relational connections. As the gatherer-nurturer, the right brain is more empathic, adaptable, explorative, and capable of a both/and approach. She writes that in these cultures, the perspective was and is more fluid, present, embodied, connected—more right-brain integrated.

The human journey changed post-alphabetic literacy, when the strengths that are attributed to the left-brain: logical, mechanistic, linear, abstract, time-bound, hierarchical became central to the discourse and structure of culture.

With alphabetic literacy came new Sky Gods and new creation stories that did not feature a woman—the Goddess—gestating and birthing all life through the birth canal and sacred yoni. With a dominance of a more left-brain perspective and the emergence of the new Sky-Gods, humans began to make abstract concepts more important than presence and connection to the world around them. The Goddess and all things female became suspect and dangerous. Women could ultimately be positioned as "non-human." The Burning Times illustrate the extremes of this imbalance.

As humans, we were designed with a balance of the left and right hemispheres. When we are in balance (as designed) the left-

---

*Learn more about Dale Allen at The Core Space (website) and In Our Right Minds (website).

hemisphere does not dominate with its either/or, separate, abstract approach, which underlies the dehumanization of others.[17]

The left hemisphere is responsible for translating our experience into words. This brings it to consciousness, rendering our non-verbal or preverbal right-brained and implicit, somatic memories accessible to understand and integrate. In relation to prenatal and birth experience as shadow, it is important to acknowledge that our right brain develops first. Our left brain is less active until about age three and is not fully online until about age seven, whereas the right brain develops rapidly in the first year. Experiences prior to left brain development are registered and remembered nonverbally, held in the body and emotions. In a culture where these feminine qualities are devalued and held captive in shadow, our earliest memories remain in the dark caverns of the unconscious mind.

SHADOW, CONSCIOUSNESS, AND ACCURATE REFLECTION

As verbal language abilities develop in toddlerhood, the child begins to be able to speak about their experiences. If adults around them ridicule or dismiss their reports, the little one quickly learns to reject them as well. This process begins very early in life. In the next chapter, we will examine preverbal, including prenatal and perinatal, intelligence, memory, and sentience. For now, consider that children up until the age of about six, are functioning, as cell biologist Bruce Lipton notes, in a hypnagogic state.[18] They soak up the world around them without question. This includes the beliefs, values, behaviors, and shadow of the family and culture they arrive in.

We retain as conscious memory what is reinforced. If you haven't thought about an event for years, you may not remember its details as well as if you have spoken about it frequently with others. This is also true for young children as their conscious mind is developing. Left hemisphere verbal and conscious memory begin functioning in the second year, altering brain organization. When toddlers have an experience that their parents or caregivers reflect to them, the experience can be stored in conscious memory. For example, a child visits the zoo with their parents. The next day, they draw a picture of the elephant with its big ears and eagerly show the drawing to their mother. The mother might respond with words that help the child to record this memory more verbally. "Oh, you drew the elephant we saw at the zoo! It has big ears. We also saw giraffes there. They had long necks." In this way, the child's experience is put into words. It's like creating a file in conscious, verbal memory for this experience. A child's drawing of being in the womb or of being born is unlikely to be received the same way. It may not even be recognized.

Similarly, a child may try to draw or tell a parent about a sexually abusive experience. If this occurred in the 50s or 60s, or in too many families even today, the most likely response would be something like, "That never happened! What a filthy mind you have that imagined that! Don't ever mention that again!" This experience is clearly not acceptable. The child learns quickly to never talk about this kind of event again. They also may have been warned by the abuser that it is their secret and to never tell anyone. It becomes safer to not think about it at all. This tendency can be augmented by the trauma response of dissociation that serves to protect the individual from intense pain of a traumatic experience.

Designating memories of such abuse as fantasy feeds and protects the shadow, along with shadow-fueled organizations like the FMSF mentioned earlier. Gradually, light is being shone on this too frequent expression of cultural shadow. Again, when the sacred feminine is rejected and forgotten, her shadow is projected onto innocent females. Those fearing this repressed aspect of themselves, often men, attack its expression in others, through abuse, rape, incest, and so on.

Relegating pre- and perinatal memories to shadow similarly expresses this fear and denial of the feminine. In that they occur within the feminine womb and the function of birth, these are also feared and demeaned. They are aspects of the Mystery, well understood in the feminine psyche but dreaded by the masculine as impossible to fully dissect, analyze, or control.

Little ones often attempt to communicate about their experience of birth and the womb. In working with babies, I have seen repeatedly how they readily demonstrate the way they moved through the birth canal.

⁓ This Baby Just Needed to Tell His Story ⁓

Many years ago I was delighted to work with a little eight-week-old boy. His parents were aware of the value of Craniosacral therapy for newborns. Although they didn't see any issues and thought the birth had been non-eventful, they wanted me to treat little George and make sure he was healthy.

In our first session, George seemed very present. He readily made eye contact and seemed to enjoy my hands holding him. Just to be sure, we arranged a second session. This time I was surprised when George suddenly started to twist in my hands. After making quick eye contact apparently to ensure that I was with him, he began to rotate toward the right, expressing some effort and then crying as he moved through a stuck place. He then emerged from an apparent birth canal and continued crying. In working with babies, it is important to help them to stay in present time. Because they are nonlinear, "left-brained" oriented, their memories are implicit, body-based, and outside of time. In this state, they don't differentiate between past and present. They just experience directly.

In this case, I could see that George was still present in the room, looking around and making eye contact every few minutes. I also realized that he had been showing us his birth from his perspective, which hadn't been as easy as his parents believed. When he was done, resting in his mother's lap and making eye contact with me, I spoke to him with what I felt in my own heart. I found myself apologizing to him. I said something like, "I'm sorry I didn't realize it was so hard for you. I missed it." After a moment, this little eight-week-old baby began to laugh and laugh! He evidently enjoyed that I was apologizing to him. He wasn't very traumatized by his birth experience, but he did need to tell his story and have it be recognized and received. Being present with him in the session, his parents were now able to understand what his body movements were about and to appreciate how he had struggled.

Toddlers frequently talk about how it was for them at birth, in mommy's tummy, or even where they were before conception, and how they chose their parents.[19] If they are lucky, their parents or others they speak to are interested in their story and ask for more details. This provides the reflection and reinforcement to establish these memories in consciousness.

∼ Stuck in a Tunnel ∼

Joey was born via emergency caesarean section. At three years old, he loved playing in boxes and tunnels. His parents were puzzled that at some point in his play he would always become frustrated and begin crying. In our work together, I supported Joey in acknowledging what was happening when he became frustrated. When asked what was happening, he explained that he was stuck. This was exactly what had happened in the birth canal. When I reflected to him, by saying, "Yes, you were stuck and you couldn't get through," he looked up at me in surprise. No one had ever acknowledged his birth history before. He was trying to express his story in his play.

We then created a soft tunnel made from blankets and cushions. When Joey came to the stuck place, he then wanted me to pull him out through the space above him between two blankets. This was a reenactment of his C-section. Once he was satisfied that this part of his birth had been recognized, Joey began to negotiate the stuck place within the tunnel. Each time he got past the stuck place, we applauded and celebrated his success. Over time, with support, he began to be able to move further in the tunnel until he was eventually able to move all the way through to the end. Having successfully now had a vaginal birth, Joey lost interest in playing with tunnels and stopped displaying frustration any time he faced a challenge. He now became interested in finding creative ways to meet whatever situation awaited and was able to appropriately ask his parents for help when he really needed it. His parents could now understand when feelings of frustration or being stuck arose, and could reflect that this is how it was in his birth.

More often, adults respond to these utterings from the innocent as nonsense. They may say or think, "Aren't they cute!" or "Yes, dear," or distract them with a different topic or activity, without appreciating that these are actual valid statements of memory. Within a culture that values "left brain," masculine analysis and denies sentience before verbal language develops, these expressions cannot possibly be valued. The child in this context learns that these are unacceptable experiences, and memories are buried in the unconscious, becoming shadow.

CULTIVATING SHADOW

What we hold in unconsciousness can profoundly affect our perceptions, choices, behaviors, relationships, personality, and health. We learn to do and be what is expected. Rejected aspects of us go into hiding, as we respond to cultural conditioning delivered via the people around us, such as parents, siblings, and teachers.

This is intelligent behavior. Our survival often depends on conformation to what is expected or demanded of us. This applies even on an embryological level. For example, you wouldn't be here reading this page if you hadn't responded to the circumstances around you by implanting, or nesting, into the wall of your mother's womb about five to seven days after conception. This is an embryological imperative. You would have starved to death if you had not implanted. Hopefully, implantation was a satisfying experience and your mother's uterine wall was nourishing. For some of us, it may have been perceived as toxic or unwelcoming. This creates a double bind. We need to implant to survive but doing so takes us directly into the toxicity that we need to feed on. That very early experience can profoundly affect our relationship to nourishment as well as to other people, intimacy, and even being able to find and settle into a safe home. We may have trouble with these aspects of life due to this unconsciously remembered experience. We might call it the shadow of our implantation.

In this way, even on an embryological level, we need to follow the rules of our surround. In the case of implantation, the rules are biological. The situation is further affected by the mother's state, including her mental and physical health, and her attitude toward her feminine body and to having a baby, which are influenced by the relationships, family, culture, and collective she lives in. For older children, following the rules might be more obvious. We need to behave appropriately in school. We need to eat at mealtimes. We may need to sit still at the dinner table. Depending on our own proclivities and the capacity for compassion and flexibility of those enforcing prominent tenets, we may suffer under the pressure of these rules.

Symbolically, children learn to fit spheres and cylinders in round holes and cubes into square holes. The process of socialization can be like fitting the roundness of a human being into a square hole. We may grow up feeling like a misfit. I was one of those children who was certain I had been adopted. Although I physically resembled my family members, I couldn't find a way to be my genuine self within the family mold. It took me years of therapy to discover and reclaim my roundness. Like many others, I learned to function well within the more mental, analytical world around me. To do so, I had to dissociate from my own feminine nature (along with its intuitive creativity and wisdom), from my body, and from memories of my earliest moments in this life.

A LARGER CONTEXT:
COLLECTIVE TRAUMA AND
INTERGENERATIONAL INFLUENCES

Collective trauma refers to trauma experienced or held by a larger group, such as a culture. Thomas Hübl, author of an essential book in this field, *Healing Collective Trauma*, writes:

My work has shown me that trauma is never purely an individual problem. And no matter how private or personal, trauma cannot belong solely to a family, or even to that family's intricate ancestral tree. The consequences of trauma—indeed the cumulative effects of personal, familial, and historical traumas—sweep across communities, regions, lands, and nations. The burden borne by a single person, family, or community invariably and inevitably reaches its larger society, touching even those who share little in the way of common identity or custom. The impact of human-created suffering extends beyond the original subject or subjugated group; trauma's legacy weaves and wires our world, informing how we live it, how we see it, and how we see and understand one another.[20]

The transfer of ancestral trauma happens both through epigenetic changes and the passing down of traditions and unconscious coping mechanisms. As you might imagine, much of this happens before birth, as embryological development unfolds.

~ Marinating in Her Mother's Shame ~

Helen came to a womb surround process workshop hoping to reduce her chronic feelings of fear, self-hatred, and anger. She didn't feel she had reasons for these strong emotions which plagued her and interfered with her relationships. As we looked at the history of her conception, Helen told us that her mother had a miscarriage as a teenager, followed not long afterward by an abortion after being raped.

As we explored this history, Helen felt apathetic. I asked her a question we often use in this work to identify when experience or emotions are inherited from an ancestor. I asked, "Who felt this apathy before you?" Helen quickly realized her mother had felt this way. Becoming pregnant again with a history of two previously traumatic pregnancies, her mother was not enthusiastic about Helen being conceived. Instead, she harbored unprocessed fear, shame, and anger from her past. Helen, as a prenate, marinated in these feelings. Again, little ones are not able to differentiate between what is theirs and what belongs to someone else. They experience it directly, as their own. These feelings became part of Helen's identity and way of meeting the world as she grew up. Her nervous system and psyche developed as genes were turned on and off in alignment with her mother's difficult emotions. In the womb surround, we identified these feelings as her mother's, then provided support for her mother that was needed back then.

My sense is that this kind of experience within a safe, compassionate group literally changes the context for the person's cells, tissues, and nervous system, which an experienced trauma therapist, Bonnie Badenoch describes as disconfirming experience.*[21] The group is a nourishing womb where the one Helen grew in offered the toxicity of her mother's unprocessed emotions. By the end of Helen's process in the workshop, she felt predictably relieved. Her body softened. She cried tears of relief. She then felt enthusiasm about going back into her life and exploring how relationships could be with her newfound differentiation and confidence. She was no longer needing to act out her mother's feelings to keep alive her prenatal memory.

Natalism, or the symbolic expression of prenatal and birth memory, is a universal experience.[22] As the unconscious cannot be perceived directly, it seeks recognition and integration through less conscious, symbolic, forms of expression, like art, dreams, myth, ritual, and dance. Because of their unconscious nature, these symbolic expressions interpret and reflect the history of their unique culture, often reinforcing generational trauma and/or resilience. For example, drumming and dancing have been used by Indigenous peoples around the world to strengthen community ties and address challenging issues.†[23] In my doc-

---

*This phrase refers to providing what was needed but not available at the time of the traumatic event.

†For a recent account of the function of ceremonies and dance in the Himba tribe in Africa, I refer you to Antonella Sansone's book, *Cultivating Mindfulness to Raise Children Who Thrive: Why Human Connection from Before Birth Matters,* inspired by her intimate time with this group that had experienced almost no contact with Westerners.

toral dissertation "Dancing Our Birth," I reviewed the global history of dance and ritual, examining how various forms and practices reflect prenatal and birth experience, and take on a symbolic healing affect that embodies the powerful forces of creation. Ritual includes initiatory rites, usually for young adolescents acknowledging their transition, or birth, into adulthood. There are also rituals to welcome, name, and acknowledge new babies arriving into the community, as well as rituals relating to death. We continue to have rituals in our modern world, such as funerals or graduation ceremonies. These also relate to moments of transition, which involve dying out of one phase of life and birthing into another state. In ancient cultures, the symbolism of birth might be more obvious, as when the dead were laid to rest in a burial mound, looking similar to the "bump" of a pregnant woman. These *tumuli* have been found around the world, including in Turkey, Siberia, and Central Asia.*[24]

Early Goddess religions centered on the mysteries of birth and death as the "Mystical Return and Rebirth."[25] These are common themes in ritual, and rebirth can be a soothing solution to fear of death. Burial rites placed the dead in the fetal position, often sent to sea in a boat, symbolizing death as a return to the fetal state in the womb, to be followed by rebirth.[26] An example is Tolland man, who was buried in Denmark in the 5th century BC.[27] Similarly, burial mounds represented a return to the pregnant womb of the earth.[28]

> Primitive peoples saw themselves as incarnations of the Great Mother's children; to them, there was no separation between the body and the world, inside and outside, this life and the next: all things were indissolubly united . . . Originally, all rituals were danced; body and mind were set in motion as a unity. Through dancing, primitive peoples expressed their natural excitement and deep emotions.[29]

---

*You can learn more about burial mounds or tumuli in the article "Tumulus Tombs: The Predecessors of Modern Mausoleums" on the Mausoleums website.

Like little children playacting in order to name and integrate what they do not yet have words for, embodied ritual symbolizes the Mystery, which can include the experience of beginning a new life. This can be soothing and healing.

> In the beginning there was not the word, rather there was the symbolic action—a union of body and psyche. In the beginning dance was the sacred language through which we communed and communicated with the vast unknown. In the earliest times the dancer was both healer and priest.[30]

Dance continues to be an important healing and uniting modality today. As a young woman, I was a folk-dance fanatic, learning, enjoying, and performing dances of peoples from around the world. As I write this, war is waging in Ukraine. I see photos of Ukrainians proudly donning their traditional clothing. Seeing them, I remember watching spellbounding dance performances by Ukrainian dance troupes in Toronto where I lived as a young folk dancer. Such traditions passed down through the generations support communities in maintaining their ties and identity, which can remind them of their strength in the face of adversity, such as invasion by a neighboring country.

Not all intergenerational experiences are performed in such positive ways. Without outlets for healing, unconscious coping mechanisms abound, often echoing cultural trauma. For example, generations of Jews descended from those who escaped the violent attacks of pogroms in Eastern Europe have carried on survival strategies of hyper-vigilance and readiness to escape at any moment. Marginalized communities are particularly at risk as repeated exposure to trauma may force them to prepare their children for interacting with a world that poses a constant threat, either real or perceived. Immigrant families may teach their children that they must be perfect in order to avoid criticism.

~ Being Perfect Is Never Enough ~

Dorothy grew up in the 1930s in one of the few Jewish families in a small town in eastern Canada where anti-Semitism was common.

Throughout her life Dorothy struggled to know and express her authentic self. Her mostly unconscious fear of attack, passed down from her immigrant parents, infused anxiety into every aspect of her life. She was a high achiever, becoming a nurse in the 1940s when it was less common for women to work outside the home. After her children left home, she went back to school to earn a degree in nursing, which hadn't been available when she began her career. She graduated with top marks in her class and went on to teach others what she had learned from her many years of practice. Even with this degree of success, Dorothy had low self-esteem and never felt like she had done enough. Her parents' fear of attack by the Goyim (non-Jews) never left her. What if they saw how imperfect she really was?

In therapy, Dorothy was able to identify her fear as belonging to her parents. She found relief in talking about what they had been through in the old country, where there was always fear that the Kozaks might come at any moment to attack and destroy their village. This may be another example of epigenetic changes in the womb, but these were reinforced by her parents' insistence that her performance always be above average. Even as a prenate, Dorothy's nervous system was developing in resonance with the hyper-vigilant anxiety of her mother and family, as she prepared to live in their world. Her own anxiety continued the neuronal tradition of many generations before her.

There are so many examples of how tribalism, strong identification with one's people and sense of separateness from all other peoples, even if a survival mechanism, can contribute to collective trauma. Later chapters address this more specifically but for now, let's acknowledge that collective trauma abounds and is inherently stressful. This stress contributes to the context in which pregnancy and birth occur, leading to, for example, higher levels of maternal and infant mortality for Black and Indigenous births.

Something in us freezes in response to trauma. Emilie Conrad, founder of the mindful movement practice of Continuum, spoke of paralysis as a shock in the system, the body tissues, nervous system, and so on, that blocks the flow of information. Where we have been injured, for example, and not able to process that injury, our tissues are held and dense. Conrad found in her work with people with spinal injuries that practicing Continuum supported them in releasing the shock that she always detected as the actual paralysis. They then had much freer movement, even if they still couldn't walk.[31]

I have often heard Thomas Hübl compare our traumatized cultures to ice. If snow falls into a flowing river, it melts and becomes part of the river. If it falls on ice, it remains on the surface, where it piles up. Gestating and being born into a culture holding undigested trauma is like snow falling on ice. Until this traumatic experience is digested, it is part of the culture, perceived as normal and will continue to recur. In other words, it is hidden as shadow.

As little ones prepare for life in the mother's world, they respond to messages of collective trauma, including remnants of the experiences of parents, grandparents, and other ancestors. Arriving in a traumatized world and developing a heightened stress response echoes the stress met by ancestors and others in their culture and is an intelligent way to prepare for living in that culture.

As Hübl notes,

When a human incarnates, a stream of light enters into and travels upward along millennia of spiraling DNA and accumulated genetic histories. Pushing through thousands of years of karmic substrate, a single human soul emerges into a world weighed down by ancient, modern, and postmodern bands of tribal pain and cultural trauma. Its light surfaces, finally, at the conception and crown of a single bawling infant.[32]

As the collective trauma is resolved, the snow can melt, and individuals can have a different experience. By the same token, doing our individual trauma work can contribute to resolution of the cultural trauma.

I am reminded here of my experience of healing sexual abuse from my childhood. In the early 90s, when sexual abuse and incest were just beginning to emerge from the cultural shadow, most people did not acknowledge its existence. As part of my healing journey, I encountered pioneers in trauma therapy, including Judith Herman and Bessel A. van der Kolk, now widely recognized as experts in this important field of therapy. Back then, members of the FMSF who knew little or nothing about trauma criticized such authorities in the field of trauma and memory as frauds. Although the organization did not deny the existence of incest, it propagated unfounded beliefs about the nature of memory. It is now well-established that trauma survivors may not consciously remember aspects of the traumatic event and they may be retraumatized by flashbacks.

Hopefully this is changing. I see abuse being named more readily than in the 50s and 60s when I was a child. Within a Me Too culture, modern children are likely to have been exposed to the topic and may be aware of resources for help. The omnipresence of the internet and social media presents new opportunities for sexual abuse as well as potential for education and protection. Modern Western culture still has a distance to go in terms of ending misogyny as it is still abundantly present in entertainment, fashion, politics, and so on. However, the awareness challenges perpetrators who are in increased danger of being exposed as the light shines on them.

Unfortunately, this is less true for prenatal and perinatal abuse. Insensitive or abusive treatment of infants at birth and even in the womb continues within a culture that still does not recognize the sentience and extreme sensitivity of little ones. Birthing babies continue to be subjected to routine abuse in the form of violent, invasive interventions without sensitivity, warning, or explanation. For example, pulling a baby out with forceps or vacuum extraction (ventouse) without telling the baby what to expect tends to be shocking for the little one. If the maneuver is not done gently and sensitively, the baby suffers with unexpected pain. This experience is even more extreme in caesarean section. Rarely are babies spoken to during this process, in which there is often a sense of extreme stress if the procedure is performed as an emergency. With communication, babies can be more prepared for what is about to happen and may suffer less shock.

Babies are believed to be incapable of understanding, despite their obvious ability to respond to what we say to them. The evidence of their trauma and shock has been considered normal. Babies who are dissociated due to trauma are often considered good, calm babies because they don't cry much. Some studies, though later questioned, suggested that babies in sub-Saharan Africa prior to Westernization were advanced in their developmental milestones compared to Western babies who at the time were routinely being born with anesthesia and other often unnecessary interventions.[33] I find it informative to read these old research reports and find that birth was never considered a possible influence. The researchers considered other less shadowy factors, such as how African babies were generally held more by their mothers.

Prenatal abuse also persists. Little ones in the womb subjected to invasive amniocentesis have been seen on ultrasound to move away from the needle or to try to bat it away.[34] They are clearly aware of the invasion and don't like it. It would be simple to explain to them why the procedure is being done and let them know the needle will be coming. They could then respond by withdrawing out of reach of the needle without being shocked or terrified for their life. Similarly, where fetal surgery is required, the little one can be supported by explaining the procedure to them and its purpose. Taking such care requires awareness and won't happen if the prenatal psyche is held in shadow.

I have had clients who as adults still resent that their mother had surgery during the pregnancy without any acknowledgment of how the baby would be affected. Elaine, a woman in her 40s, repeatedly complained in her sessions about how her sensitivity as a fetus was not acknowledged when her mother had her appendix removed during the pregnancy. She still harbored anger for her mother, the surgeon and other medical staff for their lack of consideration for how the operation would affect her.

Recognizing a harmful divide between prenatal and postnatal research and knowledge, Marti Glenn and Wendy McCarty co-founded the Santa Barbara Graduate Institute in 2000. This unusual school hosted a unique opportunity to obtain a doctoral degree in Prenatal and Perinatal Psychology. In an article published in 2008 they wrote,

> Although many fields of research were identifying the origins of later problems stemming from the prenatal, birth, and postpartum period, mainstream practice has still focused its attention primarily after birth. Even some of our most recognized researchers, educators and policy makers who recognize the value of early experience do not always include the prenatal and birth period as part of a continuum that has an effect on later development.[35]

In other words, the collective continues to deny the profoundly influential period before birth, despite increasing evidence. Prenatal intelligence and vulnerability remain largely in shadow, contributing to a continued lack of adequate support for pregnant families. Consequently, issues stemming from prenatal challenges are not addressed as early as they could be. Children may suffer from problems with learning, behavior, and other aspects of development due to this unnecessary ignorance. Continuing with the words of McCarty and Glenn,

> Clinicians working with infants from the prenatal and perinatal psychology perspective believe that the majority of infants who have traumatic experiences from the prenatal and perinatal period show traumatic imprints that largely go unrecognized as such. Most are left untreated until they become recognizable as more familiar maladies such as attachment and learning disorders and regulation issues in later infancy and childhood.[36]

What is rarely noted is that issues from prenatal experience may never be acknowledged and properly treated. They may continue to affect behavior, attitudes, and relationships throughout life. This may unfortunately be passed on to the next generation by parents and birth professionals.

I invite you to notice your own reaction to this discussion. I would expect some readers to be shocked to learn that little ones are dismissed as sensitive and treated in detrimental ways, and others to be dubious that there is reason to treat them otherwise. This speaks to a shifting shadow. The light is beginning to come through, but there is still darkness here.

I have been delighted to hear some trauma therapists, like Gabor Maté and Bonnie Badenoch, mentioning prenatal influences in their teaching, but this is still rare in our world. Please see the questions below to aid you in reflecting upon your own pre- and peri-natal experiences and the ways that these may have impacted you. These questions can help you begin to examine how your early experiences may be expressing themselves in your current life or in your tendencies. You may not yet see a connection with your prenatal or birth history, but I suggest keeping your responses to these questions in mind as we expand on how early experiences may manifest. I also recommend recording your responses in a journal where you can refer to them later.

Reflections

1. What are your intimate relationships like? Are you attracted to partners who are trustworthy, reliable, consistent, present, or not? Have you experienced betrayal by a loved one?
2. Have you ever been bullied or bullied others? Do you feel empowered and worthy in relationships with others, including your siblings, other family members, friends, co-workers, and intimate partner?
3. What helps you feel safe—at home with yourself or with others? When are you most likely to feel anxious, afraid, shy, or self-conscious?

2

Exploring Early Consciousness
The Path to Embodiment

> *Memory is truly a body-wide web. Whether or not we*
> *can consciously access a memory is not as important as the*
> *realization that we had the experience, the lived event,*
> *which has left some kind of impact, influence, mark, trace,*
> *record, or imprint on our cells and tissues.*
>
> THOMAS R. VERNY, *THE EMBODIED MIND*

Shining light on pre- and perinatal shadow requires acknowledging the experiences of little ones. Counter to modern Western beliefs, the field of prenatal and birth psychology has gathered mounting evidence of very early sentience, intelligence, learning, and memory. Alongside anecdotal accounts from clients and practitioners, research has grown, conducted by psychologists and graduate students meeting the need to learn more about this influential time of life. Researchers investigating perception, learning, and memory have also refined their methods to be more relevant for toddlers, preverbal babies, and even newborns.

The age at which we are assumed to begin learning about our environment has become increasingly younger. Shifting perspective slightly, we can now also include cellular consciousness and energetic communication to help explain how people can remember their experience of conception or even before that, being an egg or sperm, or the spirit preparing to enter the physical. These experiences are not remembered explicitly as you would a trip to the grocery store or your first romance, since they arose before the ability to translate them into words.

PRE- AND PERINATAL MEMORY

How often have you talked about what you experienced in the womb? Like with the action riding a bicycle, these nonverbal memories are recorded in the body. This is called procedural memory and allows us to perform physical tasks without conscious awareness. Pre- and perinatal memories are similarly stored in the body. These are a form of implicit memory, which, as mentioned earlier in this book, isn't held in the conscious, verbal mind. Psychologists who claim that we don't remember anything until we develop the ability to talk are focused on declarative or explicit memory, which involve conscious language and enable verbal communication. A specific form of explicit memory, autobiographical memory, does not develop until sometime after the second birthday, as the pre-frontal cortex matures. Autobiographical memory enables us to have a sense of time and sequence which finally allows the child to differentiate between history and present time. Unfortunately, in a culture that values only conscious, verbal, explicit memory, little ones learn that their earliest experiences are devalued and considered fantasy. Implicit memory may be unconscious, but nonetheless can profoundly influence our perceptions, decisions, behaviors, relationships, health, and even personality. Bringing it into consciousness empowers us to live our lives in a more intentional way.

Pre- and perinatal experience is often traumatic as well as unacknowledged. That babies remember these experiences is demonstrated by their behavior and response to words and stimuli. When I work with babies, they are very eager to tell the story of their birth or their time in the womb. They also commonly become unsettled and cry when their parents tell me about how difficult the birth was. These babies are listening, remembering, and expressing how they feel about the experience.

Birth is a big experience, whether traumatic or not. When you have a profound experience, you want to tell someone about it. Usually, when babies try to tell people through the language available to them—crying and body movement—someone tries to hush them. Soothing is helpful but acknowledgment is also essential for health. In my work with babies, I aim to offer compassionate understanding and validation of their experience. Depending on what the baby is expressing, I might reflect to them by saying something like, "I really feel how sad you are." Or "That was really hard for you!" Or "You were scared." Or "Yes, you are really angry!" Typically, the baby will stop crying for a moment and look me in the eye, as if to say, "Oh, you understand! You see me!" Then, if they have more to express, they continue, checking in with me and their mother every so often with eye contact, as if to make sure we are following the story. They demonstrate through their movement how they negotiated the birth canal. They respond to parents talking about stresses before or during the birth, often by fussing or crying. They were there, too. They also experienced the stress. Acknowledging that the baby also has feelings about this usually results in them making eye contact and either settling or completing what they need to express. This frequently appears to dramatically resolve bonding and feeding issues. Having opportunities to express and process feelings during the day also supports more sleep at night. Otherwise, these memories tend to arise in the relative quiet when the family is trying to sleep. Being left alone in bed, as occurs for so many unfortunate babies, can also resonate with a terrifying sense of abandonment or loss if mother and baby were separated for some time just after the birth.

⌁ Finding Her Way to Cuddles ⌁

Becca came to me as a six-year-old with multiple behavioral issues and trouble sleeping. Although her parents were devoted to her, she was rushed to the Neonatal Intensive Care Unit (NICU) within moments of being born where they were not allowed to cuddle her for the first month. In her sessions, Becca repeatedly played with a little stuffed dog, which she enjoyed holding closely and then pushing through small birth-like spaces. Eventually, she felt ready to take the dog's place, curling up in fetal position surrounded by cushions, where she rested deeply, assisted by Craniosacral therapy. When she finally birthed herself out from the cushions, her mother was there to receive her with abundant cuddling. Having been able to push herself out of the womb in her own timing during her play provided a more secure ground from which to act in her everyday life. This initially caused her behavioral issues to become stronger as she seemed to feel more confidence in herself. But over time, Becca was able to process her traumatic separation from her mother at birth and began to sleep more soundly and her behavioral issues began to settle.

We all have a need to tell our stories. Where there is unresolved trauma, there is a further need to integrate the experience through behavior, nervous system activation, and emotional expression. These expressions may be ignored. Babies are quieted by putting a breast or pacifier in their mouth. Toddlers are told not to talk such nonsense or are distracted by presenting an interesting toy or food. In the process, important traumatic memories may be suppressed (as well as possibly generating habits of eating or stuffing something in the mouth when upset, which can lay a foundation for later addictions).

Repressing these important memories becomes necessary for the individual to function in the shadowy culture within which they live. These excluded memories present in the body through our posture, tension, inflammation, tendencies toward injury, as well as our behaviors. We act out our unconscious history as a way to keep it alive. The Health in us is always seeking to express itself and discover pathways to healing. It is not unusual for overwhelming birth pressure on the cranium to be recapitulated through repeated injuries in the exact part of the head affected at birth.

Shadow endeavors to be acknowledged. I once knew an exhibitionist who told me that on some level he wanted to be arrested. To arrest means to stop. Each time he was arrested, it stopped him in a way he could not stop himself. It also made it less possible to ignore his addiction, which kindled his desire to heal. He could then address the early emotional wounding he was avoiding through the addiction.

Shadow material longs for the light. It yearns to be seen. The hidden parts of us are like long lost children terrified of being discovered but still craving the love they haven't received. If we were to open a door and discover one of these children, they might kick and scream if we held them close. After some time, they would settle and begin to cuddle into us. This is what they have been waiting for. What is waiting in your shadows?

PRENATAL DEVELOPMENT AND AWARENESS

What might the little one be aware of? We have already reviewed their often-unacknowledged abilities to sense and respond to their environment, which is heavily influenced by their mother's surround. Cell biologist Bruce Lipton has noted that prenates' preparation to live in their mother's world is informed by her perception, particularly her sense of threat or safety and support.[1] Cells can function in either a defensive, protective or growth mode, but not both simultaneously. This is also true for the cellular communities of which we are composed.

At the level of the nervous system, we also can be in a defensive nervous system state, usually known as fight, flight, freeze or submit/collapse. Stephen Porges, mentioned earlier, has developed polyvagal theory and identified the social engagement nervous system, associated with the ventral vagus nerve. He notes that this most recently evolved aspect of the autonomic nervous system needs to be operating for us to perceive safety.[2] Someone locked in a trauma pattern of sympathetic fight/flight or protective parasympathetic (dorsal vagal) freeze, dissociation, submit or collapse, is unable to perceive safety and, being oriented to danger, may misinterpret friendly gestures as threatening. Porges would say that our nervous system detecting danger is not actually perception but what he calls neuroception.[3] This is a neural process functioning without our conscious awareness. If it detects danger, it quickly triggers a defensive reaction. However, we can learn to consciously activate the social engagement system to establish a sense of safety.

The social engagement system is important in bonding. It facilitates self-regulation, communication, sucking, swallowing, and bonding after birth. It enables us to enjoy touch, eye contact, and other social gestures. For mothers, the social engagement system can support their relationship with their baby early on, including during pregnancy. For babies, this system is just beginning to develop late in the second trimester. Below, we will discuss the evolution of physiological components of the prenatal nervous system, and their psycho-social impact.

Components of the autonomic (automatic) nervous system arise in the embryo in order of their evolutionary development. The oldest unmyelinated vagus (parasympathetic) first appears in the brain stem at 9 weeks gestation (7 weeks after conception), with its nerve centers considered to be mature at 28 weeks. The sympathetic nervous system is believed to be active and available to do its job of accelerating the heart rate by 16–20 weeks gestation, evidenced by how heart rate increases with fetal activity at that time.[4]

The nerve center of the newest myelinated vagus appears by 8 or 9-weeks' gestation. Although its neurons mature by 12.5 weeks, they have yet to reach their target tissues in the heart, preventing their regulatory effect until myelination of these vagal nerve fibers begins at 23 weeks. Myelin is a fatty sheath around nerves that insulates the nerve rendering its conduction more efficient. Myelination, the laying down of myelin around the nerves, increases during the subsequent weeks of pregnancy and continues actively through the first year after birth.[5] This means that the social nervous system begins functioning from 23 weeks on but is still not fully developed at birth.

This reveals how the little one in the womb might be able to detect and react to safety or threat. The oldest parasympathetic system can only respond to threat by shutting down. The individual becomes less present, dissociated, less able to feel the pain in case this threat means death. Think of an animal "playing dead," when attacked. This system is present by 7 weeks after conception. This withdrawal reaction to threat is reminiscent of what is seen on a cellular level. That cells and unicellular organisms can retract from perceived danger may explain reported fear reactions long before 7 weeks. Remember that we begin at conception as a unicellular organism and that the sperm and egg uniting at that time have also had experiences in their journey as cells.

As the embryo evolves and the sympathetic and social engagement systems develop, little ones could continue to easily slip into parasympathetic states of shut down. They may try to socially engage once this system is available but too often their cries for help or contact are not understood and responded to. Babies may be left to "cry it out." When social engagement doesn't work, we humans naturally shift into a sympathetic response. Babies, even in the womb, may experience the activation of a sympathetic arousal but, being too little to fight or flee, their only option is to shut down. Similarly, they may try to communicate with their mother or others. These efforts may be missed by parents not expecting an infant capable of this.

Prenatal trauma is therefore unlikely to be processed until much later, if at all. It is held in the nervous system, accompanied by a tendency to dissociate. We might consider this an autonomic shadow. In pre- and perinatal therapy, we find that people easily enter a "little one state" where their nervous system responds as if they were still very little, as implicit memory is triggered. If they tend to withdraw, shut down, and dissociate, they need support to orient to present time, remembering their current age with all their current resources. Their social nervous system then becomes available again. Little ones who experience this kind of trauma and these nervous system responses will often tend to repeat these patterns as they grow. Their bodies hold onto the memories of the trauma and their health finds ways to express it physically.

SOMATIC EXPRESSIONS OF SHADOW:
BODY MEMORY

Carl Jung differed from his teacher, Sigmund Freud, in his views of the unconscious, which Jung perceived was held in shadow. Jung appreciated that shadow was generally not expressed or met directly through our everyday states of consciousness. He saw creative expression as a helpful way to meet shadow through what he called active imagination. My introduction to this territory was through the meditative movement practice mentioned earlier called Authentic Movement, initially developed by Mary Whitehouse and further refined by her students, Janet Adler and Joan Chodorow.[6] Whitehouse was both a Jungian therapist and a dancer. While writing my master's thesis, which involved observing prenatal and birth themes in authentic movement, I discovered that they arose frequently, both in the clients' movements and in their reports of what they were experiencing.

One of the most common positions arising from participants in my Authentic Movement groups was the fetal position. The mover would curl up on the floor, usually with eyes closed, lying still for a very long time or slowly reaching or stretching out. This fluid movement was very reminiscent of how little ones move in the watery environment of the womb. Sometimes two movers would curl up together. They would often know of having had or lost a twin in the womb or believe this was true for them. In one group, several women who had been curled up together—some next to each other and some intertwined—for most of the movement time all described a similar feeling in our discussion group after the movement. They felt they had been with their sisters in the ovary. Some felt happy to be there while others felt sad because they had to leave the ovary.

Birth also frequently presented in these groups. The mover would usually begin in the fetal position and inchworm their way across the room with eyes closed (eyes are often closed in Authentic Movement to enable listening within) to where they would begin moving under a chair. They might become stuck, as they were in the birth canal, and, with much effort, eventually find their way through with an emotional release. They would often talk about feeling like they were in the birth canal when we spoke after the movement. I was fascinated by these themes presenting every week in my groups. They also arose in individual therapy sessions, such as the one described earlier with Susan (see pages 26–28). Others, such as Tina Stromsted, have also described pre-natal and birth themes emerging in their Authentic Movement work.[7]

Our bodies hold and attempt to communicate our preverbal memories. Posture, asymmetries in face and body, gestures, and movement patterns often relate to birth. These can tell stories of challenges in negotiating the birth canal, as well as experiences before birth. These are easily visible to those trained in certain birth therapies but usually invisible to those in the person's life. These signs can present at any age.

A preborn can be observed responding to stimulation from outside the womb with body movements. Parallel to many parents' observations, research has noted that a gentle tapping on the bump can be responded to with kicking.[8] A baby in the womb may react to music with rhythmic movements, showing very different responses to classical music vs. hard rock. They may also answer maternal distress with agitated movements and quiet with maternal reassurance. They may roll in the direction of sound or light pressed against the mother's belly. Like babies after birth, little ones in the womb are learning and remembering through their body. For those who are alert to their reenactment, this is clearly demonstrated by their later behavior. For example, one fascinating study observed twins in the womb via ultrasound and continued the observation after birth. Prenatally, they seemed to be playing with each other through the membranes between them. A favorite game as toddlers was to play in a similar way through a curtain.[9]

Babies readily demonstrate how they moved through the birth canal, as well as aspects of their prenatal experience, through their bodily movement. When working with babies, I often observe them recognizing that I can understand their birth story, and they immediately communicate this with their bodies. Part of my job is to acknowledge what they are showing me, including the emotions expressed, and help the parents to also perceive and understand this as communication.

∼ It Was Hard ∼

Max was one year old when his mother, Jane, brought him to me
for Craniosacral therapy. She was concerned that he cried so much

and needed so much comforting. She told me about how Max's birth began well with the midwife present. At Stage Two, the labor became difficult. After a two-hour wait for the ambulance, they were rushed to the hospital, where a spinal block, episiotomy, and forceps were used to facilitate the birth.

We began the session, as I often do with babies, with Max on mom's lap, where he could feel safe, and me making contact with her to help her to settle. As usual, this helped the baby to also settle. Max smiled as he settled. I made some gentle contact with Max's lower back and different parts of his cranium, noting that Max was holding his head turned to the left. When I asked Jane if this was common, she told me that he slept in that position. During the session, I felt his nervous system releasing a previously held charge and further settling. Jane then described how he would cry in the late evening.

When I asked about the timing of her labor and birth, she explained that she had been pushing for about four hours when they went to the hospital at 1 a.m. Doing some quick arithmetic, we realized that the difficulties with pushing would have been happening from around 9 p.m., corelating to the time Max regularly became agitated. In response to her story, I acknowledged how hard it was to have the midwife telling her to keep pushing, and then to have to go to the hospital. Max stirred as we talked about this but did not cry. Jane reported that he was generally much more relaxed and less upset in the evenings following this first session though he still had some crying and colic at that time of day.

During the second session, we took some time to talk more about how it was when Jane was pushing hard. Jane thought resentfully that the midwife was more anxious than she was. Max watched us and whimpered as we talked. I could see that he was having some of his own emotions about this stage of the labor. As I held his head, I could feel a force releasing from the left side, where forceps would have been applied, perhaps relating to his tendency to turn his head in that direction. Max then began to cry. This cry sounded angry to both Jane and me. She acknowledged that this was what he did in the evenings.

As we talked, Max clearly responded to everything I said, as I reflected how hard it was, and how he didn't like the feeling of the forceps. I helped Jane to acknowledge it was hard for her too and supported her in talking about how she would have wanted it to be, a gentle birth at home with a supportive midwife. At this, Max began pushing with his feet. Like babies do, he was resonating with his mother's feelings as they were being spoken. I met his push with my hand, giving him something to push against, and then guided Jane in how to also do this. He settled in response and then began pushing harder, making progress across Jane's lap.

He maintained eye contact with me as I continued to reflect how he was pushing himself and moving forward. His eye contact told me he was present, not lost in the trauma he was expressing. He then began peeking at Jane and found his way to her breast. After settling there for a while, he became restless and began pushing again with his feet. When I suggested that he didn't have to do it all at once, he rested. He went through a few cycles like this and then went to sleep when I suggested that he could rest, that I would be happy to hear more of the story another time.

After this session, Jane reported that Max was much more relaxed and no longer having the evening colic and crying spells. He seemed to have been able to tell his side of the story as she told hers. She had also learned through the sessions to recognize the emotions her son was expressing and to respond by acknowledging with words what he was feeling.

Once the baby can tell their story and have it received, they are often able to rest contentedly. This is also a key to bonding. Without the reflection, they tell the story repeatedly through endless crying, restlessness, difficulty breastfeeding, and so on. Some people believe that is always due to colic or teething and therefore "normal" behavior for babies. Once one witnesses how quickly such behavior can change when the baby is seen as trying to communicate something, the belief that this behavior is normal becomes less tenable. It may be seen as an expression of a cultural shadow within a collective that doesn't perceive prenates and newborns as conscious, intelligent beings, capable of communicating.

EARLY SENTIENCE

Embryos, whose existence is often not even acknowledged until their heartbeat is detectable the fourth week after conception, are exquisitely sensitive, highly responsive beings. Even on a cellular level, there is receptivity to the surrounding environment. Every cell has a level of awareness enabling it to respond appropriately to its context. In embryology, there is an understanding that cells developing in a heart field are influenced by surrounding cells to become heart cells. Those in a different field become skin, muscle, bone, brain, or other organs depending on what is around them. Cells also remember what they have encountered. Our immune system could not function without such memory and the ability to create receptor sites in response to the experience of having met substances perceived as toxic or threatening. Unicellular organisms are also known to withdraw or contract in reaction to toxins or other dangers around them.

We begin a new life as a unicellular organism once the egg and sperm have united to become a zygote, a process involving them communicating with each other. Even before conception, the egg and the sperm are cells having experiences which can be reenacted throughout life. For example, I have encountered people born via in vitro fertilization (IVF) who were frozen as sperm or egg and always feel cold.

As gametes (sperm and eggs) are developing, they are exposed to the environment of the mother's or father's body and all that the parents carry in their minds and tissues. All the eggs in a female fetus are present by five months after conception. One of those eggs meets a sperm many years later, carrying the influence and memories of that time inside the mother.

Sperm are also affected by the father's experience. For example, paternal lifestyle choices, including alcohol, tobacco, and nutrition before conception have been associated with problems with fertility, risk of miscarriage, birth defects, and diseases like leukemia and heart disease.[10] If parents began smoking pre-puberty, their children's health can be affected, and even a grandparent's history of smoking is associated with aspects of their grandchildren's health.[11] For example, when young boys start smoking before their sperm develop in puberty, their granddaughters and even great-granddaughters tend to have excess body fat at age seventeen.[12]

These preconception influences affect the environment of the sperm and egg before conception. With conception, the sperm and egg bring these experiences together in a somatic, nonverbal memory, held in the cells and tissues. Once the zygote is formed, the sensorial experience and nonverbal memory continues to develop. I have heard that the embryo can detect sound by 22 days, long before the ears develop.[13] The faculty of hearing begins with the skin and the vestibular system.[14] The embryo is bathed in the vibrations of sound of the mother's world, resonating in the cells and influencing embryonic shaping. We are also sensitive to light before the eyes form, and scientists are discovering this sensitivity develops much earlier than previously believed.[15] Recent research suggests that senses of sight and touch are connected in the fetal brain.[16] Touch is thought to develop first, around 8 weeks.[17] Fetuses have been found to respond to invitational touch through haptomony (a practice using touch to establish relationship) as early as 5 weeks after conception (7 weeks gestational age) and may request contact by tapping from inside the womb a few weeks later.[18]

Neuropsychologists are now challenging our collective belief that we have 5 senses and suggesting that we may have as many as 22 or 33 different senses, including what we commonly call a "sixth sense."[19] If we don't even know how many senses we have, how would we know when they develop? Babies in the womb are evidently psychic or sensing the world around them in physically impossible ways. This is reminiscent of people who have survived near-death experiences reporting details of conversations about them held outside their hospital room or other medical details they could not otherwise be cognizant of. Similarly, a child might describe a house they lived in as a prenate, even though the family had moved out of it before the child's birth and had not visited it since or spoken of it to the child.[20] What else might we be sensing embryonically that we do not even have names for in our very active outer adult world?

How can so much experience be denied, ignored, relegated to unconscious shadow?

PRE-UMBILICAL TRAUMA

⌁ Remembering the Sperm ⌁

Lily, a client in her thirties, went through an egg-like phase of lying quietly in an Authentic Movement group, waiting for something important to happen. Then, as she rested, someone moving quickly across the room would suddenly crash into her before I could alert them to what was about to happen. (Since Authentic Movement is often done with eyes closed, movers are instructed to open them if they are moving quickly to avoid accidents.) Although no one was hurt, Lily found herself crying uncontrollably. She later described how she had felt violated, which she equated with how her father had imposed sex on her young mother, who hadn't been ready for it. She felt her emotional outburst was an expression of her mother's fright and hurt at the time. Lily also believed that the violent, involuntary nature of her conception helped to predispose her to being sexually abused as a child. Not surprisingly, she felt shut down sexually when she tried to have a relationship.

In our individual work together, Lily also had an opportunity to embody her healthy sperm energy. This is the original potential that had been lost in the trauma. I guided her in choosing an object across the room to aim for and put on some lively music. Lily then followed her own impulses to move in a bouncy, wriggly way across the room toward the physio ball she had chosen, representing her egg. As she danced, Lily began to giggle and enjoy herself. She had never expected to find joy associated with being a sperm. After this session, Lily began to find herself having more energy in life. She felt more present and even felt some sexual urges that had long been dormant. She began to feel hope of finally finding a boyfriend.

Even before the umbilical cord and placenta develop, little ones can have traumatic experiences. For example, it is not unusual for people to report a sense or memory of trauma at conception. A sperm may have felt engulfed by the egg, or the egg may have experienced a violent rape-like penetration by the sperm. As the unicellular organism, or zygote, floats down the oviduct, there may be a sense of obstacles to overcome or toxic maternal energy around them. As the zygote subdivides and becomes a multi-cellular blastocyst, it is contained and protected by a relatively tough membrane called the zona pellucida. By about five to seven days after conception, the blastocyst is running out of food and needs to implant, or nest into the uterine wall, to survive.

Implantation requires "hatching" out of the zona pellucida, rendering the blastocyst more exposed and vulnerable, but also capable

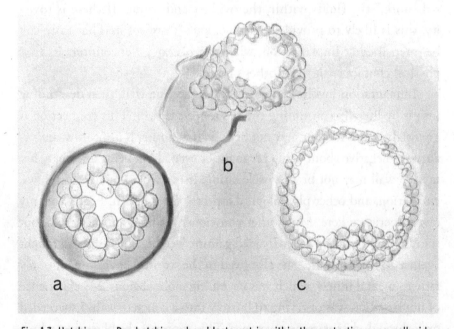

Fig. 1.3. Hatching: a. Pre-hatching when blastocyst is within the protective zona pellucida, b. Hatching out of the zona pellucida, c. Blastula (blastocyst after hatching)

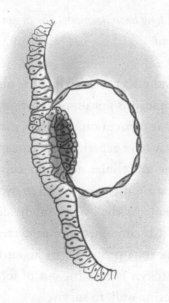

Fig. 1.4. Implantation. The embryo on the right is adhering and beginning to eat into the uterine wall on the left.

of making contact with and attaching to the uterine wall. Many people report a memory of "blastocyst bliss" prior to hatching. Then, as if their bubble has burst, they find themselves in direct contact with the maternal "milk," the fluids within the oviduct and womb. If there is toxicity, this is likely to provide a first noxious "taste" of it. That taste can be intensified at implantation, when the blastocyst encounters its first physical contact with the mother's body.

Implantation involves adhering to the uterine wall, then descending into it by literally consuming the tissues of the wall. This connection is essential for survival but may not be easy. If a mother is unhealthy, ambivalent, or negative about being pregnant or even about being a woman, her uterine wall may not be very welcoming. It is affected by her hormones, circulation, and other physiological aspects of her health. I can share my own experience here. My mother consciously wanted another child, but she also hated her body and dreaded gaining weight, which she had fought against all her adult life. She also lived in the stressful environment of my father's mental illness, which was becoming more obvious. My experience of implantation was of trying to burrow into a concrete wall. I succeeded only through desperate perseverance. This contrasts the blueprint, which is to be received by a soft, plush surface we can nest in.

It is not unusual for implantation to be difficult to achieve. Many babies die at this early time in pregnancy.

This is a good time to pause, take a breath, feel your feet, and acknowledge that you survived this time, or you wouldn't be here reading this page!

If you are interested in connecting further to your own experience of implantation, please take a moment to look at the exercise I've included below. Take this time to reflect on your experiences and reconnect with yourself before continuing.

EXPLORATION
✒ Implantation ✒

A Nourishing Home

Implantation involves the embryo adhering to and entering into the wall of the womb, which then becomes a source of nourishment and support. You can explore what implantation may have been like for you and how you would like it to be now (accessing original potential) by creating a nest and cuddling into it. You can make a comfortable womb for yourself from cushions and blankets.

Observing

Is it easy for you to connect with the soft support? Which part or parts of your body do you make that contact with? Many people experience implantation with the forehead but embryologically, we actually connect through what becomes the back side of the embryo.

How is it for you to have an intention to make contact and rest into the cushions? Do they feel welcoming? Do you feel safe there? Is there something that can help you to rest more deeply? Can you allow yourself to just be there for some time?

Explore

In that implantation is originally about finding necessary nourishment, you might inquire into any sensations of hunger or satisfaction as you explore. Perhaps you want to have some favorite food available as you rest. How welcoming and comfortable can you make this womb? How familiar is this experience?

You may want to explore the relational aspect of implantation through interacting with another person. This could be a therapist or someone else you trust and feel comfortable with. It may be helpful to have a cushion leaning against the person so that you can nestle into their support. Listen to your own timing. Again, do you feel safe? Do you feel welcomed? Perhaps your person has some welcoming words to say to you. Maybe you want them to hold or stroke you. What feels right to you?

I suggest staying in contact as long as it feels good to you. In that you are not a hungry embryo now, you are not dependent on this person or these cushions for survival. You can be in charge of the contact and how long it lasts.

Be gentle with yourself both moving into and out of contact. Take some time afterward to orient yourself to the space you are in. Look around and see the colors and shapes in the room you are in. Look out the window. Make eye contact if you are with another person, if it feels comfortable to do so.

As usual, it can be helpful to take some time to journal about your experience. What information do you receive about how your implantation was in the womb?

Some prenatal therapists consider the double bind nature of the implantation time as being the root of eating disorders and other addictions.[21] The experience of challenging, unwelcoming, or toxic implantation can also establish patterns for how we seek and settle into relationships and living situations.

Before resolving this aspect of my own history through prenatal therapy, I used to move house constantly, sometimes more than once in the span of a year. This was before the days of digital address books. My poor friends would complain about how I had filled their entire address book because I kept moving. I didn't know the feeling of having a safe, welcoming home I could relax in. Fortunately, this has changed. I am still amazed that at the time of this writing I have lived in the same house (and been in the same relationship) for almost fifteen years. This is in complete contrast to my earlier life. I have finally implanted!

One reason implantation challenges can be so traumatizing is that humans, even as little blastocysts, require connection. It may be easier to see the physiological necessity. Without the connection with mother through implantation, the embryo dies. Little ones also thrive on the emotional connection characterizing the mother-child relationship. Although at this early time of implantation, the mother is usually not aware of her baby's existence, the little one senses and responds to a sense of welcome, expectation, ambivalence, or rejection. Welcome means safety and protection ensuring survival. Little ones appropriately dread maternal ambivalence and rejection. I have worked with many adults who continue to live their lives as if in hiding, afraid to be discovered and rejected.

A more reliably supportive connection is that of Source or Cosmos. This is also essential for health and well-being, often acknowledged for adults as a need for spiritual practice. For little ones, there is the memory of where they came from. There is the fluid resonance with Cosmic frequencies, connecting them with all that is. For many with very early trauma, dissociating from their bodies has enabled them to continue in an otherwise painful life. Dissociation often includes an experience of being connected with a realm beyond the physical, characterized by love and light. This is a way to stay connected with Source, even when life in a body is unbearable. The spiritual connection may serve as a major resource where human connections are not as nurturing.

Sadly, many of us experience a loss of connection with Source as we come into the physical. This can occur as early as conception. Pre- and perinatal therapy pioneer William R. Emerson taught me about Divine homesickness, experienced by the little one missing and often reaching back toward their source. Divine betrayal is a different form of loss of connection with the Divine.[22] Here the little one feels betrayed or tricked into entering life. There may be a sense of having been promised a different kind of life. What we arrive into often isn't as welcoming or rosy as we had expected, and our families may not be people we can feel connected to or supported by. Little ones sense this very early on.

If one had a twin who was supposed to accompany them, there may resentment, or a feeling of betrayal or abandonment. In that pregnancy is usually discovered later, such early loss of a child tends to be unacknowledged. The surviving twin is usually the only one aware of the loss. The grief that often follows them through life is usually never acknowledged. This shadowy grief can understandably lay a foundation for depressive tendencies. Survivor guilt is also common. The surviving twin feels responsible for their sibling's death or is driven to live for two. They may experience gnawing guilt, shame, and grief without being able to understand its source. They may also resonate with the pain and terror their dying twin probably experienced, and confuse those emotions for their own. All these feelings tend to be greater if the twins were identical, having started out as one unicellular organism, sharing one body. The surviving twin may also tend to create twin dynamics with people in their life. For example, they may quickly attach in a romantic relationship, feeling this is the person they have been missing all their life, only to be disappointed when they discover their partner is not as they had imagined. Or they may feel more comfortable always doing things with one other person.

The shadowy effects of twin loss can also apply when a twin dies later in gestation. Even if the dead twin's existence is acknowledged, parents and medical practitioners rarely consider that the surviving twin would have feelings about this. After all, babies aren't conscious before they can speak, or before they are born, or whatever it is they believe. It is often extremely healing in therapy to create and conduct a ritual celebrating and consciously grieving the lost twin. Just acknowledging the loss can be healing. That so many of us have experienced twin loss is reflected by how frequently the issue arises in pre- and perinatal therapy. I can report that this issue arises in essentially every womb surround process workshop I facilitate, often for more than one participant.

PRENATAL DEVELOPMENTAL MILESTONES

Difficult emotions and conditions may relate to significant prenatal developmental milestones. Like milestones of postnatal development, such as lifting the head, rolling, crawling (or creeping), standing, walking, and talking, babies before birth develop through meeting challenges arising at different stages. Parents and birth practitioners appreciate prenatal development, hopefully celebrating when pregnancy is confirmed, when they can feel or see on ultrasound the baby's first movements, their positioning in preparation for birth, and so on. The little one has their own perspective. They have already passed through several developmental milestones by the time their existence is discovered.

The life-death challenges of implantation, already mentioned, are preceded by other developmental milestones laying a foundation for developing a placental connection with the mother. These include conception, successfully journeying to the womb, hatching from the zona pellucida, and cell subdivision and differentiation. As described, implantation occurs under pressure as the blastocyst runs the risk of starving to death. Each of us reading this book has passed these essential milestones and may carry imprints of difficult conditions encountered.

Once we have implanted, our next major milestone is being discovered. I often heard William R. Emerson define discovery as the time when the pregnancy is confirmed through a pregnancy test. Although some mothers or couples are aware of conception the moment it happens, most depend on a test. Discovery tends to happen around the time the heart starts beating, approximately Day 22. I have heard Emerson frequently declare that anything less than celebration at the time of discovery is shocking for the little one. This shock tends to be held in the body region developing at the time—the chest and heart.

People who met ambivalence or rejection upon discovery often develop a caved in posture, protecting their wounded heart. As an example, I would like to bring back Maria, the adopted woman described earlier. In addition to her rapid speech and tendency to breathe very shallowly, Maria held tension in her chest, which was visible in her hunched posture. Being unplanned and unwanted, her time of discovery was characterized by shock and terror. Biologically, she needed her mother to accept, welcome, and protect her for survival. Although she did survive, Maria lived with a fear of being seen and a need to be heard, which contributed to her pressured speech. The tension in her chest restricted her breath. She took in just enough breath in a way that reflected her prenatal experience of demanding just enough to get by so as not to be even more fully rejected.

Little ones may have a sense that they will be rejected and try to avoid this by staying as small as possible. This can become a personality trait. They may wonder why no one seems to listen or pay attention to them. A child with this history might avoid speaking in class or find the teacher ignores them when they raise their hand.

I frequently meet discovery issues while supervising new practitioners who are ambivalent or even terrified to let people know that they and their services exist. Exploring the source of this resistance to being seen, we often come to how they felt rejected by their parents in some way when the pregnancy was discovered. After processing this, it becomes easier to create their website, post on social media, or distribute business cards.

Those with an opposite reaction to prenatal rejection may puff their chest out as if trying to overcome their early wound. Whether the chest is caved in or puffed out, there is tension in the tissues. There is a natural tendency to want to hide, but the person defends themselves from this sense of vulnerability by tending to be or experience themselves as invincible. Some try to do this by being obnoxiously out there. We all know the type!

Discovery is one of the most important milestones and commonly is not a time of celebration. Consider that most conceptions are unplanned.[23] Even parents wanting a child may have a moment of shock, disbelief, or ambivalence upon discovering the pregnancy. I have worked with so many parents who tell me they just wanted to take that one trip to Tibet, finish their education, become more established in their work or their relationship, or be more financially stable, before having a baby.

Often parents move past their ambivalence and celebrate by the time the baby is born. This is helpful but the initial wound remains.

Babies' survival is completely dependent on acceptance, love, and protection from their parents. Without these, the embryo senses danger. The threat may be further enacted through abortion attempts or ideation, or later adoption. Survivors of abortion attempts understandably tend to live their lives in a hypervigilant state. Maria's rapid speech was an expression of this hypervigilance, involving sympathetic nervous system activation and associated difficulty in pausing or resting. Fortunately, prenatal therapy, which includes acknowledging the trauma and providing a different, safe, welcoming surround, can be profoundly healing. Repair from parents can also be helpful at any age, the earlier the better. Consider how healing it could be for an adopted person to finally meet their birth mother and learn that she regrets giving them up.

Once our existence has been discovered, development can proceed relatively smoothly. The main traumas that occur relate to the mother's challenges or other external conditions. For example, in the late 1950s and early 1960s, mothers were encouraged to take a new drug, thalidomide, to ease nausea. If taken at the time the limbs were developing, babies were born with limbs or parts of limbs missing. Other toxic substances the mother ingests or is exposed to also have their effects, contributing to umbilical toxicity, discussed in more detail later in this book. This situation creates a potentially life-threatening double bind for the baby who is completely dependent on the umbilical cord for nourishment. Food arriving with toxicity stimulates a natural repulsion. Babies have been seen on an ultrasound trying to squeeze the umbilical cord, apparently to protect themselves against this toxicity. This solution isn't tenable because they need the incoming nourishment to survive.[24] Babies also react to toxic intake in the form of alcohol or drugs, as well as very stressful events, by stopping their movement for an extended period of time.[25]

A double bind experience early in life tends to contribute to a person's perceptions and actions later on. Recapitulative forces unconsciously attempt to resolve the early trauma. This often occurs relationally, replaying the dilemma of needing love and acceptance but experiencing rejection, abuse, or toxicity. The early experience of needing to accept toxic nourishment as a fetus can establish lifelong challenges with setting and protecting personal boundaries. Again, acknowledging the original trauma lifts the double bind dynamic out of shadow, enabling conscious healing to occur.

Examples of survival-related double binds are unfortunately abundant on 21st century planet Earth. Consider our dependence on Mother Earth for food, air, water, and other resources. With human mistreatment, these have become less available or more contaminated. We begin to question how long we can survive on this planet, creating an echo of prenatal toxicity.

LANGUAGE AND PRE- AND PERINATAL SHADOW

Another way that prenatal and birth experiences are relegated to shadow is how we talk, or rather don't talk, about them in our modern culture. Babies rapidly learn about the world, even in the womb. By 20 to 25 weeks their ears and hearing are well-developed. They intelligently listen to and respond to sounds arriving from their mother's world. This includes the language she speaks. Babies at birth clearly recognize and attend to their mother's voice.[26] For example, a baby whose mother has read Dr. Seuss to them in the womb responds after birth to a recording of their mother reading this story, demonstrating preference for their mother's voice and this story by sucking more on a special pacifier that measures their sucking rate. In the study, babies sucked less with unfamiliar stories, indicating they were bored. Similarly, babies recognize music they have heard prenatally.

In age-appropriate research, like that mentioned in the previous paragraph, newborns demonstrate their preferences by sucking on a non-nutritive nipple at the speed that selects their preference.[27] As a sign of recognition, hearing the mother's voice has also been found to stabilize preterm babies' conditions.[28] Newborns also demonstrate different neurological responses to emotional prosodies in their mother's tongue compared to a foreign language. This suggests they have already learned these differences before birth.[29]

Inspired by research findings on prenatal learning, programs have been developed to teach babies before they are born, although some of the skills offered, like mathematics, are of questionable value for a prenate. The belief is that this early learning supports learning later, including in school.

As part of acculturation, children learn to not perceive certain sounds, and orient only to those of the language around them. Before about age eleven, children can readily learn any language.[30] After that, they have trouble hearing sounds of other languages that are not used in their native tongue. I remember a Chinese friend in university trying to teach me Mandarin. He would say something, and I would repeat it after him, thinking I had said it perfectly. "No, no, no!" he would impatiently respond and say it again. This would go on for a long time until we both gave up. It was impossible for me to hear the nuances he was trying to get me to copy. Even at eighteen, I was too old for this to be easy for me.

Our learning to selectively perceive does not just include sounds of languages. The way we talk about things instructs the little one about what is and is not considered reality. As mentioned earlier, toddlers often try to tell their parents their memories of being in the womb, being born, or even of pre-conception when they describe seeing and choosing or being guided toward their parents. Some also talk about past lives. In Western culture, these descriptions may be seen as cute but are not reinforced or engaged in.

Although some parents express curiosity about pre- and perinatal memories, this is much less common in the West. Dr. Ludwig Janus, a German pioneer in pre- and perinatal psychology, begins his book, *Echoes from the Womb: Enduring Effects of Prenatal Experiencing*, with the following:

One of the first big questions that a child asks is about where babies come from. The answer the parents give is crucial for the child's understanding of himself. And, as we all know, the answer is almost always unsatisfactory. Whereas in earlier times recourse was made to fairy tales or mythical powers, that, for example, the child had been delivered by a stork or had grown from a tree, nowadays, in keeping with the scientific spirit of the times, most people try to describe our coming to the light of day in purely biological or physical terms. All questions about the possible significance of the experience of being born are left unasked and unanswered.[31]

Our natural sense of the significance of our earliest experiences is usually not reflected or confirmed by those around us as we are learning to talk and to transmute our preverbal experiences into verbal, consciously accessible understandings. The mystery of our source and purpose remains nameless and readily slips into shadow.

Preverbal memory can function like a dream, as well as presenting in dreams. How often have you had a powerful dream that you couldn't imagine ever forgetting only to find that by morning or the next day it is gone? Dreams can be considered messages from the unconscious mind. Common advice is that putting them into language by writing, drawing, or speaking helps solidify the memory. They then become conscious memories, shifting from the nonverbal to verbal realm. As you read this book, you may want to pay attention to and write down or draw your dreams. The material you are reading may be processed in your dreams, colored by your personal prenatal and birth history. When you record your dreams, you may also find it enlightening to allow yourself to write about them in the form of stream of consciousness, without editing as you write. What do you think the dream means? What might different parts or individuals in the dream represent?

Nonverbal memories are processed differently than our conscious ones. For example, you might easily say, "Yesterday I went to the store and met a friend." You don't have much trouble finding words for that experience. If it is important enough, you are likely to easily recall it. Nonverbal memories are more challenging to put into words. If you know how to ride a bicycle, your body remembers, but how do you describe those instinctual movements? Unless you regularly practice putting the experience into language, you might find yourself struggling.

It is worth noting, however, that preverbal experience, including prenatal and birth memories, can be expressed through what we can call "birth language." Do you ever hear yourself or someone else exclaiming, "I feel so stuck!" "I'll never get through this!" "I'm in a very tight place." "I can't (or can finally) see light at the end of the tunnel." These are all examples of how birth memories may express themselves in language. You might recognize the metaphoric quality of the words. They function symbolically, like images in a dream. Paying attention to such phrases can provide information about the person's experience of their birth.

EPIGENETICS AND SHADOW

We marinate in the shadow (i.e. the denied aspects of the
unconscious) of our parents.
WILIAM R. EMERSON, "SOMATIC THERAPY"

Perhaps the power of these very early experiences is beginning to emerge out of shadow, supported by studies in epigenetics. As well as the influence of fathers and grandfathers, we now know a grandmother's stress can be expressed intergenerationally.[32] For example, daughters of Dutch women who were pregnant during a severe famine at the end of the second world war had a higher than usual risk of being schizophrenic.[33] This may also be true for babies gestating during war.[34]

Evidence of effects of trauma has been observed through changes to a particular gene in Holocaust survivors and their children.[35] In some cases, the second or third generation shows changes opposite to those of their parents, such as when a grandmother has endured starvation and the grandchild is obese, or children of Holocaust survivors showing abnormal stress hormone levels and greater incidence of stress disorders.[36] The child has apparently prepared for traumatic history to repeat itself. Children of drought or starvation survivors, who tend to have extra efficient metabolisms, are well-prepared for the kind of starvation their parents faced but tend toward obesity in a world where food is plentiful.

Conditions and contexts the cell meets can affect genetic activity, causing changes that are passed down for generations of cells and organisms. Sperm, eggs, and little ones in the womb are preparing to live in the world of their parents. Whether the mother perceives her life as safe and supportive or as threatening and unsupportive is communicated to her unborn baby biochemically and probably bioenergetically. The baby responds accordingly.

An essential component of our environment as little ones, and even as humans, is love. Babies and children of all ages thrive on love. Little ones can fail to thrive and even die without it. According to psychologist Dorothy Mandel, "Genetically, cells adapt to what they perceive their environment to be. Because an event experienced in the midst of a heart response will be perceived and interpreted very differently than an event experienced in the midst of a stress response, the heart can also powerfully affect genetic expression."[37]

Our collective belief is that cells cannot perceive; they simply react. The same has been said of babies screaming with pain or needing cuddles. Again, we can suspect collective shadow at work. When we look for causes, we tend to examine what is most obvious. Someone who is overweight must be eating too much. Perhaps they have a metabolic disorder. Looking deeper requires shining a light onto what may not be so obvious. Many people may be unaware of an ancestor's relationship to substance use or addiction. As well as transgenerational effects of grandparents smoking as youth, which was already mentioned, grandchildren's mortality has been found to be affected when grandparents faced food shortages, horrors of the Holocaust, or post-war trauma, as occurred for men returning home from prisoner of war camps in the American Civil War in the 1860s.[38]

Epigenetic influences are not often immediately apparent. I am often amazed by how twin studies are still used to "prove" or "demonstrate" genetic influences. Yes, identical twins have the same genes and yes, they develop in the same womb. There may, however, be less apparent differences in the conditions they experience. For example, their position in the womb may affect how much nourishment they receive and how much space they have. On a more psychological level, sometimes only one twin is detected (in ultrasound for example) and expected. The other one remains in shadow. They may feel unwanted, unseen, unimportant, second best, and feel a need to compete for attention. They may fear the reactions of those who finally discover their existence. On the other hand, the twin who is acknowledged may carry their own guilt for being the one that is seen and feel protective of the other. There are many possibilities. Identical twins are not identical. They have many similarities, and share DNA sequences, but their genetic expression may differ depending on how they each perceived their world. The two twins may also have quite different birth experiences. It is not unusual for one twin to be in a breech position. This may result in anxiety and even a caesarean section for the breech baby after the first twin has been born vaginally. These two birth experiences can have profoundly different effects on personality and responses to the world.

BIOENERGETIC DYNAMICS

Little ones in the womb are made up of more than cells and genes. Like all of us, they are also bioenergetic beings who emit energy.[39] We know that the human heart, the first organ to come online in the embryo as early as 22 days after conception, has a huge electromagnetic field. Its bio-electric field is 60 times that of the brain and its bio-magnetic field is 5000 times that of the brain.[40] When I work with pregnant women, I sense the baby inside her as a powerful energetic field, radiating out to fill the entire room. If I don't perceive this, I worry about the health of the child. Energetic radiance is a sign of health.

The massive size of the heart fields means that, when two individuals are close to each other, their heart fields overlap and influence each other. The prenate is as close to the mother and her heart as is possible for two human beings to be. The prenatal heart rate is established and regulated in relation to that of the mother.[41] Heart rate reflects emotional states. In this way, maternal stress or peace can be directly transmitted to the baby she carries. This is also true after birth, when babies tend to and need to stay close to their mother. Research from the HeartMath Institute has found that emotional states affect heart rates, and that personal coherence contributes to the coherence of others. HeartMath research indicates that "as more and more people increase their personal coherence and ability to self-regulate, they benefit themselves and others because their hearts' magnetic fields, which are radiated out into the local environment, become more coherent."[42]

Specifically in relation to babies, HeartMath research implies that "a mother in a psychophysiologically coherent state became more sensitive to the subtle electromagnetic information encoded in the electromagnetic signals of her infant."[43] This increased sensitivity is likely to support mother-infant bonding. Referring to the overlapping heart fields of mother and baby, child development expert and author Joseph Chilton Pearce notes, "The meaning of the fields shared by mother and infant contain a great deal of critical information for both." The energetic communication between them supports their bond. Pearce further explains:

That heart fields interact and entrain is a precise, measurable, scientific fact. The amplitude and the Hertz value of the two heart frequencies become coherent, creating a state of harmony, wholeness and health. When the infant's heart and the mother's heart are entrained, their brain structures also become synchronized. We refer to this balanced state as bonding between mother and infant.[44]

Most of the research refers to babies after birth, but we know that a mother's emotional state prenatally affects the health and state of her unborn baby. Although seldom acknowledged, these energetic connections are part of the mother-baby relationship and contribute to the little one's sense of safety and welcome.

PRE-CONCEPTION BONDING
AND CONSCIOUSNESS

Even before conception, there may be energetic communication between the arriving consciousness and the parents. Those who have received such messages from their yet-to-be conceived child usually have no doubt that an intelligent being has reached out to them. A fascinating book by Elisabeth Hallett, *Soul Trek: Meeting Our Children on Their Way to Birth*, offers copious reports from parents who have seen their child some time before conception. Similar stories have also been described by other authors. Commonly, the child appears as a toddler. Two or three years after the birth, the parent sees that their child looks just as they did in their earlier vision. Whenever I mention these stories in my classes, at least one student comments that they had a similar experience. The child may even have convinced the parent to conceive them. It would be difficult to not experience some sense of bonding when a child has connected in this way.

Wonderful research from the Japanese doctor Akira Ikegawa has collected reports from parents of statements their little children have made to them, usually before they are old enough to learn that these experiences are not to be spoken of. For example, a mother reports her first born telling her when her second child was born, "We were watching mommy from the sky together, and I told him, 'I'll go first' and came."[45] Toddlers also may report having chosen their parents. For example, a two-year old boy whose parents had not conceived until five years after their marriage declared, "I chose my Mummy and Daddy. I was waiting for a very long time."

～ Don't Worry! I'll Be Back! ～

Brenda was the mother of a two-year old who sadly reported a miscarriage during the time we were working together in therapy. Just after the baby died, she had a sense of its soul hovering by her side, stroking her in a soothing way, as if to say, "Don't worry. I'll be back." Some months later, she sensed the same soul floating near her body, reaching out to touch her and then her husband. She felt it getting to know them and their bodies. Not long after this, she felt cramps she associated with implantation. Her little son, who had been speaking about a new little sister for some time, now began describing the sister swimming inside mommy, while he uncharacteristically kissed her belly, as if welcoming the new sister. Note that this happened before a pregnancy test.

These reports of words and actions from innocents evinces consciousness even before conception. If this seems outrageous, please consider the growing evidence, often from medical doctors, of memories from people who have survived near-death experiences (NDEs). As mentioned earlier, survivors may accurately report what medical staff were saying down the hall from their hospital room during surgery or while technically dead.[46] Some aspect of consciousness also seems to be carried by certain organs removed and transplanted into another person, such as when a heart recipient displays changes in personality and preferences resonant with those of the donor.[47] Pre- and perinatal psychology pioneer Dr. Thomas Verny refers to this whole-body intelligence as *The Embodied Mind*, the title of his most recent book.

Evidently, consciousness, learning, intelligence, and memory are not confined to the brain and nervous system and may not even require a physical body! This can help to explain clients' memories from before they had a brain or even were conceived.

∼ Arriving from a Pleasant Space into Terror ∽

Lena had been adopted soon after birth. She was interested in re-visiting her journey into the womb and what had happened when the pregnancy was discovered. Guided to relax and let herself go back in her consciousness to this very early time, just before conception, she described a sense of other energies around her. They were not beings, but she had a sense of pleasant space around her with other energies present. There was no hint of her mother's rejection. Then she felt something like a gust of wind pulling her toward her mother.

Once inside her mother, her space felt crowded by emotions she was unfamiliar with. As an adult, she could identify these as her mother's terror pressing on her. In response, Lena felt herself curling up as small as possible in the womb and not moving, in her attempt to hide and not cause trouble. She was aware of having no escape and had the sense she had been very quiet throughout her time in the womb.

It is to this pre-body consciousness that practices of conscious conception can be directed. Parents hoping to conceive may appeal to the soul or spirit of their future child through ritual, prayer, and psychic communicators, as well as preparing a fertile physical ground by honing their diet and lifestyle.

WHO ARE WE? WHAT IS REALITY?

Learning about pre- and perinatal learning, memory, and intelligence can stimulate questions about the very nature of reality. This questioning is supported by contemporary scientific research exploring our quantum nature. The existence of time and space may be holographic. We may live in parallel universes, or a "multiverse."[48] Some researchers like Jenny Wade have been influenced by the brilliant physicist, David Bohm, declaring that an absolute order, a form of non-biological personhood, precedes and gives rise to the more explicit implicate order, including the individual. Wade writes,

> ... the absolute order is present in its entirety, interpenetrating every point of space and time, so that all of eternity and the cosmos is wholly present right here and right now. At some level then, all the previous and future states of an individual—fetus, infant, child, adolescent, adult, and corpse—coexist with (or without!) embodiment as we usually think of it.[49]

If this is our true nature, occluded by collective shadow that only believes in the material reality, perhaps we can access it more fully by acknowledging all states, including those of the preborn, perhaps even the pre-conceived.

Please be gentle with yourself while considering the questions below. Take your time and remember to breathe and be with what supports you.

Reflections

1. What knowledge do you have about your parents' relationship and life situation when you were in the womb? Where were they? What were they doing in their lives?
2. Do you have a twin? Do you have a twin who did not live. At what point in the pregnancy or postnatal time did the twin leave?
3. Were you premature. How many weeks?
4. Did you have a hospital stay after birth?

   _____ I was in a Neonatal Intensive Care Unit. Please state how long.

   _____ I was incubated. How long?
5. Consider both physical effects (maternal or paternal smoking, drinking, drugs, mom's diet), and emotional effects including absence or presence of father during pregnancy or birth, parents' relationship with each other during your pregnancy, parent loss, grief or trauma during the pregnancy. What do you know of your parents' (and grandparents') lifestyle habits and experiences before or during your time in the womb?
6. If you are adopted, what do you know about transition in hospital and new family as well as any birth history?

3

Orienting to Our Original Embryological Potential

Return to Stillness, Fluidity, and Inherent Health through Somatic Inquiry

> *God speaks to each of us as he makes us,*
> > *then walks with us silently out of the night.*
> *These are the words we dimly hear.*
> *You, sent out beyond your recall,*
> > *go to the limits of your longing.*
> *Embody me.*
> *Flare up like flame*
> > *and make big shadows I can move in.*
> *Let everything happen to you: beauty and terror.*
> *Just keep going. No feeling is final.*
> *Don't let yourself lose me.*
> *Nearby is the country they call life.*
> *You will know it by its seriousness.*
> *Give me your hand.*
>
> > RAINER MARIA RILKE,
> > *BOOK OF HOURS: LOVE POEMS TO GOD*

What is it we emerge from as we enter a new life? There is a sense for many of having come from a very vast expanse. We might call it God, Spirit, Source, Heaven, Cosmos. All of these can have resonances with the sense of existence experienced before entering human life.

When we slow ourselves down and settle our usually very active nervous system, as we do in mindful meditation or perhaps in other contemplative practices like yoga or *Tai Chi*, we tend to experience more spaciousness. We might sense the tissues of our bodies softening and spreading. We perceive more space. We come to a sense of stillness. We might consider this to be our true origin.

Out of the stillness arises an impulse, perhaps a tidal motion, as we sense in Craniosacral Biodynamics, a subtle hands-on bodywork practice evolved from osteopathy. The practice is inspired by key advice from the father of osteopathy, A. T. Still, "To find Health should be the object of the physician. Anyone can find disease."[1] This Health with a capital "H" represents our original potential, often ignored by practitioners orienting to disease and trying to fix the problems presented by their clients.

Biodynamic Craniosacral therapists, like myself, practice settling our own body into relative stillness, and widen our perception to include the client's system. We listen quietly for very subtle bioenergetic rhythms, which we call tides. These are considered expressions of ever-present Health within the system. Biodynamics pioneer Franklyn Sills writes,

If Health is truly perceived, we discover that it is never lost. We find that structure and function are mutually interdependent, that the body is self-healing, self-regulating, and self-integrating. The key to this process of discovery lies in our ability to be present, to be able to deepen and widen our fields of awareness and enter a truly receptive state. It is in the ability to be still and listen that the truth of the human system unfolds its mysteries. As we listen, a true humility arises as we meet the awesome Intelligence within the human condition. This is really the starting point in our journey.[2]

Here Sills refers to what I call our original potential. Our Health is always there, waiting to be revealed, even if it is in shadow. Discovering or supporting it requires listening, intentionally orienting to what is deeper, slower, quieter, and less obvious. Clients generally arrive requesting assistance with their aches, pains, and problems.

~ A Dramatic Return to Health ~

Many years ago an elderly woman was brought to me by her son. His mother, Elsie, had been too depressed to leave the house and needed coaxing to come to the session. She didn't expect to feel better from our work together. She had been in pain due to fibromyalgia for too long and had given up. In our first session, I supported her in being as comfortable as possible lying on the treatment table. Not surprisingly, when I first put my hands on her, I felt strong pulsations in her nervous system activation. As I deepened under these with my attention, I began to sense the pulsations calming. There was some sense now of fluid fluctuations under my hands. These also gradually settled until I began to sense the deeper subtle rhythms we orient to in Craniosacral Biodynamics.

At this point, Elsie appeared to be sleeping, something she had been having great difficulty with due to her intense pain. I could feel held energy discharging from her system during the session as we deepened further into the inherent Health that she had lost touch with. A few days after the session, Elsie's son called me. He was amazed at the change in his mother, reporting that she had felt so much better after the session that she had now gone out to play bridge with her friends. The Health was apparently still strong within her! She just needed some help to reorient to it.

Most of us focus on what is most loudly and obviously demanding our attention. We only pay attention to our bodies when they hurt. We notice our dreams when they scream at us as nightmares. We do our best to keep up with the speed of life, ignoring our inner knowing as we meet demands of work, family, relationships, and so on. What happens to our original potential amid all this activity? For most of us, it crouches in the shadow of our consciousness, perpetually seeking to be noticed, whispering as that inner voice we often are too busy to notice or honor.

My other main practice is Continuum, the mindful somatic inquiry practice developed over almost 50 years by my dear mentor, Emilie Conrad, and her curious, devoted students. I have found that Continuum naturally takes us into subtle perceptual states like those experienced in Biodynamics. Although the orientation in Continuum is not to tidal rhythms, we similarly find ourselves settling into relative states of very slow movement or stillness. Here we often perceive a sense of our original fluid potential. We may even feel like we become a tiny embryo, dissolving our habitual tensions and patterns, and re-forming our physical body. In the process, historically tight tissues soften and reorganize themselves. We may also sense our consciousness melting, as if we can return to the potent pre-brain state of the embryo, floating in a supportive fluid field, sensing vast spaciousness, like the Cosmos.

As we deeply rest in this relative stillness, impulses arise, pulsating as micro-movements, much like those of the embryo in its first dance. We emerge, feeling renewed, rejuvenated, resiliently ready to face life again. We have re-visited our original embryological potential and carry at least some of it with us out of shadow into our lives.

Conrad writes,

A living organism contains a vast potential for innovation by containing an intelligence that can elicit new pathways to optimize internal life processes. What may appear to be frozen and dormant can throb with currents of life, all of it taking place within the profundity of a fluid recapitulation.[3]

This refers to our incredible fluid potential. When we return to a relatively fluid state, as in Continuum or Biodynamics or some other practices, we can remember and access that potential. Conrad maintains that, as we adapt to our world as babies, we gradually lose touch with that "cosmic song."[4] The potential to awaken from our amnesia remains as we slow down, melt, and listen to inherent pulsations still undulating deep within our bodies.

At a simple level, we can perceive the rhythms of our days. We awake usually in the morning and become more active. At night, we go to bed, close our eyes, and return to the unconscious speaking to us in our dreams. Each day is a pulse. We also pulsate through our various activities, relationships, and breath. Between each pulse, there is stillness. Within the stillness lies immense potential. The potential to become. This represents our original potential, available for us to remember and encounter if we are willing.

Consider the complex body you now have, composed of trillions of cells, carefully formed tissues, organs, body parts, all remarkably functional, even when they aren't functioning as perfectly as you might hope. This miracle comes from one unicellular organism, the union of sperm and egg, with its amazing original embryological potential to develop into a highly complex body. That potential has not gone away. Even if we don't sense it in our everyday lives, it is still there and accessible. Our original potential is often an aspect of our shadow material, hidden away behind the form we have taken to adapt to life conditions.

I have included an exercise to help you tune in to your own "pulse" through developing a connection to the Continuum. In Craniosacral Biodynamics, we recognize that an energetic midline or core organizes our cells and tissues both in the embryo and throughout life. This is an expression of our original potential and offers a way to orient to that potential. Continuum is a natural way to explore this. In the following exploration, I have incorporated Continuum into a somatic inquiry into your own sense of midline. Continuum involves making sounds and then listening in what we call "open attention" to how our body tissues receive the gift we have just offered them through the vibrations of the sound. I consider Continuum to be a somatic mindfulness practice.

As we make the sound, we practice sensing its vibrations in our body. After making the sound, in open attention, we simply listen with our attention. What are we aware of? Can we feel sensations? breath? movement? We don't try to make movement happen in open attention, but it often arises spontaneously. The sounding (creation of voiced sound with Continuum) naturally lengthens our outbreath, which supports the rest and rejuvenation of our parasympathetic nervous system. This helps us to slow down. In the process, we begin to feel our tissues softening, returning to their original state of fluidity, reminiscent of the fluid embryo.

In this state, subtle movement arises spontaneously. These fluid movements present as spirals, fluctuations, and waves. We practice allowing these and usually enjoy them. This does not always happen for beginners in Continuum. A high degree of density in our tissues, which is common in our accelerated, over-stimulating modern world, reduces the fluidity.

Over time, as we practice, the vibrations of the sounds dissolve the density, and we can be surprised by what emerges. As our tissues melt, we may also find our history that has been held in the tissues begins to release. If old traumas arise, we practice acknowledging the feelings and orienting to what else is present. This is a Continuum way of returning to the Health. Difficult emotions and sensations tend to take over our attention, but we can practice remembering that there is more to us than the pain. We can then look for that "what else" and let it support us.

EXPLORATION
৶ Locating the Continuum ৶
Step 1: Your Starting Point: Midline Awareness

In Continuum, we generally begin any exploration with what we call a baseline. This represents our starting point. In this case, we are inquiring into our sense of midline as we begin, before we add any Continuum sounding. We all have midlines, in physical as well as energetic forms. An easy way to locate your midline is to bring attention to your spine. Can you feel it? You may want to take a few minutes to sit quietly, settle your mind, be with your breath, and allow your body sensations to come to the foreground. If you need to keep your eyes open to stay present, please do so.

Take a moment to reflect on what resonates with you. Check in with your body, is there any sense for you of being fluid like an embryo?

Do you have any sense of your center? Do you sense it in your spine or elsewhere such as your core? What are you aware of in your body as you begin to settle? What feels good? What stands out for you?

Step 2: Awakening Your Midline

Let yourself make some movement with your spine to enhance your awareness of it. Perhaps practice slowly arching and flexing forward and backward like a cat. This creates a fluid wave motion up and down your midline. Now, can you make that movement smaller? How small? As your movement becomes more subtle, you begin to sense fluidity and even wholeness. If you make a tiny movement with your spine, is there a response or resonance anywhere in your body? Allow yourself to be curious. There is no right or wrong here. In Continuum, we discover that the smaller, slower body movements enable us to return to our original fluidity whereas more active, faster, larger movements tend to increase tissue density and reduce fluid movement. Our intention with Continuum is to dissolve this density.

Step 3: Sounding Along the Midline

In Continuum we use different breaths and sounding to support our return to fluid awareness and potential. The sound of "O" stimulates a sense of elongation, augments midline awareness, and fluidity. You can make an "O" sound, like the letter O, by gently breathing in through your nose, if possible, and then allowing the sound of "O" with your outbreath. This is a very gentle, effortless process of offering the vibration to your tissues. It is different from projecting your voice outward as you would in singing. Direct your attention where you would like the vibration to go.

One option is to imagine an energetic line from the crown of your head down to the center of the perineum (between the anus and the vagina or penis). As you make the "O" sound with your outbreath, slowly lower your attention down this midline, either tracing your spine or as a straight line from top to bottom. You can pause and take a few ordinary breaths between the sounds if you need a break. Stay curious.

Can you sense the vibrations in your body? If not, what else do you notice? If you feel inspired, perhaps envision the midline continuing down into Mother Earth.

Return up the midline to the crown, continuing sounding the "O"s. When you reach the crown, you may choose to follow the midline up toward the Cosmos. Visualize reaching down into the Earth and up into the Cosmos and bringing the energy you find there back to your body. Practice this movement, completing in the downward direction to ground and energize you. Go slowly and stay curious to remain present in your body.

Step 4: Open Attention

After you are finished moving the sound and awareness through your midline, take a moment to pause. just observe what you are experiencing. We call this "open attention" in Continuum. This isn't about doing anything. Just observe what is present for you with curiosity. Orient to what feels good. You may have some sensations of warmth, softening, tingling, or even subtle or spontaneous fluid movement described above. You may find yourself feeling like a little embryo embodying its original potential.

Stay with this exploration as long as it feels interesting and beneficial to you. Feel free to repeat moving the O's along the midline and then take more time with open attention. You may also want to return to creating waves in your spine, which may be easier now with your increased fluidity. Each time you engage in this exploration, you may find your body feeling more melted and fluid. You may also find yourself becoming more fluid and resilient in your life.

Our shadow may include the potential we have forgotten about. It may also include what seems magical, ineffable, mysterious, and vast. Where and what we emerge from and the stillness in which we may reconnect with it become shadow in a fast-moving world where only scientific evidence and the material world it analyses are considered real. Again, the masculine focuses on the external reality, what can be analyzed, dissected, described, and controlled. The feminine, orienting to wholeness, includes the internal, dark, hidden, mysterious, liquid, cosmic undulations of life that are often beyond analysis, description, or control. Our modern world undervalues, or demeans the Mystery and its vast, relatively untapped potential. That masculine intelligence, which we often encounter as intellect, is in some ways limited compared to the intelligence of our potent, essential Health.

INHERENT INTELLIGENCE GUIDING OUR DEVELOPMENT

As we spiral into embodiment, we form within a much larger whole. We emerge from a vastness, an intelligence beyond our comprehension. Father of Cranial Osteopathy, William Garner Sutherland, referred to an inherent "Intelligence, spelled with a capital I" guiding the treatment.[5] In Biodynamics, we also perceive this Intelligence guiding our development. A mysterious force, the breath of life, expresses in our bodies as *potency*, a form of embodied life energy. Potency guides our formation, initially as little embryos but continuing throughout life. If you cut your finger, you can watch the remarkable effects of potency guiding the healing. The same potency that directed our embryological formation facilitates healing and re-formation later in life. When we practice sensing and listening with Biodynamics, we become aware of this aspect of our source.

Throughout our thinking lives, we may question where we come from. We embrace or denounce the Mystery, depending on our beliefs. We seem to have lost touch with a knowing we can no longer easily imagine. Like shadows passing through fog, there is something we aren't quite aware of, yet are a part of always, suggested in the following poem.

> *What is the life that brings us here?*
> *How is stray energy of the cosmos snared in tissues and*
> *   personalities?*
> *We pass through the world as shadows through fog.*

Life is around us, in us, inside our inside;
   yet we do not stave it and cannot grasp it.
As from nowhere we become alive,
   we encounter a remote apprehension of absolute existence;
   we sustain its fragile range all our days.
A chorus sings, "For all we know, this may only be a
   dream.
We come and go just as ripples in a stream."
                              RICHARD GROSSINGER, *EMBRYOGENESIS*

Our source may be said to remain in shadow as we live our lives within shades of ignorance. From reports of toddlers and others remembering their experience before or around the time of conception, we infer that we may lose knowledge from coalescing into human form and from social learning.[6] Our sense of where we come from can be intricately linked to our sense of purpose. It is not unusual for clients inquiring into their earliest history to begin to experience a sense of carrying an intention into this life. Such apparent memories often evoke tears of gratitude and tender appreciation.

⁓ Deepening into Purpose ⁓

Margaret contacted me to work with Continuum to address a brain injury and depression. The injury left her unable to engage in her work or maintain a relationship. Margaret had been adopted at birth. She had always been attracted to cigarettes, alcohol, and drugs, like heroin, which she believed her mother had used when pregnant with her. Unlike her mother, Margaret had stopped using drugs and alcohol when she became pregnant with her first child. When we met, she had already been on a healing path addressing her brain injury with dance. She found the more internal, subtle movements of Continuum helpful because, when she tried to dance, the active movement stimulated dizziness. She discovered that, listening and moving on such a deep level with Continuum enabled her to stop smoking, which she had been trying to do for over thirty years.

I taught Margaret the O's down the midline as a way to help her ground. Having had a brain injury myself many years before, I understood how ungrounding its effects can be. Margaret enjoyed the sounding and began to feel steadier on earth. This supported her in being able to begin to return to her love of dance, as well as having fewer, less severe accidents. A particular Continuum breath helped her calm herself when she felt anxious and overwhelmed by life. We acknowledged that, being separated from the familiarity of her mother and adopted at birth had also been overwhelming. The toxic surround of her mother's body had been familiar, even if it wasn't healthy. She had never felt at home or like she belonged in her adoptive family.

As she began to resolve the effects of the brain injury and her adoption history, Margaret began to think about what she wanted to do with her life. She began to feel more capable of engaging in something meaningful, where in the past circumstances had led to the next thing. She continued practicing Continuum between sessions and gradually reported feeling well again. In her practice, she could now delight in deepening into an embryonic fluidity which had previously felt frightening. She realized that she had been connecting with her prenatal experience of shock at being unwanted, leading to resistance to being in a body. She now began to enjoy her body and had a clear intention to become more embodied. She began attending dance classes regularly without feeling dizzy. At this point, she became clear that her purpose in life was to teach the form of dance she was studying. She began immersing herself in that work, using Continuum to support her journey.

What is our purpose in being here? Why is it so difficult so often to articulate? Conrad notes, "What we call our bodies are interpenetrating wave motions that have stabilized within a particular electromagnetic field called earth for a purpose that we don't know. In other words, we don't really know what the body is for."[7] We live in these physical bodies, but we don't know why. It seems that we enter at some point before birth. Clients frequently describe their experience of preparing to come into a new life, and somehow being drawn in, usually at the time of conception. Different spiritual traditions hold that the soul or spirit comes into the body at different times. In that we experience and apparently remember our early experience, why do we often not seem to remember why we are here?

In Jewish tradition, there is a belief that babies arriving into a new life are touched just above the lip by the angel, Lailah, a teacher to souls before birth. This touch creates the philtrum, the indentation below your nose above the upper lip, and causes the baby to forget everything. The knowledge is still there but needs to be reclaimed.[8] Do we know our purpose before we are born? How can we remember?

Other reasons for forgetting include early shock and trauma. This may occur as early as conception and may interfere with our ability to come fully into our bodies. I am reminded of the character, Mr. Duffy, whom James Joyce described as one who "lived a short distance from his body."[9] The combination of personal trauma history and collective distraction may cause our own physical bodies to be in shadow.

As a somatic, body-centered psychotherapist, I have seen how common this phenomenon can be. I also see myself as having spent the first two or three decades of my life not quite embodied. It has taken years of therapy and mindful body-based practices to enter my body more fully. Until then, my physicality remained somewhat in shadow. I used to say that I expressed everything in my body. When I look back, I realize that what I meant was that any intense emotion expressed itself as physical pain. I had not yet learned to identify the emotion and its sensations, to feel their subtle and not-so-subtle expressions as tensions and movement in my organs, nervous system, and other tissues. As I was able to shine light on these physical events in my own body, I had less need to be in so much pain. I was able to reclaim and heal emotions that had been established years before. These included very early wounding from birth, the womb, and even conception.

As trauma resolves, we can more easily discover and remember our original embryological potential. This includes qualities of the embryo, fetus, or newborn that we may want to resurrect or at least be able to access at times.

BEING VS. DOING

Little ones in the womb are not busy doing as you and I usually are. Settling into relative stillness, as in meditation, can help us to recover our innate capacity for being. Embryos develop and form their bodies not through active doing as we might by building a structure from Legos or a building from bricks. Their growth and development are more like that of a tree, or other aspects of nature, following and expressing an inherent intelligence. The eastern concept of *wu wei*—effortless action in accord with the natural way of the universe, or action that is non-action[10]—is foreign to our modern, masculine way of life. Our ability to restfully emerge may reside in the shadows of our experience. When we allow ourselves to consider our very early beginnings, we open a portal to return to being.

This can profoundly affect our health. Much disease has been reported to relate to autonomic nervous system disturbances, often linked to omnipresent stress, even prenatally. We spend much of our time in modern Western life in accelerated sympathetic fight/flight mode, reacting to the constant bombardment of stimuli. Electronics, traffic, movies, mobile phones, email, social media, and so on, are all over-stimulating. How can we slow down and keep up? Babies are quickly overwhelmed by speed.

The effects of electronics can be observed early in development. Toddlers exposed to mobile phones demonstrate increased risk of learning difficulties.[11] Prenatal exposure may be linked with emotional/behavioral/attention issues and spontaneous abortion.[12] Nature didn't design our nervous system for all this speed.

We might say that our natural, inherent sensitivity is occluded by the reaction to overstimulation. We are animals. Human animals. How would a deer in the forest react to the sounds of rock music or high-speed traffic or to the sight of changing colors and shapes on a screen? Babies may be fascinated and curious, but their brain and nervous system can be easily over-stimulated. Babies in the womb have been known to kick so vehemently when their mother attended a hard rock concert that she left the concert with broken ribs![13] Our animal nature, our sensitive innocence, is too often not acknowledged or respected. I cringe every time I see a tiny newborn in a supermarket, even with the understanding that this is usually not avoidable because of lack of layers of support that babies and their families need. As a result, new mothers often have to return to the overstimulating demands of work, shopping, and so on, detracting from their ability to just be present with their newborn. Little ones carry the exquisite sensitivity that is our birth right. I am reminded of my amazement the first time I heard about how elephants with their huge bodies are so sensitive that they are aware of when they are about to step on a tiny insect and adjust their footing to avoid this.

In contrast, I also remember hearing that the brain-to-brawn ratio of a person driving a car is the same as that of a dinosaur. Our bodies are made gigantic with all our technical extensions like cars and the internet. This increases our responsibility. We can step on many more creatures with such a big body. We need more sensitivity, not less. Yet we are stepping heavily on our babies, even before they are born. It is important to be aware and acknowledge the trauma we may also be imparting and the profound effects it has on both individual lives and the planet. Fortunately, awareness has been increasing about what our planet needs, as well as what little ones and birthing families require to thrive. I hope and believe we are emerging from the shadow, and that this book might help with that change.

MOTHER EARTH, RESONANCE, AND A TENDER HEART

Little ones are naturally heart centered. The heart is the first organ to come online, as a massive "heart bulge" in the center of the embryo. Our heart energy, with our potential for empathy and compassion, can become dampened through trauma and overwhelm. Yet, we begin as exquisitely sensitive beings, already receptive to learning, love, emotions, and relationships.

Perhaps our receptivity relates to being so close to Source. We have just arrived or are just arriving. Whatever you believe about where we come from, we seem to have an innate sense of a mysterious intelligence guiding our journey in life, Intelligence with a capital I, as Sutherland, called it. Scientists have been able to describe how the embryo forms in increasing detail, but they still struggle to know *how* this happens. As Thomas Armstrong describes in the beginning of life in his book, *The Human Odyssey*, prenatal development may not just be a series of biological steps but rather a journey guided by forgotten consciousness.[14] Until relatively recently, in utero development was hidden from view. I personally like that it has been shrouded in mystery for so long. I believe the miracle of how the embryo develops is the Mystery expressing its wisdom and Intelligence.

Being so close to Source is an aspect of our original embryological potential. There seems to be a resonance for little ones in the womb with that mysterious place they are emerging from. We are all energetic entities, but this may be more obvious with embryos who are still less physical. Their bodies are initially highly translucent and fluid. They are composed of even more water than we are as adults.

We know that water is a very resonant element, as illustrated for example by the work of Masaru Emoto and the less known William Tiller. The research of the late Masaru Emoto demonstrates how water responds to vibrations around it.[15] He found a way to photograph crystal formations in water as it was thawing and discovered very different patterns depending on words or intentions the water was exposed to. Words like "love" resulted in beautiful crystal formations. "I hate you" created a dark, chaotic pattern. Although Emoto's research has been questioned, another researcher, William Tiller, clearly demonstrated that the pH of water can be shifted when experienced meditators focus on this intention.[16]

As bioenergetic beings, we emit and receive vibrational frequencies all the time, and water is especially responsive to vibrations, being so resonant. Quantum physics has shown that this can occur remotely, and intention has been used for healing purposes through prayer and other healing modalities probably since humankind emerged.[17] Vibrational resonance may help to explain how babies in the womb can apparently be aware of and remember details from their parents' lives that they "should" not know about, as mentioned earlier.

I often heard Emilie Conrad declare that the embryo is spiraled water, and the Cosmos is spiraled water, with the two forms of water having direct communication through their resonance. Little ones apparently are sensitive both to Cosmos, or Source, and to the physical, human world around them. In that this awareness precedes development of physical sense organs or nervous system, they must be detecting their world in other ways. Watery resonance may be partly responsible for prenatal sentience. Cells, which we have already noted are responsive to their environment, communicate with each other in part through resonance. They are also made up primarily of water.

Outside of our own bodies, we resonate with nature itself. We are designed by nature to be vibrating in resonance with our Great Mother, the Earth. She has been found to have a rhythm, called the Schumann resonance frequency, which is about 7.8 Hz, and has also been found in the human brain.[18] This appears to be a resonance by which we biologically attune to the Earth's rhythm. Interfering with an individual's exposure to the Schumann resonance frequency can affect circadian rhythms and lead to an array of health issues. This may explain some of the developmental issues now being discovered in relation to prenatal exposure to electronics. Perhaps fetal resonance with Mother Earth is being disturbed. Perhaps maternal resonance is also being interrupted, which then affects the little one inside her.

I have heard Conrad hypothesize that the speed of modern life is one such form of interference. Supported by scientific research of Valerie Hunt, who observed and measured the electromagnetic frequencies associated with her movement practice, Conrad proposed that the way we slow down when practicing Continuum enhances health by enabling us to come back into resonance with the Schumann frequency. Hunt noted, "This is the same energy that Emilie [Conrad] activates by undulating movements."[19] Conrad later thought we might be slowing down even more to be in resonance with something much vaster and more mysterious than Mother Earth.[20] Returning to our original embryological potential puts us in direct resonance with the spirals of the Cosmos.

As I write this a major headline in the news every day is about climate change, global warming, and our need to change our ways if we are to survive. As always with shadow material, as light is shone on how we have been damaging the planet we depend on, there are those who resist and deny the obvious. If we compare modern life with Indigenous ways, a primary difference is our relative lack of reverence for the Earth. We do not live in harmony with our Mother. As Mia Kalef writes in her book, *The Secret Life of Babies*,

> When you are a baby in your mother's womb, you know life through her. Through her you learn to what degree you are in unity with or in wholeness with life. The degree to which she feels coherent about her circumstances and surroundings influences the degree to which you do. She is your first teacher, your first Earth. Her mind, her experiences, become yours. You don't even know you are separate from her until you learn to walk nearly a year after you are born."[21]

A fetus lacking resonance with the mother would not thrive and may not even survive. This can happen in challenging circumstances, such as when the mother experiences overwhelming or chronic stress, feels unsafe, struggles to survive in a threatening relationship, lives in a war zone or extreme poverty, faces racial discrimination, and so on. Considering how pregnancy and birth have been viewed and managed since being largely taken over by masculine medicine, is it surprising that we no longer live in harmony with the Earth? Are we perceiving and treating her in accordance with the relationship we experienced with our mother before or during birth, which may not have been supportive or welcoming?

One hope I hold is that bringing prenatal and perinatal experience out of shadow might serve to strengthen our relationship with the Mother we now depend on. Perhaps, returning to our original embryological potential, how we were or were intended to be prior to cultural, collective disruptions, we might again find ourselves spiraling in resonance with nature.

The heart, like all body tissues, also spirals into form. We have already touched on the vast bioenergetic fields the heart emanates. Its sensitive intelligence sends messages to the brain more often than the other way around. In the embryo, the heart is simpler. The brain may not even be developed or functioning yet. The heart beats its rhythm, listening to and regulating in relation to the maternal heart. Mother and baby are already in relationship as the heart begins to beat, long before the brain begins to function.

Consider that our survival before birth is completely dependent on mother's physiological support. Her physiology is directly affected by her feelings, emotions, moods, stresses, and sense of safety and support. Our survival is relational from the very beginning. Sperm and egg need each other and need to communicate to find and unite with each other. The embryo requires a receptive womb to ensure adequate nutrition at the time of implantation and beyond. Again, the mother's physiology affects the state of her womb. How she feels and how welcoming she is toward this baby and pregnancy can support or threaten the embryo's life.

We need to be sensitive to acquire food for the new life we have begun. Where we have encountered highly challenging conditions, we may have struggled or feared for our lives. Our open hearts may have needed to shut down in protection even as they were starting to beat. This may interfere with our ability to be sensitive and respectful to each other, to our babies, and to our Mother Earth.

Fortunately, the potential of the embryo remains available, even if it is shadow. Shining the light usually begins with awareness. We must acknowledge that little ones are having a very full and rich experience, long before we can see them, and even before we usually know that they are there.

EARTH SHADOWS

I recently listened to a beautiful panel discussion with Indigenous wise people where one of the presenters, Eriel Tchekwie Deranger, described how her father taught her to track animals. As a seven-year-old, she repeatedly asked, "What is this?" Her father responded with, "Shhhh. Just listen."[22] We all need to listen. We need to listen to the whisperings, not just the screams of our Great Mother. We need to return to the stillness in the spaces between. But how did we learn not to listen? We can blame colonialism. We can blame the industrial revolution. We can blame rampant greed for money. But where might that all come from? Important aspects of Indigenous worldview include feminine qualities of wholeness and relationship. We are in relationship with the earth that provides our food and water, as well as with other animals and humans.

As modern, colonialist ways of life emerged, they fostered separation from our intuitive knowing, our natural relationship with nature, each other, ourselves, and our own bodies. This included our ability to birth and raise our babies according to biological wisdom. Man began trying to control birth. Respect and appreciation for women and more feminine ways of relational interbeing diminished. Women began to lose connection with and confidence in their bodily intelligence. Birth became a medical emergency to be isolated in hospitals, managed by medical practitioners who were trained only in disease and usually had no experience with normal, healthy birth. Birthing within a medical context of fear is very different from nurturing natural knowing in the body. Pregnancy within an increasingly toxic, polluted, unnatural, overstimulating context contributes its stressful effect on mother and baby, as discussed above.

One perspective is that this unbalanced, unhealthy way of living, which is about being out of relationship, echoes our experience in the womb. Lloyd deMause, founder of the field of psychohistory, addresses psychological roots of historical events. He views war as caused by a "bizarre group-fantasy," where war is a metaphor for birth, relieving the build-up of pressures comparable to those in the womb just prior to birth.[23] He has recorded how poisonous blood or serpentine symbols of the poisonous placenta frequent political cartoons and language. DeMause suggests that war occurs because men are enacting their rage at how they experienced toxicity in the womb.[24]

If our relationship with our biological mother felt toxic, threatening, or unsupportive, we might withdraw and become less sensitive to protect ourselves. This can be reflected in all our relationships, including our relationship with Mother Earth, the Great Mother Indigenous peoples recognized as cradling us and all life. We might stop listening to her as we try to block out what we received from our mother in the womb. If we cannot hear her screams or sense her pain when we abuse her, we might continue this disrespect as an unconscious way to express our anger and resentment toward our biological mothers. We might similarly fail to listen to our babies.

I notice as I write this that I feel a bit nauseous. My experience in the womb was highly toxic, due to extreme chemical pollution in the town my family lived. This was augmented by a very dysfunctional family, with a mother who hated her body, in which I was trying to grow. Nausea is not unfamiliar to me. In this moment, it feels like an expression of how indigestible the way we have treated the Earth feels to me. At times, I want nothing more than to pause and sit still upon the Earth, listening.

When we slow down and listen, we may encounter uncomfortable feelings. There is so much we have tried to not perceive or been taught to not pay attention to. Our relationship with our mothers, including Mother Earth, so seldom acknowledged out loud or consciously, becomes shadow. We then unconsciously act to recapitulate what we have experienced that we have been unable to process and resolve.

PESTILENCE, TOXICITY, MOTHER EARTH, AND FERTILITY

As discussed above, babies experience and are profoundly affected by maternal stress, potentially experienced as a form of toxicity in the womb and postnatally. It is difficult to conceive, carry, and birth a baby without stress in the modern world. I write this during a worldwide pandemic. Fear, anxiety, and uncertainty abound in these times. Parents and would-be parents fear for their children's future. Will Mother

Earth provide a sustainable home as today's babies grow up? Will these children even be conceived? Stress is a major factor in infertility, as well as fertility. While birth rates in some US states went down during the pandemic, rates in other states and in Australia experienced a baby boom.[24] This seems to be evidence of how some people coped with the stress of lockdown. To what degree is omnipresent stress acknowledged by well-meaning doctors referring their patients for IVF or other medical procedures? As mentioned earlier, these procedures have major effects on the babies involved, as well as the parents. How often are these important factors appreciated? For the most part, they lurk in shadow.

Research into the effects of COVID-19 in pregnant women is revealing that babies may die due to this virus invading the placenta and reducing its blood flow. This effectively cuts off essential oxygen nourishment and detoxification for the baby.[25] A moderate to severe case of the virus has also been associated with increased occurrence of caesarean or preterm birth, maternal death during birth, as well as postpartum infection other than COVID-19, postpartum hemorrhaging, baby being small for gestational age, having congenital malformations or dying soon after birth.[26] Just gestating during the pandemic has its effects as evidenced by recent research showing that babies born during the pandemic, regardless of if their mother was infected or not, score lower on neurodevelopmental tests than those born prior to the pandemic.[27]

How can there not be fear and stress for new families living in the field of this information or the unknown—the hanging questions—pervading our world? Anxious young couples longing for a baby wonder why it is so difficult to conceive or birth a full-term baby. As well as environmental stresses, cultural stresses of racism, sexism, colonialism, and other -ism's haunt the womb and growing families.

The tendency for women to choose to have children in their late thirties due to changes in modern culture can also affect the outcome of a pregnancy attempts and the context in which a little one enters their family. Women or couples often prioritize education, career and/or adventure, or finding a loving and stable partner over parenting in their 20s. Mothers in their late 30s are considered to have "geriatric eggs," which may be less optimal for fertility. Although it may be true that eggs age with time, the woman's general health and lifestyle may help her eggs to stay healthy. She may not be a victim of her age. There may be ways to empower women to conceive and birth a healthy baby in their late 30s or early 40s Older parents may be more mature and more able to meet the needs of their children, which is also part of the picture worth acknowledging.

However, young couples do have the advantage of peak fertility in their 20s and early 30s. The downside of having a pregnancy later in life is the higher risk of birth defects and infertility, the latter of which can then lead to otherwise unnecessary medical interventions like IVF, or to the couple choosing adoption. Insofar as this is not openly discussed, it joins other secrets and omissions as shadow. Some young women and couples have not been informed of this in sex education. Some of my clients may have made different choices if this information had been readily available. They might still have wanted to complete their education and so on before starting a family, but with the additional knowledge, they could have made informed decisions.

We need to recognize what a magnificent and often perilous journey we and our children traverse before even reaching the birth canal. The reward for surviving prenatal challenges is the chance to use our inherent knowing to push ourselves out into the relative unknown, where hopefully we will be met by loving welcome and protection, offering a "womb with a view" as we continue our postnatal gestation.

Reflections

1. What thoughts, feelings, sensations, images arise for you when you consider your time in the womb? What supports you in being present with these?

2. Your Relationships: Do you tend to feel like you are missing someone, but you don't know who? Do you attach to a romantic partner very quickly and then feel disappointed by who they are as

you get to know them more? Do you expect others to understand or know what you are feeling without saying what it is? Do you tend to be early for things? Do you ever feel like you are trying to reach or communicate with someone but it's as if there is a glass wall between you? Do you tend to feel like a powerless victim, that people are doing things to you or making choices for you?

3. Your Physical Sensations: What do you sense in your breath, your body, your feet, your emotions, as you remember your current age, all that you are capable of as an adult now, knowing that you have already survived prenatal and perinatal challenges you encountered on your way to your current age? Specific practices from modern trauma work can be very helpful. These include grounding. Can you sense your feet, your seat, the support of gravity or Mama Earth under you? How is it to feel that support? Can you feel your breath? How fast or slow is it? Are you able to slow it down if it is fast? Can you take a deeper breath? Can you feel where the breath goes in your body?

4

The Experience of Being Born in Modern Society

Hospitals, Doctors, Midwives, and Prenatal Echoes

> *When children come into the world, the first thing they do*
> *is cry. And everyone rejoices.*
>
> FREDERIC LEBOYER, *BIRTH WITHOUT VIOLENCE*

Human babies are said to be born prematurely compared to other animals, all of which can walk and be more independent soon after birth. We humans have large heads to accommodate our relatively large brains. We need to pass through our mother's pelvis before our brain and head grow too big to get through. Adding to the challenge is the position and relative narrowness of the human pelvis, which facilitates walking upright. Please take a moment now to congratulate yourself! You have made it here!

For some, passage through the vagina proves too challenging and modern technology enables arrival through caesarean section. Although some imagine this route to be easier, it has its own set of challenges. Birth by any account is an initiatory rite, both for mother and baby. Awareness of baby's sentience supports the process. Too often, babies are considered passive passengers. Shadowy imprints of this important journey then include all that has not been acknowledged or properly greeted as the baby emerges, including prenatal experiences.

SHADOWY PRENATAL TRAUMA

Unfortunately, there are many potential traumas before birth. Prenates experience changes in nervous system states as their mother's system reacts to her world. Extreme or chronic stress stimulates the sympathetic systems, often to the point of overwhelm for the little one. Increased levels of the stress hormone cortisol can overwhelm the placenta's protective filtering and reduce its blood flow, contributing to health problems, including low birth weight and prematurity.[1] Babies growing within a stressed surround develop a heightened sympathetic nervous system, and more anxious reactions to events as they grow up.[2] They are ready for the stress their experience has taught them to expect. Babies whose mothers detect safety and support tend to be born with a less reactive stress response. Their social engagement nervous system is more easily online, facilitating readiness for learning within a field of safety and support. Their perceptions and behavior will tend to support thriving in the safe, supportive world of their mother.

Bearing this in mind, what could be more important than supporting and protecting pregnant mothers? I was happily surprised to read in a recent article published in an obstetrics and gynecology journal that it is important to evaluate the social context of a pregnancy as part of evaluating the baby's risk for future health conditions.[3] Social support offers the possibility of offsetting the harmful effects of racism, discrimination, poverty, war, and so much else.

Babies do not arrive at birth a *tabula rasa*. They are not a blank slate. They have already had about nine months of life inside their mother preparing to meet her environment. Babies gestating during famine tend to gain weight easily as adults.[4] Their metabolism has prepared them for a world lacking in food and makes the most of what is available. Babies of mothers addicted to drugs like heroin or cocaine suffer withdrawal at birth. Other extreme or chronic stresses include war, death of a loved one, and partner violence. On the other hand, maternal support can help to balance the effects of stress. For example, partner support for the mother can lessen the dysregulation in their infants within an otherwise stressful context.[5]

Through neuroception, the mother's nervous system may experience stress that she isn't consciously aware of. Remember that we live in an accelerated world characterized by constant overstimulation from electronics, as well as common exposure to crowds of strangers, noise and other pollution, non-biologically based mobility in cars, trains, planes, and so on, all of which the mother may consider routine rather than stressful. It is important to also include here the chronic stress created by poverty, racism, discrimination, and misogyny. A pregnant woman may think she is getting appropriate prenatal support, but her system has entered pregnancy already stressed by her life situation.

We thrive when we live and birth within *layers of support*, a phrase midwife Mary Jackson coined to describe the natural needs of babies within their family, community, and world. She worked closely with prenatal and birth therapist Ray Castellino and observed how much easier birth was when adequately supported. She concluded that everyone needs at least two layers of support to enable them to relax and feel safe.[6]

Throughout this book I have made mention of "relying on" or "checking" your supports. Now that we are beginning to have a better understanding of the support needs of the mother and neonate, let's take the opportunity to check in with your own support needs as you proceed with your shadow work.

EXPLORATION
ঞ Layers of Support ঞ

It is possible to explore our sense of layers of support, both on a somatic and an emotional/social/psychological level. This can echo our original experience in the womb. To begin the exploration, check in with yourself as to what might support you in this moment.

Physical Support

Do you need physical support to be more comfortable? Is this something you naturally look for or do you need to be reminded that you can have physical support? Are your feet on the floor? If you are sitting cross-legged or in some other position, are your feet and legs resting into or on a surface? Can you feel the sensation of that support under you? What does this feel like to you?

Scan the rest of your body. Does your back require support? Your arms? Your head? What materials or positions would allow you to rest just a bit more in this moment? Do you need a cushion or blanket, for example?

Perhaps taking a deep breath is supportive. Or maybe observing your breath for a few minutes helps you to relax and arrive into this moment more fully. As you begin to rest further into physical support, does your breath change? Try placing a hand on your heart, if that feels comfortable for you. Can you feel the sensation of your hand there? Does that give you a sense of support?

These points of support represent layers. The support under you is an expression of gravity. Mother Earth is there holding you in her lap. Can you rest into the sensation of her support?

Your breath relates to the air around you, the atmosphere which makes life possible. You bring it into your body, where it nourishes your cells. You then return your used breath out into the space around you. You are supported by your environment. It also provides food, natural beauty, water, and other essential or supportive elements. Can you sense your breath? How is that for you in this moment?

Social Supports

There may also be people or animals who support you. Do you have a pet? Do you have family, friends, neighbors, colleagues, or others who provide a cushion between you and the rest of the world? Perhaps you confide in them, feel loved and appreciated by them, are guided by their opinions or advice, or simply feel less alone and safer because they are nearby. The people, or beings (like pets), around you can serve as a layer of support. What are you aware of inside yourself when you consider this?

Less Tangible Support

There may be additional layers of support available to you. For example, you may feel supported by ancestors, like grandparents or parents. Even if these people who preceded you are no longer alive, they have left parts of their experience as a foundation upon which you have grown. Although these may not always feel supportive, there are likely to be aspects which contribute to who you are, such as genes. The culture you live in and the language you speak have been created before you. Can you sense this ancestral/cultural layer of support? What other layers of support are you aware of in your life? How is your breath and your body now as you consider these layers supporting you?

You may want to take some time to journal about your experience or at least to list the layers of support you are aware of. This process can also help you to notice where you feel a lack of support and to start looking for ways to remedy that situation.

Fig. 4.1. Layers of support: The template for this support structure is seen in the embryo, which is suspended within protective, nutritive fluid sacs, the yolk sac, amniotic sac, and chorionic sac or chorion, as illustrated in figure 4.2.

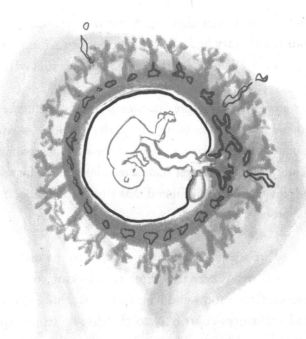

Fig. 4.2. Chorion: What do you sense in your own body as you view the embryo supported by the amniotic fluid within the nutritive tissues of the surrounding chorion?

The importance of community support systems was previously studied by developmental psychologist Uri Bronfenbrenner, who noticed differences in support systems between countries upon emigrating from Russia to the USA. His ecological systems theory proposed that children develop in relationship to five nested layers of context.[7] The largest of these he named the chronosystem, which includes major life transitions, like starting school, parents divorcing, or the historical influences of the particular time or epoch the child arrives into. Other ecosystems acknowledge attitudes and ideologies of the surrounding culture, including socioeconomic status, ethnicity, geographic location, extended families, neighbors, parents' workplaces, schools, as well as immediate family and community such as parents, siblings, church, teachers, peers and so on. We exist within so many layers of potential support and/or stress.

Events or circumstances that are stressful or traumatizing in one community or family may be less so in a different surrounding. Layers of support can make a huge difference. As Thomas Hübl writes,

> The question of precisely where the consequences of trauma become dysfunctional may lie somewhere within the container of relation that surrounds a traumatized person and their family, community, society, and culture. The longer trauma remains uncared for and/ or untreated, the higher the likelihood that a life becomes dominated by the symptoms it produces.[8]

Where there are adequate layers of support, trauma can be held and processed with others. Where this support is lacking, trauma is more likely to establish firmer roots and have farther reaching effects

Collective influences contribute to the ease or stress experienced during pregnancy and birth. The tendency to be blind to effects of beliefs or attitudes we have grown up with can augment the potential damage of these influences. Collective shadow may present as ongoing racial discrimination creating chronic stress during pregnancy. Adding to the pain of discrimination is the insult of ignorance or outright bigotry on the part of medical or birth practitioners the mother encounters.

This is true not only for BIPOC people but also for birthing parents whose gender identity differs from cultural expectations. Insensitive practices, including the language used in relation to them, may be offensive and stimulate autonomic reactions, such as fear, anger, or hopelessness.

It is natural to fear people whom we sense don't understand or accept us. The mother may conclude that she would be better off with as little help from these people as possible. Mothers may also have a pattern of being overly independent, shunning support, usually based on their own developmental history. Although this may consciously feel safer, her nervous system may feel threatened by the lack of support. On a biological level, a baby in the womb thrives on layers of support. We can look at this at an embryological level, where the placenta and umbilical cord can be seen as one layer, and the mother's healthy circulatory system interacting with it as another layer.

Beyond the womb, the maternal nervous system is most likely to settle when she has loving, supportive people around her. This may include her partner, extended family, friends, neighbors, colleagues, and other social groups, as well as hopefully her birth practitioners. Ancestral layers can also provide degrees of support, depending on how healthy the ancestors were. These layers are nested within a larger collective, cultural layer. For example, if her country is at war, her entire support system is likely to be stressed. As noted above, other collective stresses or threats, like climate change, a pandemic, economic and political crises also affect the neuroceptive and often conscious perception of support and safety or threat. The more layers of healthy support that are available for the mother, the more supported and safer the little one is likely to feel.

As well as discrepancies between conscious perception and neuroception, the fetus may have different preferences than their mother. Remember the pregnant woman suffering from broken ribs after attending a hard rock concert because their agitated fetus was kicking so hard in reaction to music the mother enjoyed? These unconscious, somatic experiences of stress can be explained by neuroception. The stress response can be triggered by neuroceptive awareness of stress or threat that is perceived differently on a conscious level. The mother, for example, is consciously grooving to the music, but her sympathetic nervous system reacts to a sense of danger in the intense sensory stimulation. If she is pregnant, this information is communicated to her baby, whose system also reacts. The baby also reacts directly to the booming sounds, which in the wild would signal danger.

A neuroceptive experience of safety has a different effect. When the mother feels safe, protected, well-supported, and well-nourished, she can experience natural states of love and protectiveness for her baby. The little one senses this and can relax and do their job of growing and developing.

Other potential sources of trauma or distress, where a prenate's experience is commonly not considered, include intrusions to the womb like ultrasound, amniocentesis, prenatal surgery for either the mother or the baby, very loud sounds, violence, and umbilical toxicity. The latter refers to toxic elements delivered to the prenate via the umbilical cord. These include chemical toxins, such as pollution, as well as the maternal intake of drugs, alcohol, and nicotine. Less commonly acknowledged is the emotional toxicity the baby receives when the mother harbors difficult emotions like anger, rage, fear, terror, hatred, or ambivalence about the pregnancy. Maternal emotional states affect her hormonal and bio-chemical states, which are communicated umbilically to the baby, even if the toxic substances don't pass through the placenta.

When a mother has experienced prenatal trauma and has not had a chance to resolve it, her body continues to carry it when she becomes pregnant. Conception, pregnancy, and birth can trigger implicit memories of the mother's own early development. These challenging memories may include later traumatic experiences, such as childhood sexual abuse that has never been acknowledged or sufficiently addressed.[9] Related maternal emotions and body reactions then become part of the field in which the baby grows. If the mother and parents can address their own early trauma, the baby has a clearer surround and is more likely to experience welcome and safety. Understandably, prenatal and birth therapists see the time before conception as ideal for education and healing of primal trauma. Unfortunately, most parents aren't aware of having these early issues because they are held in shadow. If they come for therapy, it is because they feel disturbed during the pregnancy or after the birth.

It can be highly effective to work therapeutically with this material during pregnancy or in the postpartum period because it is likely to be triggered and available. It is important in this case to differentiate for the baby, reassuring them that mommy is doing her own emotional work from when she was little, that her baby doesn't need to worry about any emotions coming up. The baby needs to know that these are not about them, and that mommy is safe. Imagine if all of us had been able to arrive with such clarity around us!

✐ Prenatal Trauma Manifesting
in Your Life Today ✐

How might your tendencies in life reflect your prenatal experience? How is it for you to ask for, perceive, and receive support? Are you aware of layers of support in your life? To what degree do you feel settled or at home in your life, in your relationships, and in your home? Do you have allergies or sensitivities to foods, chemicals, airborne particles, electromagnetic fields, and so on?

SHADOWS FROM BEFORE THE BIRTH

I am repeatedly amazed and disturbed by the lack of awareness demonstrated by birth practitioners even in the 21st century, when almost any knowledge is available through quick Google search. Consider this opening phrase from a 2022 article in the *Journal of Perinatology*.

> Many neonatal-perinatal providers are unaware that climate change-related and air pollution exposures during infancy, pregnancy, and preconception (known critical windows of vulnerability) can lead to multiple adverse health outcomes including preterm birth, poor fetal growth, abnormal lung development, and impaired neurodevelopment.[10]

This is just one form of prenatal influence birth attendants don't tend to consider. Pregnancy and birth are not just physiological processes. The psyche of both mother and baby are also involved. The baby's prenatal experience is even less likely than the mother's to be considered. We have already seen some of the challenges babies might suffer from in the womb. Their prenatal wounding or nurturing can affect how they engage with the major developmental milestone of birth.

As well as physical health, the nature of the bond between mother and baby begins long before birth. If prenatal bonding is well-established, a mother who has been sensing and communicating with her preborn can continue this process as they engage together in the dance of birth. In contrast, a mother who has been ambivalent about being pregnant or becoming a parent or has been treating her bump as nothing more than a physiological phenomenon, is less likely to sense what is needed for her little one to find their way out of the womb. The baby is less likely to feel supported and welcomed and may carry their own ambivalence about being born. They may already harbor anger, resentment, or fear toward their mother. Their birth journey is likely to be less cooperative and more challenging.

I recently spoke with an obstetric nurse who reported an interesting, disturbing phenomenon she had observed with every case of placenta previa she had encountered, (placenta previa is where the placenta grows across the uterine opening to the vagina, preventing the baby from emerging that way). In each case, the mother had been ambivalent in some way about the birth. She explained that, over time, gravity would pull the placenta down toward the opening, when the placenta was not firmly in place.

Mothers with placenta previa may not be consciously aware of ambivalence. They may be longing for a baby but carry ambivalence in their own psyche, tend toward dissociation, or be ungrounded. Babies, not differentiating between what is theirs and what is someone else's, simply take on these feelings.

In researching this topic, I was able to find only one article that provided any kind of awareness of an effect ambivalence might have on placenta previa or the birthing process. The women in the article were not yet pregnant. One link to placenta previa might be that these ambivalent women are more likely to be smokers and have a higher risk of placenta previa. They are also less likely to use contraception increasing their risk of having an unplanned pregnancy although no reasons were given for this. To me, this suggests a possibly unconscious desire or intention to have a baby, even with ambivalence present.[11] Recent research investigating risk factors for placental abruption (separation of the placenta from the inner wall of the uterus) points to prenatal maternal stresses including death of a child before or during the pregnancy and the father's loss of employment.[12] It is understandable how these factors might contribute to ambivalence. A mother might very much want her baby but be distracted by unresolved grief or worry.

Acknowledging an association like this could be used by birth professionals to reduce obstetric interventions and suffering. Helping women become clear about their feelings surrounding pregnancy, or at least acknowledging their ambivalence, can excavate it from shadow. With awareness, choices can be made. Precautions can be taken, like contraception, stopping smoking, or support for grieving. Therapy can free the potential mother to make clear choices, based on what she truly desires, rather than unconsciously acting out her history.

MATERNAL SHADOWS IN BIRTH PROCESS

Physiology responds to and is intertwined with consciousness. Our bodies express our shadows symbolically, often as bodily pain or dysfunction. Maternal shadows about motherhood, birth, being a woman, femininity, parenting, and so on, may present somatically through tighter vaginal tissues, a less than lush uterine wall, reduced blood flow to the placenta, and so on. She may also be prone to greater labor pain, or a tendency to perceive the contractions as more painful. This can be a physiological response to resistance to a natural process. Pain can lead to requests or offering of pain medication, which can initiate a cascade of medical interventions. A woman embracing the initiation of birth, who is well-supported by a gentle, quiet, sensitive surround, is less likely to run into difficulties. Layers of support can enable her to meet her initiation into motherhood with feminine power, intuition, and resilience.

Ina May Gaskin, founder and director of the Farm Midwifery Center, learned by listening to her birthing mothers that their emotions are directly associated with how their bodies open during the birth process. She writes of her early discoveries of the mind-body connections for birthing women. She describes "two healthy first-time mothers who had spent many hours with their cervices 75 percent open [who] were only able to progress further when meaningful words that addressed their hidden anxieties were spoken." One of these women had been adopted after her biological mother had died in childbirth. She writes, "Immediately after this fear was revealed and quelled, her cervix (which had felt as if it was held in place by an embedded wire), opened completely, and she was able to push her baby out."[13] Her fear of dying like her mother had been held in shadow where it had interfered with her progressing through the dreaded trial of childbirth.

~ Haunted by History ~

I worked with another woman who had been working for some time on her pre- and perinatal history. Her greatest fear was of being separated from her baby after birth as she had been from her own mother. She had been able to resolve many aspects of her history, which did not play out as she gave birth. The one remaining aspect that remained manifested as her baby needed special care after birth and she couldn't accompany them because her placenta had not yet been birthed.

Although the separation was brief, and the father was able to go with the baby for examination when they feared he had aspirated meconium (the newborn's feces) during labor, the mother experienced extreme grief and regret. She seemed to be feeling the feelings from her own birth as she saw her worst fear realized. Having already done so much work with her history, it was relatively easy to work with this piece and her baby didn't need to suffer from the separation the way she had some decades earlier. The trauma wasn't held in shadow. It could be named. The mother was able to acknowledge and feel her grief, which enabled her to be more present when she was reunited with her newborn. Together, we worked with the baby, who had the opportunity to express their feelings and have them accurately reflected before they could become more rigidly set in stony implicit memory. In this way, the birth trauma of the mother didn't have to be continued as intergenerational trauma.

It is common for mothers to re-visit their own pre- and perinatal experience during pregnancy and birth, just as parents tend to remember their own childhoods in tandem with their child's current age. This emergence of shadow, often forgotten early experience, can be a time of healing and resolution when it is welcomed and met with sufficient support. Research in attachment demonstrates that secure attachment is facilitated by how the parents relate to their own early history more than to the exact events that occurred. Developing a coherent story helps parents avoid reenacting their own history with their children.[14]

BIRTH WITH AWARENESS

Awareness enables us to treat babies not as an isolated "product of birth," as they have been considered medically, but as a member of a community, a human field, a planetary or cosmic field. Little ones need to be welcomed, included, acknowledged, accepted at birth. If they have previously experienced prenatal wounding around being less than adequately welcomed, their welcome at birth can help to heal that wound. Unfortunately, many babies have this wound reinforced at birth instead. Parents and birth attendants generally don't intend to hurt the newborn. They are often enacting the unconscious shadow of their own history.

The tendency for birth assistants to act out their own history unconsciously is demonstrated beautifully in this poem by Frederick Leboyer.

> When the infant makes its first appearance, emotion is at its height.
> And everyone's breathing—already tight—chokes, stops altogether.
> "Will the baby breathe?"
> We are all holding our own breath. Identifying with the baby, however unconsciously.
> We have all returned to our own births—fighting for breath just like this newborn baby; close to suffocation.
> And we don't have the umbilicus to supply us with oxygen.
> So things quickly become unbearable.
> It's necessary to "do something."

The easiest, the most sensible, the most obvious thing for the onlooker to do—would be simply to breathe.

Instead of which, he cuts the baby's umbilicus.

His own emotional involvement has made him irrational.

Naturally, the infant howls.

Each person present exclaims in relief: "He's breathing!"

Poor fool! It's only himself he has relieved.

What he really should be crying out is: "I am breathing!"

Because the truth is that the baby was in no hurry—its umbilicus was allowing it plenty of time.

Under the pretext of aiding this new and "other" being, the attendant has considered only himself.

Without knowing it, he has made a transference. He has rid himself of his own anguish by projecting it onto the child.

And it is this sacrificial lamb, deprived of his umbilicus, who suddenly is choking.

And howling . . .[15]

We might wonder how so many medical birth practices have arisen and been maintained despite not being evidence-based and clearly causing harm.[16] Is this an expression of unresolved birth trauma infiltrating the medical birth scene? I am reminded again of Lloyd deMause's concept of war being an enactment of men's birth trauma and feelings about toxicity they perceived in their mother's womb. Is masculinity meddling in normal birth another way for men to act out their own birth history?

Consider that historically birth was always handled by women. When male doctors began to be involved, it was only in difficult births, and hospital births were uncommon.[17] This has changed to the point where medicalized hospital birth has become the norm, with often unnecessary interventions, like caesarean, becoming popular. It is true that there are times when medical intervention can be lifesaving, for mother and/or baby. It is also clear that it can interfere with so-called "normal" birth, in which doctors generally are not experienced. Their training naturally includes observing and participating in difficult births, where medical intervention can help. Unfortunately, too many non-risky births become difficult with unneeded medical intervention.

Recently, I was deeply touched by an interview with Dr. Ricardo Jones, a Brazilian obstetrician who was horrified by the obstetric violence he witnessed as a young resident in the 1980's. He has worked to humanize birth in a country with extremely high caesarean rates. He explained that doctors go to medical school because they want to intervene through surgeries, and so on "because medicine has this masculine, you know this phallic drive to intervene, to penetrate. And midwifery is the opposite. It's to accommodate, is to respect physiology, is to understand the importance for the proper time for things to happen."[18] Doctors are not trained to do nothing as is required for supporting birth. In contrast, Dr. Jones would attend births by sitting nearby, respecting the feminine sensitivity of the midwife and doula supporting the birth, and available if needed.

♫ Echoes of Your Birth Trauma in Your Life ♫

In what ways might you act out your birth in your life? Do you reach for or depend on drugs of any kind to help you deal with challenging situations or numb difficult feelings or sensations? Do you have issues with authority? What thoughts or feelings arise for you when someone tells you what to do or tries to help you? Do you have headaches, neck pain or tension, or pain patterns in the hips, spine, shoulders, or neck?

THE SHADOW OF BIRTH:
ISOLATION, PRESSURE, DISRESPECT

How birth is perceived in our modern society affects how it happens. That birth is undervalued, often feared and isolated, like death, is an expression of its shadow. When birth happens at home, older children can be present and develop a familiarity with the process, as well as usually witnessing a happy outcome. Lack of exposure to birth can generate not only the mother's fear of the unknown but also unfounded confidence. I have heard too many horror stories from new mothers who innocently went to hospital to have their baby, believing as they had been told that it was the safest place for birth. Their stories involved how their midwives treated them coldly, sometimes brutally, without compassion. I was initially shocked by these stories of British midwives, having spent time with American home midwives who were so gentle and present and dedicated to natural birth.

What I quickly came to understand was that the chronic under-funding of the National Health Service (NHS) had led to overworked, stretched staff, including midwives. Instead of being able to be present with birthing people, midwives were under pressure to attend more births than humanly possible. Research indicates that many British midwives are affected by learned helplessness and fear of being blamed when something goes wrong. The word, midwife, means "with woman." Midwives who can't really be with the birthing women aren't able to fulfil their purpose. Continuity of care, which includes having the same familiar midwife who knows the woman, has been shown to reduce the number of medical interventions.[19]

∽ The Replacement Midwife ∽

Emma was past her due date and three days into labor. The midwife, who Emma and her partner liked and arranged to be with, was unavailable as she was needed at another birth. Emma felt ill at ease with the replacement. Then, after a day of challenging but bearable contractions, the replacement left, commenting that nothing much was happening, and she would be back. At this point, contractions stopped for a few hours, probably in response to Emma's stress at losing her support. When the midwife eventually returned, she checked Emma and announced that it would be best to go to hospital because of the chance of infection. Emma was devastated, having dreamed of and prepared for a water birth at home.

Once transported to hospital, the staff there took over, insisting on inducing the birth with drugs. Again, Emma was extremely disappointed but felt powerless to resist. The baby was born with a bruised head, apparently due to the very strong contractions caused *by the drug or the forceps used to assist the birth. The speed of the birth also caused Emma to tear, which was addressed with painful stitches. Instead of celebrating her dream birth, Emma and her baby emerged from hospital feeling battered and disoriented. The baby was not latching onto the breast and often had a far-away, dazed look. This is common in babies who are dissociated due to trauma. It took a series of Craniosacral therapy sessions to enable them to heal and enjoy each other's company.*

Perhaps all of this trauma could have been avoided if Emma and her partner had set up a birth plan with their midwife, including how they wanted things handled in case of transport to hospital. It can be helpful for parents to be forewarned about how hospital staff may be with them and what interventions may be presented. Then, they can be more prepared and more easily make choices. Even if the interventions need to happen, they can feel more empowered in relation to them.

The mothers I met suffered the effects of disempowered midwifery care, emerging traumatized and similarly unable to fully be with their newborn. The babies also felt the effects. The pressure the midwives experienced and passed on to the birthing mother and baby often led to unnecessary emergency interventions, interrupting the natural unfolding of birth, bonding, and breastfeeding. This in turn generates other unfortunate events. For example, women who don't breastfeed are more likely to develop postpartum depression.[20]

To me, this is a sad expression of cultural shadow in a society that does not value women, biology, or birth. As Dr. Ricardo Jones states, "Birth is a cultural event that happens in the body of a woman."[21] He notes that how women are treated in hospital birth has to do with their political position in society. In his webinar, he comments, "We were treating women in a way that diminishes her when compared to men." Separating women from their families and community is disorienting and disempowering. In the transition to hospital, labor often stops due to the stress of the trip, including leaving the familiar comfort of home. This can be true even for women who believe they are safer giving birth in hospital. Their bodies may not agree. Their physiology reacts to the potential for danger. Animals naturally birth in a quiet, protected location. The activity in a car or ambulance and then in hospital is the opposite of what a birthing body usually needs.

When birth is isolated in hospitals, it becomes an illness to be feared. Children do not grow up witnessing birth. When they have the chance to witness their mother engaging her feminine power to meet the contractions with good support from her partner and midwife, children learn that even intense challenges can be worthwhile. I remember a home water birth I attended where the older siblings were present. The eldest had had a traumatic birth in hospital and initially didn't want to be in the room. Just before the big moment, his curiosity overcame his fear, and he joined us. When he saw his little sister emerge, he exclaimed repeatedly, "Oh my God! Oh my God!" His excitement was palpable, and he couldn't wait to climb into the pool and join his family there. It seemed to be a healing experience for him. I can imagine he would be a supportive father when his time comes. It is important to mention that I was available as a support person for the children. If the sight and sounds become too much for a child, they need support, as well as the option to leave. This view is confirmed by Dr. Deborah Issokson's doctoral study, "A Phenomenological Study of Children Who Witness the Birth of a Sibling." Others have reported how a girl's fear of giving birth disappeared after witnessing her sibling's birth.[22] In a culture that has isolated birth, children only know that something painful happens in a hospital before a new baby comes home. First time mothers don't know what to expect. The ignorance and fear with which they approach birth can undermine their instinctual knowing of how to help their baby into the world. If they hear about birth, their fear may be buoyed by reports from friends who have already suffered in their hospital births.

Medical anthropologist Robbie Davis-Floyd describes the effects of this dynamic in the US in her important book, *Birth as an American Rite of Passage*. The women she interviewed tended to emerge from their hospital birth experience scarred, traumatized and at the very least, disappointed. How mothers feel about the birth can affect their relationship with mothering and their baby for life. Even in acknowledging challenges and traumas many birthing people endure in the medicalized birth, it is too seldom noted that mothers and their babies go through these challenges together.

I recently read an example of this where a birthing mother in Ukraine was in denial of the effects on her baby of the war around them. As this war has raged during the writing of this book, I have been feeling for the babies coming into the world surrounded by intense conditions, as exemplified by this story. The article describes how Viktoria went into labor the second day of the war. She and her husband had to drive to the hospital despite their fear of the explosions. After waiting thirty minutes to get gas for their car, they finally arrived at the hospital, where the lights were out to reduce the chance of the hospital being bombed. Sirens sounded during the labor, requiring moving to a small, stark room with minimal privacy where little Fedor was born. In the article, Viktoria states, "I hope my son will experience this war only from stories—that he will never, never feel what it's like in real life. I don't want him to know real war."[23]

I read this with amazement. How can Viktoria believe that her son has not already known real war? He went through his birth with her. Fortunately, he apparently is very loved. This can counter the effects of the extreme stress characterizing his birth, but he also experienced that stress. In so far as it is not acknowledged, his experience is likely to haunt him as an unconscious shadow acting out in the ways shadow does. Simply speaking words like, "We've been through a very difficult time but I'm so glad you are here," can be helpful in a difficult birth situation like this.

BIRTH AS INITIATION

For mothers, birth is an initiatory rite into motherhood. For babies, it is also an initiation. Although the mother has already been a mother for about nine months, most often more active parenting begins at birth. The baby obviously begins a very different phase of life.

Every initiation involves meeting challenges, which may be life-threatening. Birth is no exception. Babies often experience the pressures and sudden changes of birth as such. In that they are easily overwhelmed, birth is often a shocking experience, leaving its mark in many ways.

What may be most shocking about the prevailing often unhelpful, harmful medical practices, is that these effects have been known for many years. Typical of shadowy resistance, they continue to be promoted and applied. They are of course financially rewarding for those practicing them. I learned about this lack of evidence through the exacting work of Davis-Floyd,[24] who concluded from her research that most common hospital birth practices are part of a ritual to initiate both mother and baby into technocratic society. They disempower mothers and babies, rendering them dependent on medical authorities. This facilitates submission in other aspects of their lives.

Once again, the feminine is attacked, disrespected, and mistreated, and truth is relegated to shadow. Both mothers and babies suffer. Their traumas, though often not spoken of, are carried into every domain of modern Western society. Children who have protected themselves through dissociation at birth tend to be less present in their bodies. They then exhibit developmental and learning issues or are less able to listen to their own truth as held in their bodies. Their mothers, also traumatized through their birth, may similarly be dissociative and less present for essential bonding. As well as experiencing less satisfaction and ease with parenting, both parties suffer the absence of secure attachment in their relationship. This can lead to young children seeking relational connection they require in their peers instead of their parents.[25] These children may join gangs or be drawn to drugs or irresponsible sex in efforts to find the love they need. They may grow up to be deceitful politicians, bullying policemen, teachers, or even obstetricians. The cycle repeats itself as unacknowledged trauma is unconsciously recapitulated.

In case you think highly of medicalized birth, I want to acknowledge again that it can save lives. It is important to also recognize that most births are low risk and can proceed more safely in a natural, familiar setting, such as at home or a birth center. It is helpful for the birthing person and partner or support person to feel safe with their surroundings. According to "the sphincter law" of Ina May Gaskin, the cervix functions as if it were a sphincter and closes protectively when threat is perceived.[26] Animals during a birth process will stop pushing and run when faced with a predator. Humans have the same instinct and bodily openings react to a sense of threat or safety by closing or opening. This tends to be neuroceptive awareness of the body, rather than conscious perception.

As mentioned earlier, when transport to hospital is initiated, labor often stops or slows down. Being attended to by strangers, including a doctor, can have the same effect. This iatrogenic (medically caused) situation is generated by the perceived need for being in a medical setting or having medical procedures. Considering that such procedures are needed in only a small percentage of births, I find it sad that so many births are rushed to hospital with much speed, anxiety, and ignorance. The dangers are also evident. When a developed nation like the U.S. has one of the highest maternal mortality rates of industrialized nations (22.3 per 100,000 births in 2022), we can see that expense and technology don't necessarily reduce mortality rates.[27]

The American caesarean rate is one of the highest in the world, with 320 per 1,000 births, compared to 160 per 1,000 live births in Norway and the Netherlands. In contrast, American midwife Mary Jackson, who has worked closely with pre- and perinatal pioneer Ray Castellino to help parents process their own histories in preparing for and moving through birth, rarely transports birthing women to hospital.[28] Births at The Farm, a community established in 1971 in Tennessee where Ina May Gaskin has been the main midwife, have extremely low rates of medical intervention.[29] The lack of need for medical interventions in these practices demonstrates the value of supporting women with respectful listening in a relatively quiet, safe environment. Babies also need slow, sensitive support and communication during their initiatory journey through the birth canal. Little ones are easily overwhelmed. They need more time to process. When birth is met with the belief that the baby must be gotten out as quickly as possible, both maternal and infant nervous systems react to the stress by shifting into a protective defensive mode.

Birth interventions, no matter how well-intended, interrupt a natural movement sequence initiated by the baby and involving an intimate coordinated interactive maternal-infant dance. Interventions including medication to manage pain or induce labor may lead to assistance with forceps, vacuum extraction (ventouse), caesarean, and premature birth. Although there are times when reducing pain may be helpful, it isn't always desirable. A woman I knew chose to have pain medication when she was exhausted by five days of labor but asked to have it discontinued in time for her to be able to push the baby out. She wanted to be able to feel enough at this point to be able to meet her baby in this way. After feeling empowered to make this choice, the pain when she pushed was meaningful for her. Oxytocin, the love hormone that supports birth contractions, breastfeeding, and bonding, increases with pain. Synthetic oxytocin (brands Pitocin and Syntocinon) is often given to accelerate birth. Although the synthetic form stimulates uterine contractions, it omits the love element. It also isn't sensitive to the natural rhythm of the birth dance. Induced contractions tend to be intensely strong and fast with no pauses between them to allow the mother and the baby to rest and recuperate. This can be exhausting, disempowering, disorienting, and overwhelming. The baby and the mother are both deprived of this sacred opportunity to listen to and follow their own internal somatic wisdom. The inherent health may be forgotten. The natural moments of stillness between contractions are missing.

Even interruptions essential for survival may be experienced as traumatic or violently invasive. Simply communicating the intention and describing what is about to happen can help to reduce the harmful impact. Again, the lack of awareness of babies' sentience contributes to their insensitive treatment. Unfortunately, some medical practitioners also don't explain procedures to mothers, who are then deprived of informed consent. The shock they often experience is shared with their baby through physiology and umbilical affect. Babies not understanding that their suffering was not their mother's fault may feel angry or betrayed. Parents who are already scarred by their difficult birth experience are then further stressed by their inconsolable baby. It can be remarkable to witness the change in the relationship and the baby's countenance when their anger or other emotions are allowed to be expressed and accurately reflected in therapy. If this is not resolved in infancy, the shadowy feelings persist through life.

How we meet our lives is strongly influenced by these first moments. In that birth is relational, its echoes are often apparent in relationships. As a major transition out of the womb into the external world where we begin to breathe and eat more independently, birth also establishes a template for how we do transitions. Whenever we encounter a major change in our lives, such as starting or ending a relationship, education, or job, we are likely to experience aspects of our birth pattern. These may include physical symptoms, like a stiff neck, as well as psychological characteristics, like becoming angry, anxious, fearful, or dependent. Echoing our experience of our first transition, we may push forward in unsatisfying, exhausting ways and then energetically collapse before completing a project or tend to expect/need someone to interrupt or rescue us in transitions or other challenging moments.

COMMON BIRTH TRAUMAS AND THEIR EFFECTS

Birth trauma is unfortunately extremely common. There are several traumas frequently associated with medical interventions, as well as challenges that may lead to those interventions. Listed below are common conditions and interventions and their potential traumatic effects.

So-called "normal" birth interventions often include:

Episiotomy: This cutting of the perineum is believed to reduce the chance of tearing as the baby comes out. Instead, it tends to create pain and scarring, and the wound tends to take longer to heal than a natural tear. An alternative that is gentler on both mother and baby is to allow the baby to emerge more slowly, guiding the birthing person as necessary to help slow the process down.

Epidural: This is used for reducing pain during labor, which is at times helpful for the mother to be able to cope with contractions. Unfortunately, as it reduces sensation and presence in the tissues, it also interferes with the mother being able to feel her baby coming out as sensitively. As tone is reduced in the muscles, the baby is also met with less presence and tone. There is less resistance to push against, which can affect the baby's sense of their own power. Less sense of presence can also be perceived by the baby as mommy not being there to meet them. This undermines an aspect of the foundation for postnatal bonding. Babies may grow up to have less sensation in the lower half of their body, as if they had received the epidural. They may also tend to numb out in some way as they are completing things. This effect is stronger with general anesthesia, where the mother is unconscious. Although less common now with vaginal births than it used to be, general anesthesia may still be used in caesarean sections.

Electronic fetal monitoring (EFM): This non-evidence-based intervention can interfere with maternal mobility and comfort, both essential for labor to proceed.[30] Instead, the mother is often uncomfortably lying in one position for hours. EFM does not save lives and can lead to more interventions due to false readings. Research indicates that both EFM and epidurals can increase the likelihood of caesarean birth.[31] Labor becomes more difficult because the enforced horizontal position impedes the natural support of gravity when the woman can be in a more upright position. Being able to move also addresses discomfort, stimulates contractions, and embodies her own power and wisdom as a woman. The baby resonates with her frustration, fear, and pain, and may have their own as their passage becomes more difficult. They also must endure the shocking pain of a monitor on their scalp. Like all interventions, this could be less overwhelming if the practitioner spoke to the baby, warning them that they will feel a sensation meant to help them get out.

Other common medical interventions include the following:

Induction: Labor is induced if the birth practitioner believes it is going too slowly, based on standard schedules, if labor hasn't started and the due date has passed,* if there are concerns about the baby's or mother's health if labor doesn't begin or proceed. The results can include premature birth. Most due dates are not accurate, being based on the woman's last menstrual period rather than on the actual date of conception. Menstrual cycles are rarely as precise as the four weeks this calculation is based on. Both mother and baby may experience disorientation and disempowerment with induction. As mentioned earlier, synthetic oxytocin usually used for induction does not have the same effects as natural oxytocin. It stimulates continuous contractions, lacking the rejuvenating pauses of natural labor. They can be so strong as to rupture the womb, which obviously is traumatic for mother and baby in the womb. Synthetic oxytocin also doesn't support bonding like its natural "love hormone" counterpart. Having this hormone imposed on the system also misses the balancing endorphins that enhance feelings of ease and euphoria.

    Babies who have had their birth induced often have difficulty knowing their own timing throughout their lives. They tend to rush, and have difficulty slowing down and resting, having been denied this phase of labor. Their sympathetic nervous system is constantly on unless they collapse at some point from exhaustion. They often seem to talk without pause, never taking a breath. You might begin to feel breathless listening to them. This resonates with the lack of pause and oxygen inflicted by overly strong, incessant contractions. The challenges of induction are not necessarily worth the problems it causes. It often leads to further interventions as the baby still isn't out and now there are additional complications of stress, overwhelm, and exhaustion.

---

*Most practitioners consider two weeks past the due date to be overdue with possible dangerous repercussions.

Forceps or vacuum extraction (ventouse): Forceps began to be used frequently to assist birth as birth became increasingly medicalized. More recently, vacuum extraction has tended to replace their use, although at times both are used. These methods are generally applied as the head is emerging, purportedly to support it when it is stuck. Although skilled use of forceps with appropriate warning to mother and baby about how it will feel can be helpful when needed, the routine use, and general lack of adequate skill have resulted in forceps injuries and trauma being far too common. Babies born with this assistance often develop a resentful attitude toward authority figures in their life. They may also suffer from chronic neck tension that can be activated by stress or transitions.

Caesarean section (C-section): This surgery can be planned or unplanned in case of emergency. It may be planned if vaginal delivery is deemed dangerous or impossible for mother and/or baby. For instance, in placenta previa, where the placenta is low, lying against the cervix, the baby would not be able to get safely passed it to be born vaginally. C-sections were often assumed to be necessary if a previous birth was caesarean. This assumption has been challenged since the rise of vaginal birth after caesarean (VBAC) in the 1980s (finally recommended by the National Institutes of Health in 2010), enabling more vaginal births to follow a history of C-section. Some C-sections are planned because they are seen to be easier for mother and baby, to be healthier, or to be fashionable. For example, Brazil has an extremely high percentage of C-section births. Anyone who can afford it apparently plans a C-section party, inviting their friends to celebrate in the hospital and be the first to see the baby. Where is the honoring of the mystery of the feminine in this approach?

Emergency C-sections occur when the health or life of the mother and/or baby are assessed to be in danger if the birth does not happen quickly. Again, this is sometimes lifesaving. Unfortunately, emergency C-sections can also result after previous medical interventions don't work. Several common interventions, including fetal monitoring, and epidurals increase likelihood of C-section. Hospital birth itself increases the risk of C-section. The operation may also be administered when the baby is in a breech position because many medical practitioners these days are not trained in how to safely support a breech delivery. Despite rumors, C-section is not necessarily a healthy option. Mothers experiencing this major abdominal surgery take time to recover from the anesthesia, shock, and pain. Babies can also be more sluggish and suffer multiple health issues. They miss exposure to beneficial vaginal microbiome and the helpful squeeze of the contractions, which can be like a massage igniting all the organs. Consider that microbiome can serve as an additional layer of support, enhancing health in remarkable ways.* Where their contribution is interfered with, it is helpful to acknowledge this and compensate as possible, for example by breastfeeding.

If born by emergency C-section, babies may tend to expect or need to be rescued. With a planned C-section, they have usually missed the chance to initiate labor when it is the right time for them. They tend to be disconnected from their own timing throughout life. C-section babies were exposed to anesthesia in their birth, establishing a template for reaching for numbing drugs in times of pain or challenge. Planned C-sections often birth a baby prematurely. This may result in time in the neonatal intensive care unit (NICU), often separated from their parents and exposed to painful, invasive procedures as their main source of contact. Although skin-to-skin kangaroo care is becoming more available as understanding of its beneficial effects grows, there are still many preemies who have suffered this challenging start to life. If they are in an incubator, they may grow up feeling like they are always looking through glass

---

*The microbiome is made up of organisms in our bodies that are mostly beneficial.

at other people in their lives. Babies born early or by C-section often develop sensory integration issues, which are often accompanied by learning, behavioral, and developmental challenges. Because emergency C-sections often happen after the baby's head has engaged and they have made efforts to move through the birth canal, the baby may tend to feel interrupted by others when they are trying to express or complete something. Babies who have been assisted in their birth by caesarean, forceps, or ventouse, may feel anger and resentment about the intrusion or may feel grateful and relieved to have been rescued. These can then influence how they experience interactions with others later in life.

I am reminded as I write this of a mother and baby I worked with very soon after their caesarean birth. I went to their home where they were both very groggy. The mother was barely able to hold and talk to her baby because she was so sleepy. She was in intense pain where the scar was on her belly and could not lift her baby for care. I was there to offer Craniosacral therapy and found that it took several sessions for them both to start feeling alive under my hands. As the baby recovered, her whimpering began to sound more like angry cries, which softened as we acknowledged what she and her mom had been through. With this process, breastfeeding became easier, and the baby began to thrive. Both mother and baby clearly began enjoying each other much more.

BIRTH FROM THE BABY'S PERSPECTIVE

An important step in addressing birth trauma for the baby is to consider birth from the baby's perspective. Birth practitioners describe the birth process as occurring in three stages:

1. the cervix shortening and opening
2. descent and birth of the baby
3. delivery of the placenta

These are from the external perspective of the birth attendant and possibly the mother.

Birth as experienced from inside the birth canal is different. Informed by client work relating to the challenges birthing babies meet, my mentors in pre- and perinatal therapy, William R. Emerson with the assistance of Franklyn Sills and later Ray Castellino identified four important stages of birth from the baby's perspective. The description of the following stages is taken from their collective work, as written by Sills in *Foundations in Craniosacral Biodynamics, Vol 2*.

Stage One: Inlet Dynamics: Descent

Stage Two: Mid-Pelvic Dynamics: Rotational Descent

Stage Three: Outlet Dynamics: Anterior-Posterior Descent

Stage Four: Restitution: Head and Body Birth

Specifically, how these stages manifest and imprint upon the physical body and psyche can vary depending on maternal pelvic shape, stress, and other factors but they have general parameters. Understanding our passage through the birth canal, we see how our experiences at different stages may be reflected in our lives.

STAGES OF BIRTH

Birth Stage One: Inlet Dynamics (Descent)

Labor begins with the baby lying on one side (the lie side). The baby's head faces the side of the mother's pelvis. For a "left side lie" baby (most common), the left side of the baby is against (conjunct) mother's spine. The force of birth contractions generally affects the lie side most. Contractions have begun, but the cervix is not yet open, creating compressive forces on the baby's head (unless breech), and initiating descent toward the birth canal. In this "no exit" stage, named by pre- and perinatal therapy pioneer, Stanislav Grof, babies exert effort, pushing with their little feet, with no sense of progress or relief. Although no progress forward is possible with the cervix still closed, each baby experiences this differently, depending on many circumstances. It may be overwhelming, as Grof describes, or the baby may feel building excitement and a sense of something starting to happen. Physical pressures may generate a C-curve in the body which becomes a chronic pattern of tissue tension, with one shoulder low and the hip bone on the birth lie side rotated posteriorly (toward the back of the body). The newborn will often commonly have the leg on their lie side "pulled up in a contracted manner. It is common for people exploring this stage of birth to curl up into fetal position on their birth lie side.

The ineffectiveness of effort in this stage may be reenacted as a tendency to endogenous depression, meaning depression arising without apparent external cause. This experience of repeated non-productive pushing when the cervix is still closed can generate a "schema form[ing] the potential basis for impotence in all its various life phases, e.g., impotent action, impotent rage, impotent sexuality, impotent relating, etc." A fetus who collapses during contractions may experience schemas of victimization, denial, paranoia, or endogenous depression.

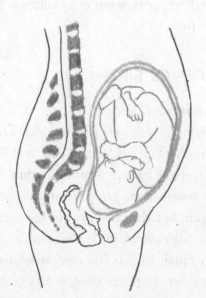

Fig. 4.3. Birth Stage One

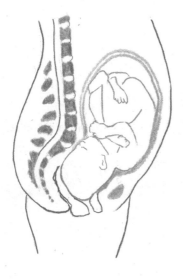

Fig. 4.4. Birth Stage Two

Birth Stage Two: Mid-Pelvis Dynamics (Rotational Descent)

After successfully moving through the pelvic inlet, baby's head rotates toward their own shoulder, usually toward mother's spine or sacrum. Rotating toward her pubic bone results in posterior or sunny side up position which can be more difficult but may be necessary for the pelvic shape involved. Rotation is needed to enter the birth canal.

Stage Two issues often generate whole body torsions, spinal rotations, and specific cranial and temporomandibular joint or jaw (TMJ) patterns. These may be enacted by twisting or turning the head, in therapy or life when Stage Two birth material arises. Depending on maternal pelvic shape, babies may struggle to find an effective way through the mid-pelvis. This may generate lifelong issues of feeling stuck, ambivalence, difficulty making decisions or committing, or directional confusion.

I am reminded of when my brother visited me after one of my many moves to a new home. To my surprise, he revealed that he found my house by following the opposite of the directions I had given him, knowing I always said left when I meant right and vice versa! Through birth therapy, I later realized my confusion in directions originated in Stage Two, further reinforced when the doctor pulled my head in the wrong direction with forceps, also creating chronic neck tension.

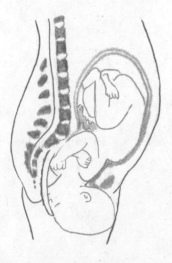

Fig. 4.5. Birth Stage Three

Birth Stage Three: Outlet Dynamics (Anterior-Posterior Descent)

In this stage the baby's face usually has turned toward mother's spine. The head is either flexed forward or aligned with the torso and extends backward to move out through the birth canal, past mother's sacrum and symphysis pubis. The baby's shoulders and torso rotate, following the path of the head. According to Sills, stage three can generate compressive patterns locked in the spine. This results when stress, trauma, or shock compounds the compression, which can be painful and frightening for babies. Depending on pelvic shape, the baby's head may turn toward the maternal pubic bone. This "posterior" position increases pain for both mother and baby as the baby's occiput is in direct contact with the mother's sacrum, creating bone on bone pressure. A resultant pattern later in the child's life may be feeling stuck or having difficulty progressing when approaching goals or completing projects in life.

Birth Stage Four: Restitution (Head and Body Birth)

In this stage the head is born and moves back to its original sideways position (restitution). The shoulders and body follow, which may be difficult and traumatic because of their size. In shoulder dystocia, a shoulder is stuck. Once the head and shoulders are born, the smaller trunk and legs tend to emerge quickly and easily. Completing this stage, the baby is "caught" and hopefully welcomed, initiating postnatal bonding.

Restitution may cause neck strain or reinforce compression and strain from earlier stages. Birth of the anterior (front) shoulder (if it is stuck while conjunct mother's pubis symphysis) may result in a low shoulder on the side opposite the birth lie side. A common practice of pulling the baby's head toward the rear of the mother's body to help clear the shoulder of the mother's pubis may injure the shoulder, clavicle, or neck on the side opposite the lie side. Babies are often born with a broken clavicle, not always recognized but painful for the baby. Difficulties delivering the other shoulder may produce similar tissue patterns on the lie side. Pulling the body out with excessive force creates rotation, torsion and compressive patterns which look like a "C" curve opposite the birth lie side. It curves away from the lie side, unlike the "C" curve toward the lie side that may be generated in Stage One.

Body movement relating to Stage Four includes "corkscrew" motion expressing twisting through the birth canal or the over-rotation imposed with forceps. Someone exploring this stage may retract their head into their shoulders, expressing resistance to forceps, vacuum extraction, or caesarean section, or having been held back until the doctor arrived. The person may turn in one direction and then the other, seeking a way out. A pattern of extension, like the cobra posture in yoga, is also

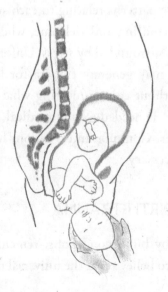

Fig. 4.6. Birth Stage Four

common. This relates to the baby being pulled out while face down. This arching pattern may also occur later in clients on their backs, sides, or standing. An individual who presented face up (posterior presentation or sunny side up) may move into a similar extension pattern relating to Stage Four but will do this lying face up.

We can see these kinds of movements in babies, children, or adults reenacting their birth. Movement relating to Stage One often involves being curled up in fetal position, pushing with feet and head, possibly against some kind of barrier, like a facilitator's hand, a cushion, or a wall. Stage Two reenactment is characterized by head rotation followed by the rest of the body also turning. Embodying Stage Three tends to involve either extending or flexing the head before shooting forward. There may be a reenactment here of feeling blocked and needing help. As mentioned above, in Stage Four, there is a tendency to extend the head as well as rotating it back to its original position (restitution). Hopefully, there is someone available to "catch" and welcome the person as they move through these stages and emerge in Stage Four. Therapy addressing birth trauma may involve moving through these birth patterns several times until a new, gentler, less impeded way is established. People often experience associated changes in their lives as they meet and integrate their somatic memories through movement and support.

Trauma and associated somatic patterns relating to each stage tend to soften or resolve with gentle handling and welcome, whereas they are reinforced and rigidified when surrounded by stress. Unfortunately, well-meaning birth practitioners may generate trauma for baby and mother by acting too quickly, without communicating what they are doing or pausing to listen to what is needed. Many medical interventions are applied in the later stages. Common interventions have been demonstrated to be only rarely necessary.

REDUCING BIRTH TRAUMA

Even without traumas imposed by birth conditions, remember that Freud and his student Rank came to believe that the universal trauma of birth resulted from leaving the relative comfort of the womb. Although this belief overlooks the frequent overwhelming conditions babies encounter prenatally, departure from the womb can engender deep feelings of loss. In the poetic words of author Martín Prechtel,

> This heaviest of losses comes to all of us when we as babies in the womb lose our mother's heartbeat when we are born. Ringing through our bodies before and during the amazing giganticness of our births, each of our mothers' heartbeats disappears when we enter into this cold, noisy, and sometimes not so friendly world. Today most people don't pay much attention to this.[32]

Prechtel, though not a birth practitioner or therapist, expresses an understanding, like Rank, that birth is a quintessential experience for babies which is generally unacknowledged. Although loss is not the only trauma possible at birth, it does need to be recognized. I recently took a wonderful course on grieving. I appreciated that there was a section on perinatal loss, but it was only from the parents' perspective of losing a baby with miscarriage or early death. The baby's perspective remains in shadow.

When looking at birth trauma, it is helpful to consider what would be less traumatizing. We know that little ones process input much more slowly than we do as adults. The speed often accompanied by fear or panic at birth is easily overwhelming for the baby, as well as stimulating the mother's stress response and therefore tightening her cervix and delivering stress hormones umbilically to the baby. We can summarize what babies need as the following:

- Slower pacing to avoid overwhelm and shut down
- Respectful, negotiated contact
- To be listened to, received, and welcomed
- To be protected
- To have their experiences, perceptions, feelings appreciated, heard, and compassionately reflected

Increasing awareness of both baby's and mother's needs can reduce trauma. Medical interventions can be done in less disturbing, more respectful, relational ways supporting trust instead of distrust, communication rather than authoritative commands or silence, with love and safety replacing fear and defensiveness.

Awareness can lift primal traumas out of shadow, rendering them less likely to be repeated in future births or in the lives of those who have been wounded during their birth. Like all developmental milestones, birth is intended to involve some degree of challenge. However, I don't believe it is meant to be overwhelming. I am sure that humans are not required to welcome other humans into their world through violence, disrespect, insensitivity, speed, fear, commercial gain, and so on. Surely, since we know that welcome can be loving, gentle, and supportive with beneficial results, we might be willing to do the healing around our own history to render us more receptive to what is needed in the moment. I think that is called compassion.

Reflections

1. Please note any interventions shortly after birth such as hospitalization for illness or jaundice, operations, illnesses or other traumas, or family upsets as an infant or a child. How old were you?

2. Did either or both of your parents lose another child to miscarriage, abortion, stillbirth, or childhood death? If yes, are you aware of how this affected you. Give dates and circumstances.

3. Please relate any other information you know concerning your conception, your parents' attitude toward having you (planned, unplanned, wanted, confused, unwanted). If unwanted, did they consider or attempt abortion?

4. How safe do you feel? How do you feel about doctors, hospitals, operations? What are your relationships like? Is it easy for you to be close to others or do you have barriers to intimacy?

5

Maternal Influences
Effects on the Prenate and Newborn

The mother gazes at the baby in her arms, and the baby gazes at his mother's face and finds himself therein . . . provided that the mother is really looking at the unique, small, helpless being and not projecting her own expectations, fears, and plans for the child. In that case, the child would not find himself in his mother's face, but rather the mother's own projections. This child would remain without a mirror, and for the rest of his life would be seeking this mirror in vain.

DONALD WOODS WINNICOTT

Sensitive, compassionate welcome is part of the original blueprint for human birth. How the baby experiences their first moments as they arrive into the world outside the womb either meets their evolutionary based expectations or falls short in some way. Liedloff describes the effects of not meeting "the inherent expectations of [our] species." She sees change, unlike evolution, as "replac[ing] a piece of well-integrated behavior with one that is not. It replaces what is complex and adapted with what is simpler and less adapted. As a consequence, change places a strain on the equilibrium of all the intricately related factors inside and outside the system."[1]

When the natural expectations are not met, the usually traumatic experience imprints can occlude the blueprint. Echoes of these first moments resonate in how the child and later adult manages transitions of any kind.

Consider that each moment is a new birth, different from the previous moment. What was has died? What is now is new? How do we meet the new moment, so very different from the last one? Birth is our first major transition and requires adaptation. Inside the mother's body temperature is regulated for us; food and oxygen are provided without our active participation, sounds are muffled, and we are cushioned by the amniotic ocean surrounding us.

Outside the womb we suddenly need to breathe on our own, suck and swallow to receive nourishment, as we are simultaneously adapting to relatively loud sounds, changes in temperature, hard, dry surfaces, and often startling contact and handling by the people around us. Too often, those people include strangers. We are separated to some degree from the familiarity of having our mother's fluids, tissues, heartbeat, hormones, and emotions all around us.

This again may be an adjustment, trauma or shock that is never acknowledged, particularly if it happens too quickly. Without acknowledgment, it cannot be fully processed and tends to linger in the unconscious, leaking out through our attitudes, behaviors, and reactions to change and transition. For example, a baby may cry when being picked up without warning. A toddler may resist going out the door. Challenges can be expressed in everyday transitions like getting out of bed, going to school, or later getting to work on time or starting a new job or relationship. These can echo the dramatic shift occurring at birth.

Reflections

You may want to take a pause here to journal about your own experiences of transition. I invite you to also observe what arises for you emotionally and somatically as you think about transitions in your life. In that your breathing began at birth, how is your breath as you read about this time?

1. How are you at initiating projects, activities, events? Do you feel able to initiate or complete tasks independently or do you feel a need for help?

2. What is your sense of timing like? Are you habitually late or early for appointments or events? Do you procrastinate and then feel rushed at the end? Do you tend to feel pressured to meet deadlines?

3. Do you like to do things your own, unique way (often a trait with breech birth)?

4. How is it for you to get up in the morning or go to bed at night? How are other transitions for you, like starting a new job, beginning a relationship, graduating from a course or from school, traveling, or moving to a new home?

5. If you have given birth, how was that experience?

6. Do you tend to feel depressed?

7. How do you support yourself with what arises?

UMBILICAL AFFECT

Another major transition concerns the umbilical cord. The link between mother and baby is an essential connection—both the experience of receiving nutrients and information from the umbilicus, as well as the transition away from this source. Umbilical affect is an important concept in pre- and perinatal psychology. The term was originally coined by pre- and perinatal psychology pioneer Francis Mott and developed further by Frank Lake. Mott defined *umbilical affect* as the "feeling state of the fetus as brought about by blood reaching him through the umbilical vein."[2] The fetal emotional state is affected by the source of nourishment, the umbilical vein, which carries not only nutrients, but also bio-chemical expressions of the mother's emotional experience.

Specifically, umbilical affect refers to the inflow through the umbilical cord of maternal emotions (affect), feelings and experience on prenates, ranging from positive to highly toxic. Although it refers to umbilical inflow, umbilical affect can include postnatal maternal influence due to the close connection between mother and infant. This implies communication beyond the physiological via umbilical blood vessels. There is clearly also an energetic connection between mother and baby, as represented by their overlapping bioenergetic heart fields.

Most important to understand here is that babies tend to be happier, feel safer, and calmer when their mother feels the same. Via the umbilical vein, babies develop prenatally under the influence of their mother's hormones as bio-chemical communications and through resonating with energetic transmissions from the mother and with her emotional states. Infants will continue to experience an echo of this influence after birth. I have frequently seen a young baby calm when I support their mother in settling through Craniosacral therapy. Returning to the HeartMath research, we see that heart rhythms are directly affected by emotional states. For example, feelings of anger create incoherent heart rhythms. Orienting to gratitude and appreciation quickly creates coherence, which influences other aspects of the person's bioenergetic body. Remember that every organ, tissue, and cell emit bioenergetic fields. These all communicate with each other. The heart's powerful fields have a particularly strong effect. When the mother feels love, joy, peace, or other positive states, she increases her heart coherence, which resonates in her baby's heart.

As mentioned earlier, little ones are not able to differentiate between the emotions of someone else and their own. They perceive and learn through their whole body. They experience the emotion directly and become the anger, fear, joy, and so on. They need others to tell them that a difficult emotion isn't theirs. For example, when a pregnant mother or one with a young baby is upset about something, it can be helpful to explain this to her little one. Babies listen and respond with relief when their mother tells them something like, "Mommy is upset just now, but it's not about you. You don't need to do anything about it. Mommy is ok and taking care of it." Differentiating, for them, in this way has proven repeatedly to be helpful. Without this kind of communication, babies suffer with the heavy load of their mother's emotions, which may be challenging for an adult but can be overwhelming for a little one.

If as a fetus or infant you didn't receive that kind of differentiating communication, you may find that, even as an adult, you tend to take on others' emotions without realizing it. You may for example feel very sad or depressed without an apparent reason. You may have difficulty setting personal boundaries in your relationships or have a tendency to have to take care of others, because you tried to do that when you were very little. Like a baby, you may tend to become easily overwhelmed by emotions without knowing how to regulate your nervous system. You may tend to isolate yourself or find intimate relationships overwhelmingly challenging.

Lake divided umbilical affect into positive, negative, and strongly negative, each with differing effects on the developing attachment style and personality of the little one. As you might imagine, positive umbilical affect generates an experience of safety, trust, and confidence, supporting social engagement and a secure attachment style. Negative umbilical affect isn't necessarily problematic. A certain amount of negative affect prepares the baby for uncertainty and challenges in life, supporting resilience, but if the negative affect becomes extreme, insecure attachment styles are likely. The fetus can respond to maternal emotions arriving umbilically by accepting them as their own, opposing them, becoming overwhelmed by them, or becoming a "fetal therapist" who tries to support their suffering mother.[3]

The child marinates in these feelings, which strongly influences their sense of self, the world, and their relation to others, providing a basis for personality development. Mother's ambivalence or negativity toward her partner or her life may become ambivalence to one's own life.[4] Little one feels bad without knowing why, without being able later in life to identify the source of depression, anger, mistrust, grief, and so on. These feelings persist in peeping out of the shadows, seeking recognition and healing. Below is an exercise designed to assist you in processing umbilical affect.

EXPLORATION
♃ *Working with Umbilical Affect* ♃

Take a little time to settle into a comfortable position, sitting or lying down, perhaps in the fetal position. Please take some time to let yourself be aware of what helps you to be comfortable and to know that you are. What sensations speak to you of comfort or discomfort? If you are uncomfortable in some way, can you allow yourself to move or support yourself with cushions or blankets until you find more comfort. Is there something that enables you to rest just a bit more in this moment? What are you aware of in your body as you begin to rest?

When you are settled and resourced, place a hand over your navel; notice how it feels to have your hand there. Is it comfortable? Does it feel nurturing? Perhaps it feels uncomfortable, intrusive. You may find yourself feeling a bit nauseous. Or there may be a warm, fuzzy feeling, as if you are being held and met by a loving presence. That presence is you! If it feels uncomfortable, you may want to shift your contact to make it firmer or lighter or even suspend your hand just above your navel without touching it. The idea is not to overwhelm yourself but to get to know and heal this territory.

As you hold yourself with your hand over your navel, what do you sense? Whatever you experience is valid. There is no right or wrong way to do this. The intention here is to be with whatever arises. If you feel nauseous, spacey or as if your space is being intruded upon, you may be touching on early umbilical memories of your experience before birth. They could relate to having the cord cut at birth, receiving anesthesia, or other medications administered to your mother reaching you via your umbilical cord.

It can feel remarkably empowering to be able to begin to push these uncomfortable sensations out through your navel. It is like returning them to their source. They are not yours. They are not inherently you, although they may feel that way because of their very early establishment. When you were little, you had no choice but to receive what came to you. You depended on the nourishment arriving via the umbilical cord. Whatever else came with it needed to be accepted, too. Now, you are no longer dependent in that way. You can begin to differentiate between what is actually nutritive and supportive for you and what is toxic or not useful. The latter can be returned now. You won't die by rejecting it, as you would have in the womb or even at birth.

Some people like to create a symbolic representation of the cord. For example, you might want to twist a sheet or blanket and stretch it out with one end connecting to your umbilicus. Check in with what feels interesting and right for you. You are empowered to explore this as you wish, but please do it gently, remembering to stay connected with your resource, what feels good or ok and supportive to you.

Stay with this process as long as it feels useful. It may be quite intense when you first start working with it. In that case, it can be helpful to practice it for short periods of time frequently. The idea is to give yourself a chance to touch on your umbilical feelings without becoming overwhelmed by them. Be sure to transition gently out of the exploration. For example, dismantle your symbolic cord slowly, with sensitivity.

You may prefer to do this exercise with a trusted friend or therapist present support you. Over time, the feelings can be processed and become more tolerable. Eventually, they can be increasingly replaced by warm, nurturing sensations. You may have a sense of not only a soothing kind of warmth, but also of a delicious filling, softening, release, spreading, perhaps a sense of light. You may begin to sense these pleasant sensations spreading throughout your body, moving down into your legs, up to your heart, chest, shoulders, and arms.

Your heart and umbilical experience are intimately connected. As a little one, you receive not only nutrients, but also hopefully love through your umbilical cord. Birth is meant to be accompanied and supported by what is known as the love hormone. Oxytocin is an important hormone supporting bonding and attachment, which also stimulates the uterine contractions required after the baby is born to eject the placenta. This powerful hormone is also present for both mother and baby during breastfeeding. You may begin to feel some of it as you reclaim your umbilicus, filling it with love and appreciation from the one to whom you most matter—you!

When you feel like you are done with holding your umbilicus, take some time to look around and slowly start moving your body. Move around the room, sensing your feet on the floor, how your legs and arms are moving, and any sense of your torso, heart, chest, throat, belly and navel. Let yourself be curious about what you sense. How familiar or new are your sensations? How does it feel to have spent time loving your own navel, and your own little one—the little one who you were?

SEPARATION, ATTACHMENT, BREASTFEEDING, AND CONTINUITY

By the time a baby is born, they have already spent about nine months within their mother, in the closest proximity that is possible between two human beings. Inside the mother, the fetus is completely dependent on the maternal heart and umbilical connection for taking in food, expelling wastes, maintaining homeostasis, and learning about and preparing for life in her world.

Birth is meant to be a continuation of this connection. According to the blueprint, the transition is relatively gentle. The cord is allowed to stop pulsing before being cut and the baby can continue sensing mom's presence through physical contact. The umbilicus through which the baby has rooted into mother prenatally continues to be a point of orientation for the neonate. Babies can't stand on Mama Earth with their two feet. According to the blueprint, they gradually transition from rooting into mother to rooting into the earth below them. Without support for umbilical or "tummy" rootedness, breastfeeding can be more difficult than necessary. Dr. Suzanne Colson, founder of Biological Nurturing, or "laid back breastfeeding," recognizes that babies latch on and feed more easily when they have tummy contact with their mother who is resting into support.[5] Both mother and baby can relax into this support.

From a somatic perspective, belly rooting into mother and breastfeeding ensure an essential continuity of the prenatal reliance on maternal nourishment and support. This softens the postpartum transition for both mother and baby. Remember that humans are born a year prematurely compared to other animals, which begin to walk within minutes or hours of birth. We take a year to catch up.

EXPLORATION

✨ *Newborn Bonding (Postpartum)* ✨

There are many ways to explore and re-create your experience of bonding just after birth. It can be particularly helpful to do these kinds of activities with a person you trust and feel comfortable with, like a therapist, close friend, or intimate partner. You can also explore on your own.

Begin by setting up a comfortable receiving station for yourself and your inner little one. This might be similar to the nest you created for the implantation exploration. You may even want to do this piece as an extension of the implantation exploration, after spending as much time in your womb/nest as you want. The next step is to find your way out of the nest in a satisfying way. Have a soft, supportive surface available for you when you emerge. Then, take some time to settle yourself on this surface. Can you feel its support under you? Are you warm enough? Do you need or want a blanket covering you? Do you have a sense of the presence of a supportive person, whether someone who is physically there with you or someone in your imagination?

Do you feel like you want some contact? This can come from the person with you, from your mother, someone else in your imagination, or from your own hands. It can be soothing to gently stroke your body, being sure to include your face. This awakens the social engagement nervous system and can help to calm the more defensive fight-flight or freeze reactions. You may want to talk to yourself softly or ask the person with you to do so.

Can you sense yourself, or the little one that you were, being welcomed? Can you sense love? What are you feeling in your body? What sensations draw your attention? What feels nourishing, resourcing, or supportive to you? Can you allow yourself to focus on these nurturing feelings?

You may discover that, as you rest with this kind of support, your body begins to move, perhaps like that of a newborn baby. This may be little wiggles of toes or fingers. It may be a feeling of wanting to be on your tummy, inchworming your way toward a breast, which you probably will need to imagine. When you reach the breast, notice how that feels, your instinct to latch onto it. To have a more somatic experience, you may find it helpful to have something to suck on. Personally, I have found the back of my forearm or hand to be most satisfying as a surrogate nipple. A participant in a womb surround exploring this territory found sucking on her little finger to be just right. You can be creative about what you use. Some colleagues and I once ordered special nipples made for calves. They were about the right size for us, but they tasted terrible!

Take as long as feels right to you to explore this territory. You can re-visit this as often as you like. If you are practicing in your imagination, you can imagine holding little you, speaking to him or her softly, falling in love with little you. If you are doing this with someone else, speak from your adult self to let them know what you need. You may want to practice on your own for some time and then ask someone else to do this with you.

I encourage you to listen to what feels right to you. This is your time to heal and to experience what may have been missing back then. When you feel complete, or you run out of time, please make the transition back into your life gently. Take some time to slowly look around the room you are in. If you are with someone, make some eye contact. Speak a few words.

Throughout the exploration, practice remembering that you have already been born, and already survived the early days after your birth. You can differentiate between the helpless little one you were back then and the comparably very capable adult you are now. Even if you don't think of yourself as a very capable person, you have all kinds of skills and abilities that you didn't have as a newborn. It may help to simply remember your current age. From that place, you can welcome, hold, and protect the little one that you were, who still lingers within you. You can make new choices, like the choice to receive the welcome offered to you by another person, or the support provided to you by the cushions. You can also make choices to move slowly from your lying down position to sitting to standing and walking. Please be gentle with yourself. Observe how that feels.

I recommend taking some time when you are done to journal or do some integrative artwork, possibly with your non-dominant hand. Allow yourself some creative integration time. This can also be useful to refer back to for further insight and learning.

In the embryo, the legs and feet develop in relation to the umbilical cord. They grow around it, in contrast to arms and hands that bud on either side of the heart and embrace it as they grow. Babies are born with their legs abducted and externally rotated, having been originally separated by the umbilical cord. They need to come into a more forward-facing position at midline to enable standing and walking. Until this function is well-established, they depend on mother for grounding. Any separation from her soon after birth tends to be shocking, disorienting, and ungrounding. This can be reflected throughout life in a less grounded gait, where the feet appear to be hesitant to make full contact with Mother Earth. Physiotherapy, chiropractic, and so on, do nothing to address the shadow of premature disconnection from mother that is indicated. Once again, the feminine is rejected or ignored in the common hospital practice of separating babies from their mothers at birth which has only recently begun to change.

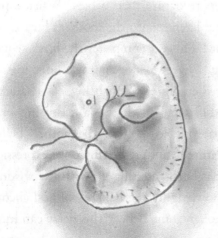

Fig. 5.1. Embryo with legs and arms

Fig. 5.2. Bonding

Fortunately, the work of Klaus, Klaus, and Kennell starting in the 1970's drew attention to the importance of the first hour after birth as a sensitive period, a time when bonding is facilitated by biology.[6] Natural hormones like oxytocin and noradrenaline support breastfeeding and bonding, enhancing the sense of smell by which babies recognize mother and find her breast and mothers recognize their babies.[7] When unmedicated, the baby crawls up to and latches onto the mother's breast, which has been called self-attachment.[8] This act completes the birth sequence, guided by an innate knowing.[9] "Every nerve ending under his newly exposed skin craves the expected embrace, all his being, the character of all he is, leads to his being held in arms."[10] There is a reassuring sense of completion of birth when the baby is able to rest on the mother's belly and find their way to the breast. Nature is finding her intended expression.

More recently, medicine has been catching up with the wisdom of traditional midwifery by acknowledging the benefits of and encouraging delayed cord cutting. Although some believe this delay can increase risk of jaundice, research indicates that, not only is this not the case but that jaundice may be avoided with the delay.[11] In some traditions the cord is not only allowed to stop pulsing but is reverently carried around with the baby until it naturally dries up and falls off. Modern hospital practices have begun to allow one or two minutes before cutting the cord to enable the baby to receive the oxygen it offers. The World Health Organization recommends sixty seconds to three minutes, although a study from 2018 found benefits for delaying cutting by at least five minutes.[12] Previously it was common to cut the cord immediately within the first twenty seconds.

Nature has designed the first breath to be relatively relaxed because the cord continues to provide oxygen as the baby begins to breathe through their lungs. As Leboyer points out in his poem (quoted in chapter 4), the shadow of birth attendants' own birth compels them to cut the cord prematurely, passing on a tradition of unnecessary trauma.

A baby connected to mother by the umbilical cord stays close to her familiar heartbeat and her nourishing breasts. Consider breastfeeding from the perspective of shadow. Breasts can be understood to represent the feminine, frequently clearly depicted in the art of ancient Goddess cultures. An example is the ancient Venus of Hohle Fels, dated 40,000 to 35,000 years ago.*

Modern distrust of the feminine recommends bottle over breast and formula over mother's milk, continuing the dominance of masculine technology over feminine trusting and listening. Research is now increasingly demonstrating the dangers for health in these modern practices. Mother's milk, as well as enhancing needed microbiome for baby, changes constantly to meet the immune needs of the baby and facilitates alertness during the day and sleep at night.[13] We also know that bottle feeding alters jaw formation, which is supported by the forces involved in natural breast suckling.[14] The rapidly growing jaws and airway in the young baby can be deformed by the altered forces involved in bottle feeding, as well as sucking on a pacifier or finger.

On another level, we understand in bodywork practices that

---

*Watch "Mother Goddess: When Women Were Worshipped" (available on YouTube) and learn more from Dale Allen at the In Our Right Minds (website).

the mouth and jaw are energetically related to the pelvis and hips. Supporting continued rooting into mother with breastfeeding may lay an essential foundation for rooting into the earth through the pelvis and hips as the baby begins to stand and walk. Breastfed babies are reportedly more active, less likely to develop motor delays, and may begin walking sooner than bottle-fed.[15] Preventing breastfeeding can undermine grounded living in trusting connection with our Great Mother, the earth we stand on and eat from as we grow up.

Some babies are unable to breastfeed, although laid back breastfeeding can solve many of the usual problems, even enabling some very premature babies to breastfeed if they are stable enough. Maternal emergency, illness or death, adoption, and other extreme situations of separation at or just after birth pose difficult challenges to establishing breastfeeding. Separation after birth may be unavoidable, as when one or both lives are in danger and urgent care is needed. At times, even this care can be done with mother and baby together. Certainly, the baby can usually be assessed on mother's belly. Cleaning that often occurs across the room or even in another room is generally unnecessary and may be harmful, depriving the baby of a protective coating on the skin called vernix.[16]

Understanding and acknowledging the multiple benefits of breastfeeding is not about judging situations where it is not possible. On the contrary, shining the light on the mysterious and scientific gifts of breastfeeding can help us to have compassion for those who are deprived of it, as well as for mothers who find themselves unable to breastfeed or chose differently in the past when their children were little. With acknowledgment, babies who were bottle fed can have extra support in finding their ground, addressing potential motor development issues and other aspects of the maternal-infant relationship that can easily thrive with breastfeeding but may be thwarted without it. As always, support for the mother or parents can be helpful.

One more essential function of breastfeeding relates to the location of the breasts on either side of the mother's heart. Remember that the fetal heart regulates in relation to the mother's heart.[17] This is meant to continue after birth. A baby lying on mother's chest with breasts available as desired continues to sense mother's heart. According to Pearce, babies need to sense their mother's heart to settle the stress hormones naturally involved in pushing through the birth canal.[18] This settling of the nervous system supports bonding as the social engagement nervous system can come online.

Science now demonstrates that the heart has powerful energetic fields. This field has been observed to have three parts, the first being very close to the heart, the second extending three feet out, and the third to fifteen feet. When a baby is nestled on mother's chest, with the breasts available for breastfeeding, baby's and mother's heart fields overlap. Mother's coherent emotional state, as reflected in her heart rhythms and fields, supports coherence for baby through entrainment, affecting both their heart rhythms and brain development.[19] This early mother-infant bonding lays a foundation for the child being able to entrain with others and their society as they grow up.

It is no mistake that the breasts are located on either side of the heart. Nature has designed us to bond with our babies through breast-feeding, as a continuation of the prenatal connection and dependence. As Montagu wisely stated,

What the newborn is looking forward to, and has every right to expect, is a continuation of that life in the womb—to a womb with a view—before it was so catastrophically interrupted by the birth process. And what it receives in our highly sophisticated societies in the Western world is a rather dusty answer.[20]

Mothers and babies need to be together after birth. They have both been through a profound initiatory journey together. They need time to integrate and digest it together. The baby's and mother's physiology influence each other in beneficial ways. For example, breastfeeding stimulates maternal oxytocin that facilitates uterine contractions to expel the placenta, as well as assisting bonding. There is some indication that not breastfeeding may be associated with postpartum depression, although it may not be the cause. Unfortunately, being together is not always possible.

Gabor Maté points out that it is not just what happened to us that affects us but also what didn't happen.[21] If we didn't receive the welcome and holding that we needed as little ones coming into the world, we may struggle to experience it throughout our lives. Even as trauma therapy has become increasingly popular and elegant, it often does not acknowledge what didn't happen, what we didn't receive. It seems to be taking longer to shine a light on this aspect of the shadow of trauma.

As light begins to shine, many are drawn to the work of Jonice Webb, which she calls Childhood Emotional Neglect (CEN).[22] She emphasizes the traumatic effects of not receiving the support, protection, reflection, and affection we need as children, and how this affects our relationships and other tendencies as adults. This can begin as early as a baby's first days.

THE MOTHER-CHILD CONNECTION

Modern Western culture produced many ideas about how to treat babies, including removing newborns from their mothers so the mothers could rest after the ordeal of birth! It was not until the 1970s that Klaus, Klaus, and Kennell, mentioned earlier, researched and promoted the importance of mother and baby being together immediately after birth. Even today, parent's needs are given priority in various sleep training systems, which involve leaving the baby to cry. A baby may eventually fall asleep after crying for hours, but this is not a restful sleep. This is the sleep of a child exhausted from evolution-based demand for parent comfort and soothing.

Babies cannot soothe themselves. Their nervous system is not mature enough to do this. This ability develops through nurturing parental connection. When it is missing, babies can learn to shut down and dissociate. Babies depend on others for safety. A baby crying in the jungle on their own becomes easy prey for hungry animals. Becoming quiet can be protective. Submitting and shutting down can support survival but down does not support thriving. This kind of stress can lead to all kinds of later health issues.

Maté emphasizes how we all have two basic needs, connection and authenticity.[23] Connection is about survival. Human babies cannot survive on their own. When little ones fear their authenticity will result in being rejected, they need to do what they can to foster connection. This often means giving up their true self and needs. For a baby left alone to sleep, authenticity is crying to express their need for connection. They cannot feel safe alone. As they experience their parents not responding to their cries and neglecting them more if they cry, they learn to suppress their authentic need. They can only do this by shutting down and dissociating from their natural fear of being alone.

This experience is common for premature babies, who usually are tended to through the glass walls of an incubator. As mentioned, skin-to-skin care is fortunately becoming more common but consider that babies born prematurely are born with stress and fear. There is usually fear that they will not survive, and other emergencies may accompany their birth. Parents already shocked by the threat of losing their baby may have trouble bonding with one they don't expect to live. They may also experience a sense of being rejected if their baby is born so early that their social engagement nervous system is not yet online. These tiny babies cannot smile and offer the sweet response parents crave. Both baby and parents may feel the desperate angst of being unable to connect with each other. The baby is also subjected to frequently painful, invasive medical procedures, often without adequate sensitivity and communication. These babies may feel that their attempts to cry are neglected, that they miss the response they need to feel safe and welcomed.

Neglected babies often become "good babies." I was one of these. After the first few months of expressing my pain, I learned to be quiet. Unlike my more unruly older brother, I never rebelled. I knew how to gain my father's affection, instead of just his abuse. My relative shut down response may have been established during my first few days of lying (and crying) alone in a nursery full of other desperate newborns, tended to by a few probably well-meaning nurses. At appointed times, we were taken to our mothers who, fortunately, were encouraged to breastfeed us. Unfortunately, a few minutes of being with mother a few times a day is not enough for a young baby. The time alone in the nursery feels like an eternity. This is evolution-based as already noted. Becoming quiet is relatively safer in the wild, less likely to draw predators but also less likely to receive needed attention of caregivers.

One of my early memories that I have always had was of my father yelling at me to shut up when I called out for my mother from my bed at around age four. Too young to reason that the growl I heard from down the hall was my father rather than a wild animal, I remember spending the rest of the night completely paralyzed in terror. This experience solidified what I had learned as a baby. I was on my own. There was no one who could hear me or protect me when I needed them. I retreated out of my body into my head. This enabled me to excel in school and gain the respect and appreciation of the adults around me, including my parents. My deeper emotional needs were put on hold. It took about 30 years to start to recover or uncover them and come back into my body.

For many of us, these early experiences of neglect or abuse remain stored in our bodies, without conscious awareness. Such somatic shadow material tends to eat away at our bodies, seeking expression. They might emerge as sudden bursts of anger from someone who otherwise is quiet and charming. In my personal therapy I discovered an aspect of myself I called "Ms. Nice." She was brilliant at being nice. The rage at how I was treated early in life rarely found its way to the surface. Pounding and screaming into pillows loosened some of the defenses and helped to dissolve ongoing depressive tendencies. These storms were not easy to integrate and recover from and I was grateful when I encountered more sophisticated modern forms of trauma therapy that I now use with my clients and students.

Catharsis may have its place in therapy, but it is also important to acknowledge and respect the defenses we have established early on. Approaching them more slowly and sensitively can engage the frightened little one within who tends to retreat further with sudden loud eruptions of rage. Supporting the person in orienting to the now, and their current ability to sense safety, can lay the groundwork for the inner little one to start to peek out and begin to receive what was missing back then. An adult who senses present-day safety can then reassure their own little one. As the inner little one perceives this safety, they may at times have anger to express, but the powerful energy of rage can be discharged in contained ways that can be easily integrated. The individual can then sense the strength in their muscles associated with anger and allow it to buoy them. They can gradually return to authenticity as they increasingly experience safe connection which welcomes who they truly are. Lost or hidden aspects of oneself can thus emerge from shadow.

SHADOWS OF GRIEF

Not all shadowy emotions derive directly from the mother and umbilical affect. As mentioned earlier, unacknowledged twin loss is one form of grief and loss that little ones can experience before birth and are likely to be troubled by throughout life. There are also other sources. In pre- and perinatal psychology, haunted womb syndrome describes how babies in the womb are affected by previous deaths or losses related to that womb. These are usually the death of siblings who have died through miscarriage, stillbirth (pregnancy loss after 20 weeks gestation), or abortion. Due to the collective lack of acknowledgment of prenatal consciousness or their status as people, these deaths tend to be less processed than would be true for an older child.

Even though miscarriage is remarkably common, it is usually not expected by the pregnant parents or family unless there have been previous miscarriages. It could be a sudden, shocking end to hopes and dreams held for the baby that has now died. Losing a child, even at the embryonic stage, must be one of the most difficult human experiences. I recently read an article promoting a paid three-day leave for both parents after a miscarriage.[24] Although that is better than no recognition of their tragic loss, I immediately wondered how parents could be expected to process their grief and loss in just three days. This to me is another example of modern cultural shadow.

Death and dying at any age tend to be isolated, as when the elderly are relegated to care homes or people die alone in hospitals. Those who have lost a spouse or family member are expected to grieve for a short time, often a week or so, and then return to work and active life. The intense emotional pain of this kind of loss is not given the space and time it needs to be met, received, supported, processed, and completed to the degree it can ever be completed. These feelings are likely to fester in the shadows of the unconscious mind. They may express themselves as physical symptoms, depression, and so on. Without being processed, they can haunt the womb into which a new little one has arrived.

Babies gestating in such a womb resonate with the grief. Again, little ones are not able to differentiate between their own feelings and someone else's the way adults do. They experience the feeling directly in their body. It is as if they become the grief that they marinate in. This is less likely to occur when parents do their grief work before becoming pregnant, or at least communicate with the fetus and let them know what the grief is about and that they are working with it. The fetus needs to know that they don't have to take it on, that it isn't theirs. Supporting couples in processing their feelings about previous loss before becoming pregnant again can be extremely helpful.

Babies who have been rejected also carry heavy feelings of grief, often accompanied by fear, terror, confusion, anger, and/or rage. This is true for babies who have survived abortion attempts or ideation (thinking about having an abortion) or have been adopted. Parents who considered or attempted abortion may have changed their minds later and even fallen in love with their baby. The little one, however, will not have forgotten the life-threatening rejection.

Women tend to carry mixed feelings about past abortions for years. This aspect of their psyche becomes part of the context if a new pregnancy occurs. Where little ones marinate in the unconscious of the parents, unprocessed abortion trauma or experience can be part of the mix. Besides affecting the mother's experience of the new pregnancy, her shadow can be felt by the prenate. I have encountered so many clients who have discovered the source of their lifelong depression, fear, or anxiety when a previous abortion had been acknowledged. So many other clients express their unprocessed feelings of guilt, shame, and confusion left over from an abortion experienced when they were much younger.

As I write this, abortion is returning to being illegal in some American states. this is not about being for or against abortion. It is about acknowledging what has been held in shadow, unspoken. In modern, Western culture, abortion and other prenatal or perinatal deaths can carry shame and confusion that is not easily discussed. It represents cultural as well as personal shadow and can be another aspect of repressing feminine wisdom. Being unwanted is also painful without abortion, as when the child is rejected and abused. Even ambivalence upon discovery of the pregnancy can be shocking for a baby whose survival completely depends on being welcomed and protected. Imagine if all pregnancies could occur within a field of welcome and readiness. This requires shining light on shadow that otherwise leads to unconscious repetition of parental or ancestral trauma histories. I believe this welcome is our human potential.

Adoptive parents are generally excited to receive their new baby and have no conscious awareness of the intense feelings the child carries after the dual experience of rejection by the mother and then the loss of the person they have been so close to for so long. The adopted baby may also have protected themselves by separating through their own dissociation from the pain of their first mother's dissociation or other extreme reactions. Additionally, adoptive parents have often tried unsuccessfully to conceive their own biological child. They are likely to hold grief, stress, disappointment, and even resentment about their failure to conceive even after extreme and often uncomfortable or invasive efforts. The adopted child comes into this emotional context, not knowing the history, but feeling the feelings. They may even assume they are responsible for the disappointment, resentment, and so on, adding to shame already established when rejected before or at birth.

Babies conceived through assisted reproductive technology (ART) (including in vitro fertilization (IVF)) may have other reasons to grieve, as well entering a womb often haunted by previous loss. They have often gone through strenuous, dangerous, unnatural means of conception, and may have lost multiple siblings in the attempt to achieve fertilization and implantation. Parents' happiness at finally having a baby sharply contrasts with their baby's grief and shock from all they have gone through and lost.

None of this is intended as judgment of the technologies supporting fertility or the parents delighting in finally having a baby. My message is about what is not acknowledged. These deep feelings are hidden in shadow, both for parents and the children conceived or adopted. These shadows can interfere with living their full potential. Simply naming what happened can be remarkably healing. Repair can further the healing. For example, "I'm sorry I couldn't welcome you back then." "I'm sorry this happened for you." "I'm sorry your mother/parents weren't able to take care of you." It can also be helpful to appreciate, hold, and reflect any emotions being expressed. "Yes, you are angry!" "I'm sorry you are so sad." Essentially everyone I have worked with or communicated with about prenatal and birth experience carries some degree of grief in relation to very early loss. Often there are layers upon layers of buried, unacknowledged, unexplained grief.

Grief expert David Kessler states, "All grief is not trauma, but all trauma has grief in it."[25] Considering how much trauma little ones often endure in their journey into form and family, we need to acknowledge the likelihood of them carrying grief. Mothers interact with their baby in the shadow of their own griefs, both from their own experience as a baby and if the pregnancy, birth and postpartum period deviated from what they hoped or expected. Where baby or mother has experienced previous loss—of a twin, another baby through miscarriage, stillbirth, or abortion, or a loved one such as a parent, older child, or spouse—grief may be triggered by birth and any associated separation. If these previous losses are not recognized, they express as unnamed ambiguous or disenfranchised grief.

Acknowledging such early relational wounding can be remarkably healing for the mother-child relationship, even years later. I am inspired by the work of clinical psychologist Tony Madrid, who supports repairs in mother-child bonding, usually through hypnosis.[26] When parents present an issue with their child, he explores if there has been an interruption in maternal-infant bonding. Through a series of questions, he identifies the disturbance, often an early separation between mother and baby or a prenatal event. He then works with the mother to address the non-bonding event and to imagine how she would have wished it to be, usually supported by hypnosis or EMDR. Even if the child isn't present, this usually resolves or dramatically improves the issue.

One issue Madrid has successfully addressed is childhood asthma, which has been seen as a suppressed cry for the mother.[27] Both child and mother usually are not consciously aware of the event that caused the rift in their bond. It remains in shadow until the therapy uncovers it. Then, it may be discovered to be that bonding was impaired by the presence of other emotions. For example, if the mother was grieving the death of her own mother or was angry at her husband's betrayal, these emotions could impede her desire to be close to her new baby.

POSTPARTUM DEPRESSION

A particularly challenging issue for new mothers and babies is postpartum depression, defined as a major depressive episode within the first twelve months of giving birth. Mothers suffering from this condition may feel unable to love, enjoy, attend to, or care for their baby, although they may be tending to the baby very well. They may not sense the love from their baby and feel they are unworthy, unknowledgeable, or somehow inadequate as a mother. In extreme situations, they may have violent intrusive thoughts toward themselves or their baby, or even become psychotic.

Babies of mothers with postpartum depression (or postpartum fatigue) may perceive their mother as not fully present or responsive, which generates a survival-based sense of danger. A defensive fear response arises in baby's nervous system as mother is apparently not there to protect them. One factor may be evidenced in research into changes in maternal-infant heart rates. Following distress, mothers who were not depressed were able to soothe their baby, calming their own heart rate first: their baby's heart rate synchronizing with theirs. Where mothers were depressed, the baby's heart led this "soothing dance" until these mothers received treatment and were less depressed.[28] In other words, the depressed mothers had difficulty self-regulating. They followed their baby's physiological lead. If the baby was upset, the mother was less able to soothe them. If the baby calmed, the mother could calm. In that we develop the ability to self-regulate through interacting with our primary caregiver, usually mother, we might expect these children to have challenges in this area as they grow older.

A baby's sense of their own body and who they are develops in relation to their mother's responsive reflection. The baby smiles and mother smiles back. Depressed mothers may have dampened facial expressions. Social nervous system is less online. The baby smiles and doesn't perceive mother smiling back. There is a sense of absence. It's like looking at yourself in the mirror and seeing a blur. Where am I? Babies experience themselves and their social nervous system is stimulated by eye contact, heart contact, and physical contact. As author and activist Eve Ensler eloquently declares, "The absence of a body against my body made attachment abstract, made my own body dislocated and unable to rest or settle. A body pressed against your body is the beginning of a nest."[29]

Newborn babies need to experience a nest, preferably the continuation of the one they gestated in. Understandably, postpartum depression can interfere with bonding, and may contribute to later behavioral, emotional, learning, and psychiatric disorders.[30] Babies of mothers with postpartum depression may also show delays in speech perception, an early foundation for speech development, possibly because these mothers may be less verbal and interactive with their baby, with less infant-directed speech and less varied pitch in their speech.[31]

It is important to note that fathers, as well as mothers, can experience postpartum depression. Although most of the literature refers to the mother and her relationship with the baby, both parents are highly influential. Paternal postpartum depression is not uncommon and has been associated with increased risk of behavioral, emotional, and social issues for their children.[32] Remember the significance of layers of support. Given the father's biological and social relationship with the baby, he, or the mother's partner, is also ideally a support for her and the baby, as are members of the extended family, friends, community, and so on. Parents are particularly influential and connected. If one partner is depressed, the other is likely to feel less supported by them and is more at risk for also having depression. If both parents are depressed, there is less resource available for the baby, which can amplify challenging effects. Depression for both parents can begin prenatally and have effects on the birth.

The psychosocial factors associated with increased risk of perinatal depression may also contribute directly to developmental issues for the child. These include stress, limited support, partner violence, marital distress, unintended or unwanted pregnancy, and intense physical pain or discomfort during pregnancy.[33] The parents' own early trauma may also contribute. For example, maternal childhood trauma has been found to be associated with premature birth and weight gain for the baby over the first year after birth.[34] Trauma held in the mother's nervous system can affect levels of stress hormones in her baby.

Previous maternal trauma and her own relationship with her mother may also contribute to postpartum depression.[35] She may also have more difficulty with challenging aspects of pregnancy and birth, which may trigger implicit somatic trauma memories.[36] For example, a woman who has experienced sexual abuse may be upset by vaginal examinations, positioning for birth, or even breastfeeding.[37] She may react by dissociating due to her trauma history. Mothers with an insecure, anxious attachment style are also at higher risk of prenatal and postpartum depression.[38] Her transition to motherhood through pregnancy and birth may trigger her own attachment system as she becomes intimately connected with her baby.[39] Her oxytocin levels may be lower, reducing hormonal support for bonding with her baby. Prenatal bonding establishes a foundation for bonding after birth, which further supports the mother-child bond. In that children of parents with insecure attachment styles tend to also have them, one possibility is that the challenges for the new mother interfere with the sense of safety that contributes to secure attachment.

Maternal trauma and stress may be transmitted both directly through her physiology and behavior, and epigenetically, carrying ancestral influences from previous generations. The mother may or may not be aware of the trauma she carries and its potential to be triggered. Very early trauma, such as that from her own prenatal and birth experience are seldom consciously remembered but can be particularly resonant with the events of pregnancy, birth, and the postpartum period. It is not unusual in the Womb Surround process workshops I facilitate for the group to have a clear sense of an ancestral mother line with generations of trauma standing behind the person we are working with. The person may have been aware of challenges with her own mother in the womb, at birth, and throughout life, but how her mother took on the traumas of her own mother, grandmother, and so on, becomes apparent. This can enable the person to experience the lifting of a burden she has carried since conception.

Another potential factor in postpartum depression is birth trauma and mother-baby separation, which can leave the mother feeling like she has missed an important opportunity, she has failed, or she is incompetent and incapable as a mother. As mentioned earlier, the use of synthetic oxytocin to induce labor does not produce the loving feelings associated with the natural "love hormone." This may impair bonding or contribute to postpartum depression.[40] Synthetic oxytocin may have very profound effects, not just for the birthing mother and her baby, but also, as French obstetrician Michel Odent warns, for humanity. Suspecting that, with this overuse, women may lose the ability to produce natural oxytocin, he writes,

We therefore have reasons to anticipate a weakening of this physiological system. This may have far-reaching consequences, since oxytocin is involved in all aspects of our reproductive/sexual life, in socialization, and in all facets of the capacity to love, which might include respect for "Mother Earth."[41]

We return here to our relationship with our Great Mother. Ironically, synthetic oxytocin omits the pauses between contractions, bringing us again to the significance of being able to rest in stillness to be able to listen to the earth, to nature, to our inherent Intelligence. The infant-directed speech mentioned above as being less present with postpartum depression is characterized in part by its relatively slow pacing, which naturally characterizes how mothers speak to their babies, according to the blueprint.[42] What happens for infants exposed too early to too much speed and too few pauses? Little ones are relatively raw, vulnerable, sensitive beings. They are easily overwhelmed and traumatized.

As mentioned earlier, adverse childhood experiences (ACEs), have been found to be associated with numerous physical and psychological conditions. Medical doctor, Veronique Mead, has taken this research one step further back to identify adverse babyhood experiences (ABEs)* These include prenatal and perinatal experiences, such as maternal stress, bonding disruption, and maternal-infant separation. Very early adverse experiences can contribute to numerous physical, developmental, and emotional issues. As Mead emphasizes, these ABEs are not the fault of the parents. They happen. Life happens. We all do our best, within the parameters of our knowledge and ability. Drawing attention to the effects of very early experiences can help to bring them out of shadow, into awareness. Then, we can make choices in relation to the experiences, rather than unconsciously reenacting them and passing them onto our children.

Circumstances arise that are beyond the mother's control. Examples include the collective trauma field around her, ancestral influences from her parents or grandparents, or from even farther back. Research focusing on the COVID-19 pandemic suggests that one in three new mothers had postpartum depression once the pandemic began compared to one in eight before it arose. Those mothers worried about contracting COVID-19 were even more likely to develop depression. Other factors in this study included formula feeding and having had their baby

---

*The research of Dr. Mead is available on the Chronic Illness Trauma Studies website.

in the NICU. A further complicating influence was the difficulty of being able to access breastfeeding support during the early days of the pandemic.[43] As a further important complication, people with a background of childhood trauma have been found to be more likely to develop long COVID.[44]

CUDDLES AND CONTACT

We have already looked at some important benefits of breastfeeding and challenges when it is replaced by formula. One of the benefits is the physical contact and closeness of mother and baby, which helps them both. In nature, babies cannot survive away from their mother. In Indigenous cultures, babies often are held or "worn" for an extended time after birth. Many modern women are reclaiming this practice through wearing a special sling or fabric wraps to hold their baby close to their body during their daily activities. As well as feeling safer when held close, newborn babies are accustomed to being in a moving environment, reminiscent of the mother's womb. This contributes to sensorimotor development, as baby senses and adapts to positional changes. Being carried continues this process, as the baby is exposed to subtle movements of the mother's body, including the reassuring movements of her heart and breath. Traveling in a stroller or car seat is a different experience, involving support from a relatively hard, unresponsive surface, and lacking the warm aliveness of the mother.

Separation, although not always avoidable, can interfere with bonding and attachment, potentially generating a sense of disorientation, loss, and depression for both mother and baby. Bonding following a time of early separation may be more difficult, lacking the natural hormonal support especially present in the first "golden hour" after birth. This may result in mother experiencing less pleasure in being with her baby and interfere with her natural instinct to protect the baby.

Longer separation may generate a physiological reaction to the loss. The mother's body acts as if her baby were dead. When the baby is finally available, she no longer has easy access to the hormones facilitating bonding and may struggle with feeling that the baby isn't really hers. Postpartum depression is not uncommon in these situations.[45] Breastfeeding also may be more difficult if it is not enabled early, and supported by skin-to-skin contact, with the critical period being the first two hours after birth.[46]

When the connection between mother and baby is disturbed and not repaired or compensated for, it can affect their relationship for life. It can also establish a foundation for the child's relational attachment styles as an adult. A secure attachment style is based on the early experience of a being adequately met and reflected, usually by the mother. Prenatal and birth trauma can interfere, affecting the baby's sense of safety in relationships. This translates into how they engage with intimate relationships later.

∿ First Cuddles at Nine Years Old ∿

Abby was nine years old when her adoptive mother brought her to me for Craniosacral therapy, hoping this might help to calm her anxiety and reduce her behavioral problems. Abby had been unable to get along with other children and could become violent in reaction to their efforts to be friendly. Fortunately, she enjoyed the soothing experience of our work together. At the end of one session, she crawled to the end of the treatment table and reached over to where her mother was sitting. She then found her way into her mother's lap and cuddled in with a look of contentment. Her mother reported that Abby had never cuddled with her before.

Where closeness and touch are possible between mother and baby, their brains and hearts mutually adapt, coming into sync, potentially alerting mother to soothe an upset or uncomfortable baby.[47] Babies also respond to cuddles and contact from others, such as siblings and grandparents, who can serve as additional layers of support.

In some situations, conditions interfere with essential contact and closeness. Emergency medical needs of mother and/or baby often separate mother and baby in ways that are distressing and shocking for both.

The baby is unlikely to understand why the separation is necessary and may feel rejected, abandoned or simply terrified. They may believe their mother has died or they will never see her again. The effects of prenatal lack of welcome can be reinforced by this separation. Explaining to the baby what is happening and how it will help them, or their mother, can be remarkably helpful. Mothers may also be confused by the severity of feelings evoked by the separation or may not have been told why their baby is not with them. The pain of their biological imperative being interrupted may be further augmented if it echoes their own early history of separation, abandonment, or rejection.

The most severe form of separation occurs with death or adoption. If the baby or mother dies, the object of their longing will never return and may be missed eternally. The adopted child tends to have a similar experience, although it is seldom named. Often the adoptive parents have no understanding of the baby's grief and trauma. They are just so happy to finally have a child, and everyone thinks it is so wonderful that the child has a home. Of course, it can be a wonderful thing for the adoptee to have warm caring parents, and for the parents to have a child, but that does not erase the baby's shocking experience of having been separated, often suddenly without explanation, from the person who has been most familiar to them for months.

Additionally, there have usually been shocking experiences of rejection in the womb, which leads to a lack of support for mother and baby, and possibly abortion ideation or attempts. The dynamic may be different in some cases, such as where the mother who wanted her baby was forced to give them up, or if she died unexpectedly. Often, the pregnancy and the rejected child's existence have never been acknowledged to anyone in the mother's world. This induces rage and terror as well as grief at not having their mother's love. The baby arrives into a new, unfamiliar family where usually no one speaks of the challenges that the child has already faced. Adoption may not be mentioned until many years later, or sometimes not at all. Stories may be concocted to protect the mother and/or child. For example, a child may be raised by the grandparents as the mother's little sister to hide a teen pregnancy.

Babies know what they have experienced even if they don't understand or remember it consciously as we would. The body holds the memories even when the history is never spoken. Adoptive children are understandably prone to depression. Often, they are on good behavior in childhood, trading in authenticity for connection they are desperate to establish or preserve after experiencing rejection by their birth mother. The emotion held in shadow may suddenly erupt when they hit adolescence. Their confusion and disorientation of adapting themselves to a world that doesn't naturally resonate with them is augmented by pubescent hormones and the natural tendency to establish one's own identity and autonomy at this age. The result may be rebellious behavior that may even be criminal or dangerous.

Adoptive parents who have tried hard to welcome and meet the baby's needs may also feel rejected or frustrated. Their efforts may be met by an infant that has spent months dissociating to defend against the intolerable pain of their mother's rejection. Adoptive parents are not supported by natural birth hormones and lack a bonding history of nine months gestating and of the birth journey together. They need additional support and education to enable them to meet and understand the special needs of a baby who has just lost their mother. The blueprint has been altered. As usual, experiences and feelings need to be acknowledged to bring them out of shadow.

Use the reflections included below to examine your relationship with your caregivers, both pre- and perinatally, and the influences that those interactions may have had on your development.

Reflections

1. Who raised you? Were your parents your natural parents? Were you raised by a single parent? If your parents split up, how old were you? Did you have other major primary caregivers like grandparents, aunts and uncles, guardians or adoptive parents? If you had older brothers and sisters, what was their attitude toward your birth? Indicate your sibling(s)' ages relative to you and the nature of your relationship as children.

2. Were you separated from your mother at birth (sent to a nursery or neonatal intensive care unit)?

    How bonded did you or do you feel with your mother? Did/do you trust her? Do you resent her or feel anger toward her? Do you feel abandoned, alone in the world, unsafe, anxious, depressed? Do you know how to ask for and receive support? Do you feel welcomed? Do you feel like you belong?

3. Were you breastfed? If yes, how long?

    What is your relationship with food and eating like? (This could also relate to prenatal experience, implantation, or umbilical affect.) Do you have allergies? Do you enjoy physical contact? If you have given birth, how was breastfeeding for you, if you did it?

4. Where was your father during your birth?

    What is your sense of being supported in your life? What is your sense of male support? What thoughts or feelings do you have toward your father?

5. Were you circumcised as an infant? If so, What is your relationship with sexuality? How do you feel about being a man? How trusting are you? How grounded and comfortable in your body are you? What is your relationship like with you mother and/or other females?

6

Shining the Light on Prevention and Healing

Healing the Collective

> *Shadow is created by arrested energy and is bound to vertices in the living matrix. But the fullness and beauty of what we are as an organic web of light, vibrating with information and potential, isn't diminished by these places of contraction, disunity, and devolution.*
>
> THOMAS HÜBL,
> *HEALING COLLECTIVE TRAUMA*

Throughout this book, we have been shining a light on prenatal and birth trauma and how it might resonate with our lives, bodies, and consciousness now. By this time, you may have had moments of recognizing or at least wondering how some of your own early history may have impacted who you are and how you engage with others and your life. This is how we shine light on shadow. Aspects of ourselves that have been relegated to the unconscious corners of the mind tend to draw attention toward themselves in unsavory ways. Like naughty children, they act out of their need to be seen and loved. If we see them as monsters, they will continue to behave as such. What they want is love. Wholeness. Integration.

179

How do we embrace the monsters within? The tools I find most effective are the triad of awareness, acknowledgment, and appreciation.

As in facing any trauma, it is important to meet it from a stable, regulated state where we can perceive our safety in present time. Mindfully meeting our monsters requires presence. As in meeting anyone, it is helpful to be in our social engagement nervous system. If we approach them from a state of fear, based on our past experience, they will snatch and swallow us whole, devouring our essence as well as possibly our authentic self. If we can face them with mindful curiosity, they will respond in kind. Monsters are like that. They like to be treated as human! Our shadow aspects are like that too. Like anyone, they want to be recognized and heard with compassion, not judgment.

Compassion involves being able to sympathetically understand the suffering of another along with a desire to help. Learning about prenatal and birth trauma supports our understanding of what at least some of our shadow aspects may have experienced and what they may be feeling. They exist as part of a what was needed to adapt to the conditions they met. This awareness is the first step in healing. Without awareness, we will not be inspired to address the issue. As awareness grows, it tends to ignite a desire to help or to evoke change.

In that implicit memory feels like it is happening now, it can be helpful to differentiate between your past and present by thinking about what you know about your history, from birth for example, by identifying ways you may be reenacting it, and appreciating or supporting the little one who you were, who is still acting as a part within you. The following exercise is about premature birth, but you can adapt it for what you have experienced if you were not born prematurely. Trust what you experience as you read this.

༄ Premature Birth Healing ༄

This is an example of how to meet and support a prenatal or birth shadow aspect, an inner little one. If you were born prematurely, you may tend to always be early to appointments or complete assignments before they are due. In recognizing this tendency, you could ask yourself, "What thoughts or feelings do I have when I am early for something?" Your answer might be a feeling of intense anxiety and a need to rush. These are expressions of implicit memory. The little you who was born early would have had those feelings or may have felt a need to get away from your mother's intense anxiety in the womb. By acknowledging these emotions as belonging to your inner little one, you can then differentiate your adult self. Remember your current age and all your resources, support, safety, and abilities in the present time.

Often, as people remember their current age, their anxiety, or other feelings from the past, immediately calms down. From anchoring in the present, what do you perceive this inner little one shadow as needing or wanting? Would you be willing to offer it to them? How might you do that? Perhaps you want to hold them, reassure them, let them know that you survived this time, explain that the anxiety belonged to your mother, and you are safe now, whatever feels right to you. This is a place to trust yourself and your intuition. What are you aware of in yourself, in your body, as you do this?

In this exploration, you might also be curious about the intelligence or wisdom of having been born early. How did this help you? Do you have a sense of having chosen? Perhaps it was an expression of an intention to relieve your suffering at the time. What happens inside you as you begin to seek appreciation for what happened?

You can use this process whenever you suspect implicit memory may be expressing. This tends to be the case when you have strong emotional reactions to people or circumstances, particularly if they are out of proportion to their stimulus. When in doubt, be curious! Even if you don't believe your early history is relevant, working with your inner little one can be a powerful healing metaphor.

REMEMBERING OUR INHERENT NATURE

Early trauma tends to have a profound effect on every aspect of our lives but, as Peter Levine notes, it does not "have to be a life sentence."[1]

Addressing the vestigial feelings held in shadow can free us to remember who we truly are.

As we practice welcoming our shadows, both individually and collectively, we can begin to emerge from the experience of darkness into the light that is our inherent nature. People remembering or visualizing their conception or journey to being conceived frequently describe intense light. There is often a longing to return to that brilliant source. It is so common that it has a name in pre- and perinatal therapy—Divine homesickness (see page 71). As mentioned in chapter 2, I learned this term from William R. Emerson. He observed through countless therapy sessions the regressor's tendency to reach behind themselves with one arm, as if trying to touch again that beautiful source they experienced before crash landing into the womb and life they experienced as traumatizing. Emerson also did research with children he had worked with and discovered that children who had resolved their primal trauma tended to display remarkable talents and qualities. He wrote:

> When there were no unresolved traumas to obscure their expression, latent talents and abilities surged into consciousness where they could be acknowledged and acted upon. Because of this, treated children were more likely than untreated children to have "found themselves" and to have identified their unique qualities, frequently without parental support or encouragement.

Once free of the hold of their early traumas, these children also frequently showed more empathy, and described experiences of radiance, clairvoyance, or conversations with God. These transpersonal experiences were considered expressions of "dimensions of Self."[2] These children were accessing their true essence, which had been waiting, like the sun behind the clouds.

As noted earlier, it is not just our so-called badness that is held in shadow. We may also protect our goodness there, until it is safe for it to re-emerge. Then, we discover our natural compassion, empathy, generosity, and more. Under the crust of cultural definitions, our true nature awaits. How do we access that original potential?

Again, we begin with awareness. This involves acknowledging what we know and being willing to look at and acknowledge how our own history may have affected us. We then usually need support to repair our relationship with what happened in the past. Remember that trauma is not the event. It is how we are still reacting to it in the present. Our nervous system continues to act as if it were still facing an overwhelming situation. In the case of primal trauma, we may still be perceiving and reacting to relationships defensively, due to rejection, umbilical affect or toxicity, and so on. Letting go of this trauma stance requires being in present time and differentiating between then and now.

In that little ones are not able to differentiate between past and present, the shadow aspects of ourselves representing little ones usually need help to do so. We can learn to mindfully orient to our current age and present time and, from there, reassure the little one within us, the shadow aspects from that early time, that we have already survived and are safe now. As we emerge from the hauntings of our prenatal and birth traumas, we can begin to embrace our full potential that may have been hidden and protected behind the clouds.

Developing the ability to compassionately acknowledge and appreciate the little one that that has been held in shadow can happen in different ways. Usually, it is facilitated through therapeutic help.

I am reminded here of the power of Authentic Movement, mentioned earlier. This spontaneous movement practice involves a witness who represents the ideal mother unconditionally viewing and supporting the mover.[3] The mover discovers that they can express anything and not get in trouble, be judged, or rejected (if they follow agreements to maintain safety for themselves and others). This form of active imagination invites the unconscious to express itself, to be seen and welcomed. Gradually, the mover learns to internalize the witness, just as a child learns to internalize the mother.

I believe it would be helpful if every therapist offered unconditional witnessing for their clients. Unfortunately, therapists who have not done their own work to integrate pre- and perinatal shadow aspects are likely to be unconsciously meeting and evaluating their clients from the perspective of the little one still inside them. Clients easily project onto their therapist (or others in their lives) their unintegrated experiences with authority figures from their past. These could include parents, doctors or other birth assistants, teachers, and so on. In therapy, this is called transference. The client sees or reacts to the therapist as if they are their mother, doctor, teacher, and so on. Psychodynamic therapy includes awareness and exploration of the client's transference.

Therapists can also project onto their clients. Their unconscious history-based reaction to their clients and the clients' projection is called countertransference. A therapist who is ruled by prenatal shadow might react to their client's anger like a helpless prenate sensing their mother being attacked by their angry father. The client needs their anger appreciated and explored within a safe relational field. The therapist bound to their own early history may be unable to meet their client's anger with healing curiosity and non-judgment. They may tend to either judge it or to withdraw from it like a helpless child.

～ Prenatal Resonance ～

Kimberly came to supervision one day describing how difficult it was for her when clients stopped coming for therapy sessions before she felt they were ready to complete. She felt unable to ask them why they were not coming back. As we explored the situation, her own familiar feelings of having done something wrong presented. We looked at how her experience of her violent father constantly criticizing her mother when Kimberly was in the womb might be resonating with the history and associated emotions the client could be running away from by not returning to therapy.

We then invited forward the aspect of Kimberly that represented the baby she had been, who may have also wanted to escape but could not. I encouraged Kimberly to give her inner little one the support she needed. Instead, Kimberly began to feel her mother's unacknowledged grief and anger at how she had been treated. After we gently supported safe expression of some of this anger, Kimberly was able to release her intense grief. She could now differentiate between her mother's emotions and her own, which she couldn't do in the womb. She then felt her heart open and was able to consider ways she could work with clients who held similar anger and grief. She suspected the clients' need to avoid feeling these difficult feelings were responsible for them leaving therapy prematurely.

My hope is that every therapist can acquaint themselves with and come to terms with their own prenatal and birth history enough to be able to hold a compassionate field of inquiry when their clients present this kind of material. Awareness is the first step in healing. A therapist who isn't familiar with prenatal and birth trauma will have trouble recognizing it. The first step may be missed.

This is not to say that prenatal and birth therapy is the only therapy, or that it is required for everyone. In that it so often lays a foundation for later wounding, it can be and often is key to deep healing. Being aware of this territory enables recognizing and addressing it when it arises in therapy or in life.

HEALING WITHIN THE COLLECTIVE

I want to take a moment here to acknowledge that, although personal healing is important, it is not everything. As mentioned earlier, prenatal and birth experience is relegated to shadow within a larger collective field. In a culture that denies or belittles preverbal consciousness, experiences of little ones are not deemed real or important. In our times, babies are seen as learning and as needing love and attention from their parents or primary caregivers. That this is also required for babies in the womb is not as widespread a belief. Prenates are still not generally believed to be aware. Implicit memory is still not widely appreciated or understood.

Much to my chagrin, I still encounter people who consider therapy to be limited to talk therapy. My field of somatic psychotherapy has been emerging for many years and had been when I trained in it in the early 1990s, but people still don't recognize it as psychotherapy!

Fortunately, this attitude is beginning to change in response to modern trauma therapy embracing the importance of including the body in therapy, popularized by the work of Bessel A. van der Kolk.

Clearly, preverbal memories held in the body need to be addressed in other than strictly verbal terms. As far back as Freud, there was an understanding that the unconscious would express itself in dreams. Jung saw that creative process, like artwork, was a way to access the nonverbal. Mary Whitehouse took this further, seeing that the unconscious is expressed naturally through movement and the body. In a disembodied culture, these truths are still not common knowledge. The cultural shadow engenders denial and dismissal of the obvious. Listening to our bodies and acknowledging our early trauma can be disconcerting and uncomfortable, upsetting the status quo. Cultural mores protect against facing the unacceptable.

Bearing this in mind, the primary intention of this book is to enhance awareness, facilitating the initiation or deepening of this healing journey. The work of my colleagues in the field of pre- and perinatal psychology is also helping to disseminate knowledge of the significance and effects of experience during this initial phase of life. A major movement in this field is to educate birth practitioners, healthcare personnel, teachers, therapists, parents, and anyone who may come in contact with birth or babies so that they will be less likely to cause traumatization to our babies (or our next generations). I hope you might join in this venture through your own healing and any ways you are able to share this important information.

With this goal of intergenerational healing in mind I will take a moment to address the parent readers among you. As you explore your own prenatal shadows, you are likely to become more aware of what your own child might have experienced. You are also likely to be able to access more of your own potential for compassion, empathy, and love. Please consider how you might share these with the child. The first step is to share them with yourself, the little one you were who is still within you. It can be helpful to remember that you are not and were not alone in your parenting. You are immersed in collective fields around you, affected by cultural shadow as well as, hopefully, layers of support. By addressing the needs within ourselves, we can become a stronger force for healing future generations.

We are all interconnected. Thomas Hübl, who works with links between personal and collective trauma writes,

> There can be no independent, individual shadow or unconscious self; there is only the collective shadow. We are intimately tied to the social environment, which informs and shapes us. The shadow needs investors, people who share a stake in its continued existence. When those who surround us are clear, forthright, and self-aware, a kind of developmental momentum can be felt in the field. This force is like sunlight; in its glow, inertia is challenged, and it becomes harder to avoid growth, clarity, and consciousness.[4]

Like cells influencing and communicating with each other through resonance, we humans also interact in subtle, energetic ways. Someone acting from a prenatal stance may radiate vibrations of fear, helplessness, or anger. These are communicated to people around them. With increased awareness, we can have more agency as to what we radiate or resonate with. We can contribute to a collective field of love and coherence, or one of fear and judgment. In the words of Dr. Deborah Rozman of HeartMath Institute:

> Every individual's energy affects the collective field environment. This means each person's emotions and intentions generate an energy that affects the field. A first step in diffusing societal stress in the global field is for each of us to take personal responsibility for our own energies. We can do this by increasing our personal coherence and raising our vibratory rate, which helps us become more conscious of the thoughts, feelings, and attitudes that we are feeding the field each day. We have a choice in every moment to take to heart the significance of intentionally managing our energies. This is the free will or local freedom that can create global cohesion.[5]

Our collective field includes not only influences from those currently in our lives or society, but also our ancestors. Although we may tend to focus on the trauma our predecessors passed down to us, what we receive from our ancestors is not all detrimental. Trauma therapist Resmaa Menakem points out, "Besides trauma, there is something else human beings routinely pass on from person to person and from generation to generation: resilience."[6] Our ancestors all had enough resilience to have survived at least long enough to enable us to come into this life. As well as whatever trauma they carried, we inherited that potential for resilience.

It can be helpful to remember that we have all survived our own early experiences. As well as being sensitive and vulnerable, little ones are remarkably resilient. Within a field of love, they can thrive. With support, they can recover from trauma, as exemplified by the children Emerson studied who displayed special talents and qualities when they resolved their birth trauma. We all can.

LIGHT AS SHADOW

Teachers of mysticism and spirituality often remind us that we are not what we think we are. We are not the successful or unsuccessful businessman, the overworked, overwhelmed mother of too many hungry, needy young children, the student, criminal, therapist, teacher, laborer, and so on. Nor are we the identity we have been taught to associate with our race, religion, culture, gender, social class, nationality, and such. We are more than that.

What if we were, we are, beyond what we think we are? What if we are pure light, as we tend to discover in various meditation practices? What if our very light were hidden from us by our needs to adapt to the world we have been born into?

When we think of shadow, associated as it is with darkness and even blindness, we tend to equate it with unacceptable qualities. Surely shadow represents greed, jealousy, anger, resentment, and violence. We might even include vulnerable qualities seen as weak, such as fear, keeping ourselves small or hidden, lacking confidence, or being self-deprecating.

Yes, all of these can be in shadow, meaning they are aspects of ourselves we are not fully conscious of. But what if our shadow also included our human capacity for love? What if we are innately loving, tender, non-judgmental, compassionate, welcoming beings? Is that not also who we are? Is that not also who you are?

We learn early on, even in the womb, that it is not enough, not safe, not appropriate in some way to fully embody this love. Over time, we forget. Our light, our love, moves into shadow. Is it your time to retrieve it?

Our healing journey is not just an individual process or limited to the present. We are a part of the collective, informed and formed in relation to our parents, family, community, culture, and planet. We inherit trauma, as well as resilience from our ancestors. These layers are all interconnected. In the words of Thomas Hübl,

> We might envision our ancestors as a great and ancient forest whose living roots we share. Those ancestral roots connect us to one another and to the Earth, as they have since long before our species first emerged. Indeed, our roots connect us to the planet, to life itself. They belong to our collective nervous system, and no matter how far apart we live or die, or how distantly related, no two humans across space or time can be thought wholly unconnected. We are bound together by our common origin.[7]

We are connected to our Great Mother just as we were one with our mother in the womb. Recapitulating our earliest traumas impacts how we treat the Earth and experience this connection. Instead of living harmoniously, we have become monstrous expressions of shadow, blighting her beauty. Changing this requires changing our ways. This isn't just about using less plastic or keeping energy bills down. Awakening requires awareness. It is time to return to the stillness we emerged from, and to listen. We don't have all the practical answers, but we can ask. We can live the question. As Rainer Maria Rilke advised, "Do not now seek the answers, which cannot be given you because you would not be able to live them. And the point is, to live everything. Live the questions now. Perhaps you will then gradually, without noticing it, live along some distant day into the answer."[8]

This is a receptive way of being. Babies in the womb are naturally in a receptive state. Like any organism, they contract and withdraw when sensing threat. This reduces receptivity. When we learn to live defensively so early, our personality and relational tendencies form around this need. Rilke's advice suggests a return to our original embryological potential, an ability to be, to live the question, "What will *I* become?" while practicing being grounded in the now.

As a collective, we also ask, "What will *we* become? What will become of *us*?" We need to pause and listen for the wisdom that can guide us. The Earth speaks. The trees communicate. The oceans express what is needed. These messages are everywhere. How do we need to adapt to meet the current challenges? *Do* we have the courage to change?

Having an intention to live these questions raises them to consciousness. Allergies, immune disorders, inflammatory conditions all indicate the awareness our cells and tissues carry, a form of implicit memory. Living the questions, we can listen to these messages from our bodies, as well as our emotions, and make new choices.

Reflections

1. Consider the journaling work you have done thus far. How do you think/sense these aspects of your history may have affected you and your relationships?

2. How might your early experience have been reinforced in childhood or later relationships?

3. What feels most important for you to acknowledge in relation to this territory for you personally?

4. What arises for you when you consider Mother Earth? Do you see any relationship between how you feel about the planet or environment and what you now understand about your earliest experience with your mother in the womb?

5. What thoughts or feelings arise in relation to answering these questions? What supports do you have that you can use as you continue on your journey? What new choices would you like to make?

Notes

INTRODUCTION

1. Johnson, *Owning Your Own Shadow*, 39.
2. House, "Primal Integration Therapy," 213–35.
3. Freud, *Introductory Lectures*, 493, 506.
4. Herman, *Trauma and Recovery*, 11–12.
5. Fodor, *The Search for the Beloved*.
6. Lieberman, "Introduction," ix.
7. Chamberlain, *The Mind of Your Newborn Baby*, xxiv.
8. Chamberlain, "Babies Don't Feel Pain."
9. Hepper, "Fetal Psychology," 129–56.
10. Somé, *Of Water and the Spirit*, 20.
11. Sansone, *Cultivating Mindfulness*, 11.
12. Partanen et al., "Learning-Induced Neural Plasticity of Speech Processing before Birth."
13. Nantel, "Conscious Abortion," 13.
14. Kelland, "Babies Feel Pain 'Like Adults.'"
15. Monell, "Living out the Past: Infant Surgery Prior to 1987," 160.
16. Williams and Lascelles, "Early Neonatal Pain."
17. Edwards, "The Long Life of Early Pain;" Mathew and Mathew, "Assessment and Management of Pain in Infants."
18. Filippa et al., "Maternal speech decreases pain scores."
19. Anbalagan et al., "Music for Pain Relief."
20. Filippa et al., "Maternal speech decreases pain scores."

CHAPTER 1. WHAT IS PRENATAL AND
BIRTH SHADOW AND WHY DOES IT MATTER?

1. Ring, McHugh, Reed, Davidson-Welch, Dodd, "Healers and Midwives Accused of Witchcraft (1563–1736)—What Secondary Analysis of the Scottish Survey of Witchcraft Can Contribute to the Teaching of Nursing and Midwifery History," 106026.
2. Jung, *Collected Works*, 13, 365.
3. Harvey, "An Ecological View of Psychological Trauma and Recovery."
4. Porges, *Polyvagal Safety*.
5. Siegel, *The Developing Mind*, 281.
6. Ogden, Minton, and Pain, "Trauma and the Body," 27.
7. Thai, "Traumatic Stress and the Nervous System."
8. Felitti, et al., "Relationship of Childhood Abuse."
9. Felitti, "Profound Effects of Early Life Experiences," (video).
10. Herman, *Trauma and Recovery*, 11.
11. Maté in Hübl and Avritt, *Healing Collective Trauma*, 58.
12. Campbell, "The Pope's Non-apology to Indigenous Canadians."
13. Carpenter, "What's Killing America's Black Infants?"
14. Barclay et al., "Maternal Early Life Adversity and Infant Stress Regulation."
15. Centers for Disease Control and Prevention, "Working Together to Reduce Black Maternal Mortality."
16. Flanders-Stepans, "Alarming Racial Differences in Maternal Mortality."
17. Allen, *In Our Right Minds*.
18. Lipton and Bhaerman, *Spontaneous Evolution*, 172.
19. Ikegawa, *I Remember When I Was in Mommy's Tummy*.
20. Hübl and Avritt, *Healing Collective Trauma*, xvi–xvii.
21. Badenoch, *The Heart of Trauma*, 13.
22. Irving, Natalism as Pre- and Perinatal Metaphor, 83.
23. Vinessett, Price, and Wilson, "Therapeutic Potential of a Drum and Dance Ceremony."
24. Britannica, "Burial Mound."
25. Ripinsky-Naxon, *Sexuality, Shamanism, and Transformation*, 15; Janus, *Enduring Effects*.
26. Eliade, *Rites and Symbols of Initiation* and *Myth and Reality*.
27. Sjoo and Mor, *The Great Cosmic Mother*.
28. Martin, "Tollund Man."

29. Al-Rawi, *Grandmother's Secrets*, 29.
30. Chodorow "To Move and be Moved," 267.
31. Conrad, *Life on Land*, 249.
32. Hübl and Avritt, *Healing Collective Trauma*, 12.
33. Warren, "African Infant Precocity."
34. Chamberlain, "The Sentient Prenate," 12.
35. McCarty and Glenn, "Investing in Human Potential," 7.
36. McCarty and Glenn, "Investing," 7.

CHAPTER 2. EXPLORING EARLY CONSCIOUSNESS

1. Lipton, *The Biology of Belief.* 186.
2. Porges, *The Polyvagal Theory* and *Polyvagal Safety*, 12.
3. Porges, "Play as Neural Exercise."
4. Porges and Furman, "The Early Development of the Autonomic Nervous System."
5. Porges and Furman.
6. Pallaro, *Authentic Movement*.
7. Stromsted, "Authentic Movement: A Dance with the Divine."
8. Sallenbach, "Claira: A Case Study in Prenatal Learning."
9. Piontelli, *From Fetus to Child*, 146.
10. Macdonald, "Let's Talk Periconception Health Care with Men," 71.
11. Golding et al., "Ancestral Smoking and Developmental Outcomes," 625.
12. Golding et al., "Human Transgenerational Observations of Regular Smoking Before Puberty."
13. Mines, *The Secret of Resilience*, 8.
14. Chamberlain, "The Sentient Prenate" and "Communicating with the Mind of a Prenate."
15. Sanders, "Babies in the Womb May See More Than we Thought."
16. CSIC, "Touch and Sight are Linked Before Birth."
17. Morgan, "Womb With a View."
18. Nantel, "Conscious Abortion," 9.
19. Crable, "Exactly How Many Senses Do We Really Have?"
20. Verny, *The Secret Life of the Unborn Child*, 23.
21. Terry, "Implantation Journey," 9.
22. Menzam-Sills, *Spirit into Form*, 151.
23. Turner and Turner, "Chapter 5: Prebirth Education Begins Before Conception."

24. Habek, Habek, Barbir, Barbir, and Granić, "Fetal Grasping of the Umbilical Cord and Perinatal Outcome."

25. Chamberlain, *Windows to the Womb*, 44–45.

26. Mehler et al., "A Precursor of Language Acquisition in Young Infants."

27. DeCasper and Fifer, "Of Human Bonding."

28. Filippa et al., "Systematic Review of Maternal Voice Interventions."

29. Zhang et al., "Near-Infrared Spectroscopy Reveals Neural Perception."

30. Ghasemi and Hashemi, "Foreign Language Learning During Childhood."

31. Janus, *Echoes from the Womb*, xiii.

32. Serpolini et al., "Grandmaternal Stress During Pregnancy."

33. Thomson, "Study of Holocaust Survivors."

34. Malaspina, Corcoran, Kleinhaus, et al., "Acute Maternal Stress in Pregnancy," 71.

35. Thomson, "Study of Holocaust Survivors."

36. Yehuda and Lehrer, "Intergenerational Transmission of Trauma Effects;" Van den Berg and Pinger, "Transgenerational Effects."

37. Mandel, "Spirit and Matter of the Heart."

38. Bygren, Tinghög, Carstensen, et al., "Change in Paternal Grandmothers' Early Food Supply Influenced Cardiovascular Mortality of the Female Grandchildren," 12; Henriques, "Can the Legacy of Trauma Be Passed Down the Generations?"

39. Rubik et al., "Biofield Science and Healing."

40. McCraty, *The Energetic Heart*, 1.

41. Ivanov, Ma, and Bartsch, "Maternal-Fetal Heartbeat Phase Synchronization," 13641.

42. McCraty and Deyle, *The Science of Interconnectivity*, 23.

43. HeartMath Institute, "Mother-Baby Study Supports Heart-Brain Interactions."

44. Pearce, "Mother-Infant Bonding and the Intelligence of the Heart."

45. Ikegawa, *I Remember When I Was in Mommy's Tummy*, 45.

46. Moody, "The Experience of Dying;" Osis and Haraldsson, 1982; Sabom and Kreutziger, 1982; Garfield, "The Dying Patient's Concern with Life after Death;" Lundahl, "Near Death Experiences of Mormons;" Grosso, "Toward an Explanation of Near-Death Phenomena;" Moorjani, *Dying to Be Me*; Alexander, *Proof of Heaven*; Parnia and Young, *Erasing Death*; Pearsall, *The Heart's Code*.

47. Pearsall, Schwartz and Russek, "Changes in Heart Transplant Recipients."

48. Dobrijevic and Stein, "Do Parallel Universes Exist?"

49. Wade, *Changes of Mind*, 13.

CHAPTER 3. ORIENTING TO OUR
ORIGINAL EMBRYOLOGICAL POTENTIAL

1. Still, *Philosophy of Osteopathy*, 28.

2. Sills, *Foundations in Craniosacral Biodynamics, Vol. 1*, 10–11.

3. Conrad, *Life on Land*, 262.

4. Conrad, *Life on Land*, 7.

5. Sutherland, *Contributions of Thought*, 14.

6. Ikegawa, *I Remember When I Was in Mommy's Tummy*.

7. Conrad, "Continuum: An Introduction," (video).

8. Armstrong, *The Human Odyssey*, 367.

9. Joyce, *Dubliners*, 89.

10. Stefon, "Wuwei."

11. Walters, "Tablets and Smartphones May Affect Social and Emotional Development."

12. Ashrafinia et al., "Can Prenatal and Postnatal Cell Phone Exposure Increase Adverse Maternal, Infant and Child Outcomes?" Birks, et al., "Maternal Cell Phone Use During Pregnancy and Child Behavioral Problems in Five Birth Cohorts."

13. Chamberlain, *The Mind of Your Newborn Baby*, 23.

14. Armstrong, *The Human Odyssey*, 367.

15. Emoto, *Hidden Messages in Water*.

16. Tiller, *Conscious Acts of Creation*, 19–20.

17. Pereira, "Quantum Resonance and Consciousness."

18. Kozlowski and Marciak-Kozlowska, "Schumann Resonance and Brain Waves."

19. Hunt, *Infinite Mind*.

20. Conrad, *Life on Land*, xv.

21. Kalef, *The Secret Life of Babies*, 5.

22. Deranger, "Climate Crisis, Fragmentation and Collective Trauma."

23. deMause, "Childhood and Cultural Evolution." and *Foundations of Psychohistory*, 36.

24. You can learn more about the unusual views of deMause in his groundbreaking book, *Foundations of Psychohistory*.

25. Lewis, "The Pandemic Caused a Baby Boom in Red States and a Bust in Blue States."

26. Schwartz et al., "Placental Tissue Destruction and Insufficiency from COVID-19," 661.

27. Metz et al., "Association of SARS-CoV-2 Infection with Serious Maternal Morbidity."

28. Shuffrey et al., "Association of Birth During the COVID-19 Pandemic with Neurodevelopmental Status."

CHAPTER 4. THE EXPERIENCE OF BEING BORN IN MODERN SOCIETY

1. Thornburg, Boone-Heinonen, and Valent, "Social Determinants of Placental Health."

2. Luecken et al., "Prenatal Stress, Partner Support, and Infant Cortisol Reactivity."

3. Thornburg, Boone-Heinonen, and Valent, "Social Determinants of Placental Health."

4. Tolkunova et al., "Transgenerational and Intergenerational Effects of Early Childhood Famine Exposure."

5. Luecken et al., "Prenatal Stress, Partner Support, and Infant Cortisol Reactivity."

6. Highsmith et al., *Supporting Families to Integrate Their Birth Experiences*, 212.

7. Guy-Evans, *"Bronfenbrenner's Ecological Systems Theory."*

8. Hübl and Avritt, *Healing Collective Trauma*, 25.

9. Hansard, *Supporting Survivors of Sexual Abuse Through Pregnancy and Childbirth*.

10. Leong et al., "Before the First Breath," 1059.

11. Patel, Laz, and Berenson, "Patient Characteristics Associated with Pregnancy Ambivalence," 40.

12. Kawanishi et al., "The relationship Between Prenatal Psychological Stress and Placental Abruption in Japan."

13. Gaskin, *Birth Matters*, 546.

14. Siegel and Hartzell, *Parenting from the Inside Out*.

15. Leboyer, *Birth Without Violence*, 104.

16. Davis-Floyd, *Birth as an American Rite of Passage*.

17. Johanson et al., "Has the Medicalization of Childbirth Gone Too Far?"

18. Jones, "What Obstetrics and Gynecology Should Mean in Our Society," 30:58 (video).

19. Johanson et al.: Mengjie Xia et al., "Association Between Breastfeeding and Postpartum Depression."

21. Jones, "What Obstetrics and Gynecology Should Mean in Our Society," 50:08 (video).

22. Mandel, "The Benefits of Having Siblings Present at Childbirth."

23. Bartholemew, "Giving Birth in a Bunker in Kyiv."

24. Davis-Floyd, *Birth as an American Rite of Passage.*

25. Maté and Neufeld, *Hold On To Your Kids.*

26. Gaskin, *Birth Matters,* 575.

27. CNN, "US Maternal Mortality Rate Declines, but Disparities Remain, New CDC Data Shows."

28. Cerelli, "Bridging Midwifery Practice and Pre- and Perinatal Insights."

29. Gaskin, *Ina May's Guide to Childbirth* and *Birth Matters.*

30. Sartwelle and Johnston, "Continuous Electronic Fetal Monitoring During Labor," e24.

31. Goer, "Epidurals: Do They or Don't They Increase Cesareans?" Wolf, "American Women Are Having Too Many Caesareans at Too Much Risk."

32. Prechtel, *The Smell of Rain on Dust,* 10.

CHAPTER 5. MATERNAL INFLUENCES

1. Liedloff, *The Continuum Concept,* 24–26.

2. Maret, *The Prenatal Person,* 23.

3. Maret, *The Prenatal Person.*

4. Sills, *Being and Becoming.*

5. Colson, "A Non-prescriptive Recipe for Breastfeeding."

6. Klaus, Klaus, Kennel, *Bonding.*

7. Odent, "Stress Deprivation in the Perinatal Period."

8. Righard and Alade, *Delivery Self-Attachment* (video).

9. Castellino, Takikawa and Wood, *The Caregiver's Role in Birth and Newborn Self- Attachment Needs.*

10. Liedloff, *The Continuum Concept,* 36.

11. Qian, Lu, Shao, Ying, Huang, and Hua. "Timing of Umbilical Cord Clamping and Neonatal Jaundice in Singleton Term Pregnancy," 104948;

Millar, Muralidhar, Bruce, et al., "323 Neonatal Jaundice and Delayed Cord Clamping," A230.

12. Mercer et al., "Effects of Delayed Cord-Clamping."

13. Saxby and Hahn-Holbrook, "Breast Milk's Unique Composition."

14. Page, "Breastfeeding is Early Functional Jaw Orthopedics;" Grace et al., "Breastfeeding and Motor Development;" and Hernández-Luengo et al., "The Relationship Between Breastfeeding and Motor Development in Children."

15. Sacker, Quigley, and Kelly, "Breastfeeding and Developmental Delay."

16. Singh and Archana, "Unraveling the Mystery of Vernix Caseosa."

17. Ivanov, Ma, and Bartsch, "Maternal-Fetal Heartbeat Phase Synchronization."

18. Pearce, *Evolution's End*, 111.

19. Pearce, "Mother-Infant Bonding and the Intelligence of the Heart."

20. Montagu, *Touching*, 70.

21. Maté, *The Myth of Normal*, 370.

22. Webb, *Running on Empty*.

23. Maté, *The Myth of Normal*.

24. Johnson, "All Parents Affected by Miscarriage Should be Given Paid Leave."

25. Kessler and Ross, *On Grief and Grieving*.

26. Madrid, *The Mother and Child Reunion*.

27. Madrid et al., "Does Maternal-Infant Bonding Therapy Improve Breathing in Asthmatic Children?"

28. Krzeczkowski et al., "Follow the Leader."

29. Ensler, *In the Body of the World*, 2.

30. Morales-Munoz, "Maternal Postnatal Depression and Anxiety," 82–92.

31. Schaadt et al., "Association of Postpartum Maternal Mood with Infant Speech Perception."

32. Pinar and Ozbek, "Paternal Depression and Attachment Levels;" Scarff, "Postpartum Depression in Men."

33. Smythe et al., "Prevalence of Perinatal Depression and Anxiety in Both Parents."

34. Apanasewicz et al., "Maternal Childhood Trauma is Associated with Offspring Body Size."

35. Stone, "How Your Own Mother and Childhood Trauma Can Impact Postpartum Depression."

36. Bailey, "Previous Trauma Can Impact Expectant Mothers."

37. Hansard, *Supporting Survivors of Sexual Abuse Through Pregnancy and Childbirth*, 21–22.

38. Eapen et al., "Separation Anxiety, Attachment and Inter-Personal Representations."
39. Bianciardi el al., "The Anxious Aspects of Insecure Attachment Styles," 2.
40. Bell et al., "Beyond Labor."
41. Odent, *Childbirth and the Evolution of Homo sapiens*, 18.
42. Schaadt, "Association of Postpartum Maternal Mood with Infant Speech Perception," 9.
43. Bailey, "A Third of New Moms During Early COVID Had Postpartum Depression."
44. Villanueva Van Den Hurk et al., "Childhood Trauma Exposure Increases Long COVID Risk."
45. Pearce, *Evolution's End*, 124.
46. Karimi et al., "The Effect of Mother-Infant Skin to Skin Contact."
47. Nguyen, "Proximity and Touch."

CHAPTER 6. SHINING THE LIGHT ON PREVENTION AND HEALING

1. Levine, *Waking the Tiger*, 2.
2. Emerson, "Somatic Therapy," 84–85.
3. Pallaro, *Authentic Movement*.
4. Hübl and Avritt, 98.
5. Rozman, "Global Coherence," 1085.
6. Menakem, *My Grandmother's Hands*, 50.
7. Hübl and Avritt, 85.
8. Rilke, *Letters to a Young Poet*, 18.

Bibliography

Alexander, Eben. *Proof of Heaven: A Neurosurgeon's Journey into the Afterlife.* London: Piatkus, 2012. Kindle.

Al-Rawi, R. *Grandmother's Secrets: The Ancient Rituals and Healing Power of Belly Dancing.* Translated by Monique Arav. New York: Interlink Books, 1999.

Anbalagan, S., J. H. Velasquez, D. Staufert Gutierrez, et al. "Music for Pain Relief of Minor Procedures in Term Neonates." *Pediatric Research*, (August 29, 2023).

Apanasewicz, A., Danel, D., Piosek, M., et al. "Maternal Childhood Trauma is Associated with Offspring Body Size During the First Year of Life." *Scientific Reports* 12, (2022): 19619.

Armstrong, Thomas. *The Human Odyssey: Navigating the Twelve Stages of Life.* New York: Ixia Press, 2019.

Ashrafinia, F., S. Moeindarbari, P. Razmjouei, et al. "Can Prenatal and Postnatal Cell Phone Exposure Increase Adverse Maternal, Infant and Child Outcomes?" *Federação Brasileira de ginecologia e obstetrícia* 43, no. 11 (2021): 870–77.

Audette, John R. "Historical Perspectives on Near-Death Episodes and Experiences." In *A Collection of Near-Death Research Readings: Scientific Inquiries into the Experiences of Persons Near Physical Death,* ed. Craig R. Lundahl, 21–43. Chicago: Nelson-Hall, 1982.

Badenoch, Bonnie. *The Heart of Trauma: Healing the Embodied Brain in the Context of Relationships (Norton Series on Interpersonal Neurobiology).* New York: W. W. Norton & Company, 2017.

Bailey, Laura, "A Third of New Moms During Early COVID Had Postpartum Depression." *Neuroscience News* (website), March 14, 2022.

———. "Previous Trauma Can Impact Expectant Mothers During Pregnancy and Beyond." University of Michigan News (website), November 23, 2021.

Barclay, Margot E., Gabrielle R. Rinne, Jennifer A. Somers, et al. "Maternal Early Life Adversity and Infant Stress Regulation: Intergenerational Associations and Mediation by Maternal Prenatal Mental Health." *Research on Child Adolescent Psychopathology*, December 12, 2022.

Bartholemew, Jem, "Giving Birth in a Bunker in Kyiv: 'I Said to Him You're a New Ukrainian.'" *The Guardian* (website), March 2, 2022.

Bauer, Dietrich, Maz Hoffmeister, and Hartmut Goerg, *Children Who Communicate Before They are Born: Conversations with Unborn Souls*. London: Temple Lodge, 2005.

Bell, Aleeca F., Erickson, Elise N. and Carter, C. Sue, "Beyond Labor: The Role of Natural and Synthetic Oxytocin in the Transition to Motherhood." *Journal of Midwifery Women's Health* 59, no. 1 (2014): 35–42.

Bianciardi, Emanuela, Cristina Vito, Sophia Betrò, et al. "The Anxious Aspects of Insecure Attachment Styles are Associated with Depression Either in Pregnancy or in the Postpartum Period," *Annal of General Psychiatry* 19, no. 51 (2020).

Birks, Laura, Mònica Guxens, Eleni Papadopoulou, et al. "Maternal Cell Phone Use During Pregnancy and Child Behavioral Problems in Five Birth Cohorts." *Environment International* 104 (July 2017): 122–131.

Bowman, Carol. *Children's Past Lives: How Past Life Memories Affect Your Child*. New York: Bantam, 1997.

Bygren, L. O., P. Tinghög, J. Carstensen, et al. "Change in Paternal Grandmothers' Early Food Supply Influenced Cardiovascular Mortality of the Female Grandchildren." *BMC Genet* 15 (2014): 12.

Cable News Network (CNN), "US Maternal Mortality Rate Declines, but Disparities Remain, New CDC Data Shows," May 2, 2024.

Campbell, Lori. "The Pope's Non-Apology to Indigenous Canadians Furthers a History of Abuse." *Yes! Solutions Journalism* (website), August 5, 2022.

Carpenter, Zoe, "What's Killing America's Black Infants? Racism is Fuelling a National Health Crisis." *The Nation* (website), February 15, 2017.

Castellino, Raymond, Deborah Takikawa, and Samantha Wood. *The Caregiver's Role in Birth and Newborn Self-Attachment Needs*, 1997. Castillino Training (website).

Centers for Disease Control and Prevention, "Working Together to Reduce Black Maternal Mortality." CDC (website), April 6, 2022.

Cerelli, Kerry. "Bridging Midwifery Practice and Pre- and Perinatal Insights." Interview, Mary Jackson, Certified Professional Midwife, *Journal of Prenatal and Perinatal Psychology and Health* 28, no. 1 (2013): 72–90.

Chamberlain, David B. "Babies Don't Feel Pain: A Century of Denial in Medicine." Presentation at *Second International Symposium of Circumcision*, National Organization of Circumcision Information Resource Centers (NOCIRC website), May 2, 1991.

———. *Babies Remember Birth: And Other Extraordinary Discoveries about the Mind and Personality of Your Newborn*. New York: St Martin's Press, 1988.

———. Communicating with the Mind of a Prenate: Guidelines for Parents and Birth Professionals. *Journal of Prenatal and Perinatal Psychology and Health* 18, no. 2 (2003): 95–108.

———. *The Mind of Your Newborn Baby*. Berkeley, CA: North Atlantic, 1998.

———. "The Sentient Prenate: What Every Parent Should Know." *Journal of Prenatal and Perinatal Psychology and Health* 9, no. 1 (1994): 9–31.

———. *Windows to the Womb: Revealing the Conscious Baby from Conception to Birth*, Berkeley, CA: North Atlantic, 2013.

Chodorow, Joan, "To Move and be Moved." In *Authentic Movement: Essays by Mary Starks Whitehouse, Janet Adler and Joan Chodorow*, ed. Patrizia Pallaro, 267–78. Philadelphia: Jessica Kingsley, 1999.

Colson, Suzanne, "A Non-Prescriptive Recipe for Breastfeeding." *The Practicing Midwife* 10, no. 9 (2007): 42–48.

Conrad, Emilie. *Life on Land: The Story of Continuum, the World-Renowned Self-Discovery and Movement Method*. Berkeley, CA: North Atlantic, 2007.

———. "Continuum: An Introduction with Emilie Conrad." YouTube, January 23, 2013.

Consejo Superior de Investigaciones Científicas (CSIC). "Touch and Sight are Linked Before Birth." *Neuroscience News* (website), August 18, 2022.

Costa, Dora L., Noelle Yetta, and Heather DeSomer. "Intergenerational Transmission of Paternal Trauma Among US Civil War Ex-POWs." *Proceedings of the National Academy of Sciences of the United States of America* 115, no. 44 (2018): 11215–20.

Crable, Margaret. "Exactly How Many Senses Do We Really Have?" *Neuroscience News* (website), January 19, 2023.

Davis-Floyd, Robbie E. *Birth as an American Rite of Passage*. Berkeley, CA: University of California Press, 1992.

DeCasper, Anthony, J. and William Fifer. "Of Human Bonding: Newborns

Prefer Their Mother's Voices." *Science* (website) 208, no. 4448 (June 6, 1980): 1174–76.

DeMause, Lloyd. *Foundations of Psychohistory*. New York: Creative Roots, Inc., 1982.

DeMause, Lloyd. "Childhood and Cultural Evolution." *The Journal of Psychohistory* 26, no. 3 (Winter, 1999): 642–723.

Deranger, Eriel, T., "Climate Crisis, Fragmentation and Collective Trauma" Wisdom of Trauma, Part 2, YouTube, November 3, 2021.

Divan, Hozefa A., Leeka Kheifets, Carsten Obel, and Jørn Olsen. "Prenatal and Postnatal Exposure to Cell Phone Use and Behavioral Problems in Children." *Epidemiology* 19, no. 4 (2008): 523–29.

Dykema, Ravi. "How Your Nervous System Sabotages Your Ability to Relate: An Interview with Stephen Porges about His Polyvagal Theory." *Nexus: Colorado's Holistic Health and Spirituality Journal*, Acusticusneurinom dk (website), March/April, 2006.

Eapen, Valsamma, Marl Dadds, Bryanne Barnett, et al. "Separation Anxiety, Attachment and Inter-Personal Representations: Disentangling the Role of Oxytocin in the Perinatal Period." *PLoS One* 17, no. 9 (2014): e107745.

Editors of Encyclopedia Britannica Article History, The, "Burial Mound." *Britannica* (website), n.d.

Edwards, Scott, "The Long Life of Early Pain." *Harvard Medical School* (website), April 29, 2011.

Eliade, Mircea. *Rites and Symbols of Initiation: The Mysteries of Birth and Rebirth*. New York: Harper & Row, 1958.

———. *Myth and Reality*. New York: Harper & Row, 1963.

Emerson, William R. *Infant Birth Re-facilitation: A Script*. Petaluma, CA: Human Potential Resources, 1984.

———. "Somatic Therapy," *Journal of Heart-Centered Therapies* 5, no. 2 (2002): 65–90; Emerson Birth RX: Somatotropic Therapy (website).

Emoto, Masaru. *Hidden Messages in Water*. New York: Pocket Books, 2005.

Ensler, Eve. *In the Body of the World: A Memoir of Cancer and Connection*. New York: Picador, 2013.

Felitti, Vincent J., Robert F. Anda, Dale Nordenberg, et al. "Relationship of Childhood Abuse and Household Dysfunction to Many of the Leading Causes of Death in Adults. The Adverse Childhood Experiences (ACE) Study." *American Journal of Preventive Medicine* 14, no. 4 (1998): 245–58.

Felitti, Vincent J. "Profound Effects of Early Life Experiences," *The Biology of*

Trauma 2.0, Health Means summit presentation, August 8, 2022.

Filippa, Manuela, Costantino Panza, Fabrizio Ferrari, et al. "Systematic Review of Maternal Voice Interventions Demonstrates Increased Stability in Preterm Infants." *Acta Paediatrica* 106, no. 8 (August 2017): 1220–29.

Filippa, Manuela, Maria G. Monaci, Carmen Spagnuolo, et al. "Maternal Speech Decreases Pain Scores and Increases Oxytocin Levels in Preterm Infants During Painful Procedures." *Scientific Reports* 11 (2021): 17301.

Flanders-Stepans, Mary Beth, "Alarming Racial Differences in Maternal Mortality." *Journal of Perinatal Education* 9, no. 2 (2000): 50–1.

Fodor, Nandor. *The Search for the Beloved: A Clinical Investigation of the Trauma of Birth and Pre-natal Conditioning.* New York: Hermitage Press, 1949.

Frellick, Marcia, "Trump Signs Historic Bill to Cut Maternal Mortality Rate." *Medscape* (website), December 27, 2018.

Freud, Sigmund. *Introductory Lectures on Psychoanalysis.* New York: W. W. Norton & Company, 1966.

Galoustian, Giselle. "Breastfeeding Status and Duration Significantly Impact Postpartum Depression Risk." *Neuroscience News* (website), September 30, 2021.

Garfield, C. A. "The Dying Patient's Concern with Life After Death." In *A Collection of Near-Death Research Readings: Scientific Inquiries into the Experiences of Persons Near Physical Death*, edited by Craig R. Lundahl. 160–4. Chicago: Nelson-Hall, 1982.

Gaskin, Ina May. *Ina May's Guide to Childbirth.* London: Vermilion, 2008.

Gaskin, Ina May. *Birth Matters: A Midwife's Manifesto.* Kindle, 2011.

Ghasemi, Babak and Masoud Hashemi. "Foreign Language Learning During Childhood." *Procedia: Social and Behavioral Sciences* 28 (2011): 872–76.

Goer, Henci. "Epidurals: Do They or Don't They Increase Cesareans?" *The Journal of Perinatal Education* 24, no. 4 (2015): 209–12.

Golding, Jean, Marcus Pembrey, Yasmin Iles-Cavenn, et al. "Ancestral Smoking and Developmental Outcomes: A Review of Publications From a Population Birth Cohort." *Biology of Reproduction* 105, no. 3 (2021): 625–31.

Golding, Jean, Steve Gregory, Kate Northstone, et al. "Human Transgenerational Observations of Regular Smoking before Puberty on Fat Mass in Grandchildren and Great-Grandchildren." *Scientific Reports* 12, no. 1 (2022): 1139.

Grace, Tegan, Wendy Oddy, Max Bulsara, and Beth Hands, (2016). "Breastfeeding and Motor Development: A Longitudinal Cohort Study." *Human Movement Science* 51 (January 2017): 9–16.

Grof, Stanislav. *Beyond the Brain: Birth, Death and Transcendence in Psychotherapy*. Albany, NY: State University of New York Press, 1985.

Grof, Stanislav. *The Adventure of Self-Discovery: Dimensions of Consciousness and New Perspectives in Psychotherapy and Inner Exploration*. Albany, NY: State University of New York Press, 1988.

Grossinger, Richard. *Embryogenesis: Species, Gender, and Identity*. Berkeley, CA: North Atlantic Books, 2000.

Grosso, Michael "Toward an Explanation of Near-Death Phenomena." In *A Collection of Near-Death Research Readings: Scientific Inquiries into the Experiences of Persons Near Physical Death*, edited by Craig R. Lundahl, 205–30. Chicago: Nelson-Hall, 1982.

Guy-Evans, Olivia. "Bronfenbrenner's Ecological Systems Theory." *Simply Psychology* (website), November 9, 2020.

Habek, D., J. C., Habek, A. Barbir, M., Barbir, and P. Granić. "Fetal Grasping of the Umbilical Cord and Perinatal Outcome. *Archives of Gynecology and Obstetrics*, 268 no. 4 (2003): 274–7.

Hallett, Elisabeth. *Soul Trek: Meeting our Children on the Way to Birth*. Hamilton, MT: Light Hearts, 1995.

Hansard, Kicki. *Supporting Survivors of Sexual Abuse Through Pregnancy and Childbirth: A Guide for Midwives, Doulas, and other Healthcare Professionals*. London: Singing Dragon, 2020.

Harvey, Mary R. "An Ecological View of Psychological Trauma and Recovery." *Journal of Traumatic Stress* 9, no. 1 (1996): 3–23.

HeartMath Institute. "Mother-Baby Study Supports Heart-Brain Interactions." *Science of the Heart*, HeartMath (website), April 20, 2008.

Henriques, Martha. "Can the Legacy of Trauma Be Passed Down the Generations?" BBC (website), March 26, 2019.

Hepper, Peter. "Fetal Psychology: An Embryonic Science." In *Fetal Behavior: Developmental and Perinatal Aspects*, ed. J. G. Nijhuis, 129–56. New York: Oxford University Press, 1992.

Herman, Judith L. *Trauma and Recovery*. New York: Basic Books, 1992/2015.

———. *Father-Daughter Incest*. Boston: Harvard University Press, 1981/2000.

Hernández-Luengo, Monserrat, Celia Álvarez-Bueno, José Alberto Martínez-Hortelano, et al. "The Relationship Between Breastfeeding and Motor Development in Children: A Systematic Review and Meta-Analysis." *Nutrition Reviews* 80, no. 8 (2022): 1827–35.

Highsmith, Susan, Tara Blasco, Kate White, et al. *Supporting Families to*

Integrate Their Birth Experiences: The BEBA Clinic Retrospective Study. Independently published, 2022.

House, Simon H. "Primal Integration Therapy: School of Lake." *Journal of Prenatal and Perinatal Psychology and Health* 14, no. 3 (March 2000): 213–35.

Hübl, Thomas, and Jordan J. Avritt. *Healing Collective Trauma: A Process for Integrating Our Intergenerational and Cultural Wounds.* Louisville, CO: Sounds True, 2020.

Hunt, Valerie V. *Infinite Mind: Science of Human Vibrations of Consciousness.* Brattleboro, Vermont: Echo Point Books & Media, 1989/2023.

Ikegawa, Akira. *I Remember When I Was in Mommy's Tummy.* Translated by Kamako S. Bondet and Seikei Marie Smith. Lyon, 2002.

Ikegawa, Akira. *Parenting Begins From a Baby's Time in the Womb: What We Know From Prenatal Memories.* Art Print, 2006.

Irving, Michael. "Natalism as Pre- and Perinatal Metaphor." *Pre- and Peri-natal Psychology Journal* 4, no. 2 (1989): 83–110.

Ivanov, P. C., Ma, Q. D. Y., & Bartsch, R. P. (2009, August). "Maternal–Fetal Heartbeat Phase Synchronization." *Proceedings of the National Academy of Sciences* 106 (33) 13641–42.

Janus, Ludwig. *The Enduring Effects of Prenatal Experience: Echoes From the Womb.* Northvale, NJ: Jason Aronson, 1997.

———. *Enduring Effects of Prenatal Experience: Echoes From the Womb.* Translated by Terence Dowling. Heidelberg, Germany: Mattes Verlag, 2001.

Jirásek, Jan E. *Human Embryo and Fetus: A Photographic Review of Human Prenatal Development,* Nashville: Parthenon, 2001.

Johanson, Richard, Mary Newburn, and Alison Macfarlane. "Has the Medicalization of Childbirth Gone Too Far?" *British Medical Journal* 324, no. 7342 (2022): 892–5.

Johnson, Becky, "All Parents Affected by Miscarriage Should be Given Paid Leave, Say Campaigners, as Bill Introduced to Parliament." *News Sky* (website), September 13, 2021.

Johnson, Robert A., *Owning Your Own Shadow: Understanding the Dark Side of the Psyche,* 2013. Kindle.

Jones, Ricardo, "What Obstetrics and Gynecology Should Mean in Our Society, and How it Needs to Change. Interview by Kathy Fray," IIMHCO, YouTube, February 20, 2022.

Joyce, James. *Dubliners.* London: Penguin Classics, 2014.

Jung, Carl G. *Collected Works 13: Alchemical Studies*, Princeton, NJ: Princeton University Press, 1970.

Kalef, Mia, *The Secret Life of Babies: How Our Prebirth and Birth Experiences Shape Our World*. Berkeley, CA: North Atlantic, 2014.

Karimi, Fatemah Zahra, Ramin Sadeghi, Nahid Maleki-Saghooni, and Talat Khadivzadeh. "The Effect of Mother-Infant Skin to Skin Contact on Success and Duration of First Breastfeeding: A Systematic Review and Metaanalysis." *Taiwanese Journal of Obstetrics and Gynecology* 58, no. 1 (January 2019): 1–9.

Kawanishi, Yasuyuki, Eiji Yoshioka, Yasuaki Saijo, Toshihiro Itoh, et al. "The Relationship Between Prenatal Psychological Stress and Placental Abruption in Japan." *The Japan Environment and Children's Study* (JECS)." *PLoS One* 14, no. 7 (2019).

Kessler, David. "On Grief and Grieving." *PESI online course*, Psychotherapy Networker (website), February 19, 2019.

Khandoker, Ahsan H., Steffen Schulz, Haitham M. Al-Angari, Andreas Voss, and Yoshitaka Kimura. "Alterations in Maternal–Fetal Heart Rate Coupling Strength and Directions in Abnormal Fetuses." *Frontiers in Physiology* 10 (April 26, 2019): 482.

Klaus, Marshall H., Phylis H. Klaus, and John H. Kennell. *Bonding: Building the Foundations for Secure Attachment and Independence*. New York: Addison-Wesley Publishing Company, Inc., 1995.

Kozłowski, Miroslaw, and Janina Marciak-Kozlowska. "Schumann Resonance and Brain Waves: A Quantum Description." *NeuroQuantology* 13, no. 2 (May 2015): 196–204.

Krzeczkowski, John E., Louise A. Schmidt, Mark A. Ferro, Mark A., and Ryan J. Van Lieshout. "Follow the Leader: Maternal Transmission of Physiological Regulatory Support to Distressed Infants in Real-Time." *Journal of Psychopathology and Clinical Science* 131, no. 5 (2022): 524–34.

Lake, Frank. *Tight Corners in Pastoral Counseling*. London: Darton, Longman and Todd, 1981.

Larken, Marilynn "Legacy from Young Boys' Smoking: More Body fat in Granddaughters, Great Granddaughters." *Medscape* (website), February 03, 2022.

Leboyer, Frederic. *Birth without Violence*. New York: Alfred A. Knoff, 1975.

Leong, Melanie, Catherine J. Karr, Shetal I. Shah, and Heather L. Brumberg. "Before the First Breath: Why Ambient Air Pollution and Climate Change

Should Matter to Neonatal-Perinatal Providers." *Journal of Perinatology* 43 (August 29, 2022): 1059–66.

Levine, Peter A., and Frederick, Ann. *Waking the Tiger: Healing Trauma.* Berkeley, CA: North Atlantic, 1997.

Lewis, Tanya, "The Pandemic Caused a Baby Boom in Red States and a Bust in Blue States." *Scientific American* (website), May 26, 2023.

Lieberman, E. J. "Introduction to the Dover Edition" in *The Trauma of Birth*, by Otto Rank. Mineola, NY: Dover Publications, 1929/1993.

Liederman, Herbert P. et al. *African Infant Precocity: Some Social Influences During the First Year.* New York; Carnegie Corp. and Grant Foundation, 1972.

Liedloff, Jean. *The Continuum Concept: Allowing Nature to Work Successfully.* New York: Addison-Wesley, 1985.

Lipton, Bruce, and Steve Bhaerman. *Spontaneous Evolution: Our Positive Future (and a Way to Get There from Here)*, 2009. Kindle.

Lipton, Bruce H. *The Biology of Belief: Unleashing the Power of Consciousness, Matter and Miracles.* Carlsbad, CA: Hay House, 2015.

Lowth, Marcus. "10 Organ Recipients Who Took on the Traits of Their Owners," ListVerse (website), May 14, 2016.

Luecken, Linda J., Betty Lin, Shayna S. Coburn, David P. MacKinnon, Nancy A. Gonzales, and Keith A. Crnic. "Prenatal Stress, Partner Support, and Infant Cortisol Reactivity in Low-Income Mexican American Families." *Psychoneuroendocrinology* 38, no. 12 (September 14, 2013): 3092–101.

Lundahl, Craig R. "Near Death Experiences of Mormons." In *A Collection of Near-Death Research Readings: Scientific Inquiries into the Experiences of Persons Near Physical Death*, edited by Craig R. Lundahl, 165–79. Chicago: Nelson-Hall, 1982.

Macdonald, Jacqui. "Let's Talk Periconception Health Care with Men." *Medicine Today* 22, no. 9 (2021): 71–73.

Madrid, Antonio. *The Mother and Child Reunion: Repairing the Broken Maternal-Infant Bond.* Self-published, 2011.

Madrid, Antonio, Ralph Ames, Susan Skolek, and Gary Brown. "Does Maternal-Infant Bonding Therapy Improve Breathing in Asthmatic Children?" *Journal of Prenatal and Perinatal Psychology and Health* 15, no. 2 (Winter 2000): 90–117.

Mahmoudabadi, Fatemeh Shamsi, Saeidah Ziaei, Mohammad Firoozabadi, and Anoshirvan Karazemnejad. "Use of Mobile Phone During Pregnancy and the Risk of Spontaneous Abortion." *Journal of Environmental Health Science and Engineering* 13 (April 21, 2015): 34.

Makichen, Walter. *Spirit Babies: How to Communicate with the Child You're Meant to Have.* McHenry, IL: Delta, 2008.

Malaspina, D., C. Corcoran, K. Kleinhaus, et al. "Acute Maternal Stress in Pregnancy and Schizophrenia in Offspring: A Cohort Prospective Study." *BMC Psychiatry* 8, no. 71 (2008).

Maltz, Wendy. *The Sexual Healing Journey: A Guide for Survivors of Sexual Abuse.* New York: William Morrow, 3rd revised ed., 2012.

Mandel, Bethany. "The Benefits of Having Siblings Present at Childbirth." *Deseret* (website), Sept 9, 2023.

Mandel, Dorothy. "Spirit and Matter of the Heart: Interview with Dorothy Mandel." *Grace Millennium* 1, no. 3–4 (Winter, 2001). Creation-Designs (website).

Maret, Stephen M. *The Prenatal Person: Frank Lake's Maternal-Fetal Distress Syndrome.* Lenham, MD: University Press of America, 1997.

Martin, Roland, "Tollund Man." *Britannica* (website), July 20, 2024.

Maté, Gabor. "Gabor Maté: How to Build a Culture of Good Health." *Yes! Magazine* (website), November 16, 2015.

Maté, Gabor. *The Myth of Normal: Trauma, Healing and Illness in a Toxic Culture.* London: Ebury Digital, 2022.

Maté, Gabor, and Gordon Neufeld. *Hold on to Your Kids: Why Parents Need to Matter More than Peers*, 2nd ed. London: Vermilion, 2019.

Mathew, P. J., and Joseph L. Mathew. "Assessment and Management of Pain in Infants." *Postgraduate Medical Journal* 79, no. 934 (August 2003): 438–43.

McCarty, Wendy Anne, and Marti Glenn. "Investing in Human Potential From the Beginning of Life: Key to Maximizing Human Potential." *Natural Family Living*, 2008. Chrysalis Counseling Services (website) Accessed January 31, 2023.

McCraty, Rollin. *The Energetic Heart: Bioelectromagnetic Interactions Within and Between People.* Boulder Creek, CA: Institute of HeartMath, 2003.

McCraty, Rollin and Annette Deyle. *The Science of Interconnectivity. Exploring the Human-Earth Connection.* Boulder Creek, CA: HeartMath Institute, 2016.

McLeod, Lin. "Tumulus Tombs: The Predecessors of Modern Mausoleums," Mausoleums (website), May 24, 2023.

Mehler J., P. Jusczyk, G. Lambertz, N. Halsted, J. Bertoncini, and C. Amiel-Tison.

(1988). "A Precursor of Language Acquisition in Young Infants." *Cognition*, 29 (1988): 143–78.

Menakem, Resma M. *My Grandmother's Hands: Racialized Trauma and the Pathway to Mending Our Hearts and Bodies*, 2017. Kindle.

Mengjie Xia, Mengjie, Jing Luo, Junqiang Wang, Yong Liang, "Association Between Breastfeeding and Postpartum Depression: A Meta-Analysis," *Journal of Affective Disorders* 308 (2022): 512–19.

Menzam, Cherionna. "An Authentic Birth: Pre and Perinatal Issues in Authentic Movement." Unpublished master's thesis. Boulder, CO: Naropa Institute, 1996.

———. *Dancing Our Birth: Prenatal and Birth Themes and Symbols in Dance, Movement, Art, Dreams, Language, Myth, Ritual, Play, and Psychotherapy*, Unpublished Doctoral Dissertation, The Union Institute, 2002.

Menzam-Sills, Cherionna. *Spirit into Form: Exploring Embryological Potential and Prenatal Psychology*. Self-published, Cosmoanelixis, 2021.

Mercer, Judith S., Debra A. Erickson-Owens, Sean C. L. Deoni, Sarah Joelson, Emily N. Mercer, and James F. Padbury. "Effects of Delayed Cord-Clamping on 4-month Ferritin Levels, Brain Myelin Content, and Neurodevelopment: A Randomized, Controlled Trial." *The Journal of Pediatrics* 203 (July 6, 2018): 266–72.

Metz, Torri D., Rebecca G. Clifton, Brenna L. Hughes, et al. "Association of SARS-CoV-2 Infection withSerious Maternal Morbidity and Mortality from Obstetric Complications." *JAMA* 327, no. 8 (February 7, 2022): 748–59.

Millar, A., D. Muralidhar, E. Bruce, et al. "323 Neonatal Jaundice and Delayed Cord Clamping." *Archives of Disease in Childhood* 108 (2023): A230.

Miller, Alice. "Depression and Grandiosity as Related Forms of Narcissistic Disturbances." *International Review of PsychoAnalysis*, 6 (1979): 61–76.

Mines, Stephanie. *The Secret of Resilience: Healing Personal and Planetary Trauma Through Morphogenesis*. Rochester, VT: Healing Arts Press, 2023.

Monk, Catherine, Michael M. Myers, Richard P. Sloan, Lauren M. Ellman, and William P. Fifer, William P. "Effects of Women's Stress-Elicited Physiological Activity and Chronic Anxiety on Fetal Heart Rate." *Journal of Developmental & Behavioral Pediatrics* 24, no. 1 (February 2003): 32–38.

Monell, Terry T. "Living Out the Past: Infant Surgery Prior to 1987." *Journal of Prenatal and Perinatal Psychology and Health* 25, no. 3 (Spring 2011): 159–72.

Montagu, Ashley. *Touching: The Human Significance of Skin*, 3rd ed. New York: Avon, 2018.

Moody, Raymond. "The Experience of Dying." In *A Collection of Near-Death Research Readings: Scientific Inquiries into the Experiences of Persons Near Physical Death*, ed. Craig R. Lundahl, 89–109. Chicago: Nelson-Hall, 1982.

Moorjani, Anita. *Dying to Be Me: My Journey from Cancer, to Near Death, to True Healing.* Carlsbad, CA: Hay House, 2012.

Morales-Munoz, Isabel, Brookly Ashdown-Doel, Emily Beazley, Camilla Carr, Christina Preece, Steven Marwaha. "Maternal Postnatal Depression and Anxiety and the Risk for Mental Health Disorders in Adolescent Offspring: Findings from the Avon Longitudinal Study of Parents and Children Cohort." *Australian & New Zealand Journal of Psychiatry* 57, no. 1 (January 2023): 82–92.

Morgan, Jamie. "Womb with a View: Sensory Development in Utero." UT Southwestern Medical Center Medblog (website), August 1, 2017.

Myers, Sarah, and Sarah E. Johns. "Postnatal Depression is Associated with Detrimental Life-Long and Multi-Generational Impacts on Relationship Quality." *PeerJ* 6 (2018): e4305.

Nantel, Claudette. "Conscious Abortion: Engaging the Fetus in a Compassionate Dialogue." *Journal of Prenatal and Perinatal Psychology and Health* 35, no. 2 (Summer 2021).

Nguyen, Trinh, Drew H. Abney, Dina Salamander, Bennet I. Bertenthal, and Stephanie Hoehl. "Proximity and Touch are Associated with Neural but Not Physiological Synchrony in Naturalistic Mother-Infant Interactions." *NeuroImage* 244, no. 118599 (December 1, 2021).

Noble, Elizabeth. *Primal Connections: How Our Experiences from Conception to Birth Influence Our Emotions, Behavior, and Health.* New York: Simon & Schuster, 1993.

Odent, Michel. *Childbirth and the Evolution of Homo sapiens*, 2nd ed. London: Pinter & Martin, 2014.

Odent, M. "Stress Deprivation in the Perinatal Period." *Midwifery Today* (website), 116 (Winter 2015): 25–27.

Ogden, Pat, Kekuni Minton, and Clare Pain. *Trauma and the Body: A Sensorimotor Approach to Psychotherapy (Norton Series on Interpersonal Neurobiology).* New York: W. W. Norton & Company, 2006.

Office of Minority Health, "Infant Mortality and African Americans."

U.S. Department of Health and Human Services Office of Minority Health. Minority Health HHS (website), Accessed August 13, 2022.

Osis, Karlis and Erlendur Haraldsson. "Deathbed Observations by Physicians and Nurses: A Cross-Cultural Survey." In *A Collection of Near-Death Research Readings: Scientific Inquiries into the Experiences of Persons Near Physical Death*, ed. Craig R. Lundahl, 65–88. Chicago: Nelson-Hall, 1982.

Page, David C. "Breastfeeding is Early Functional Jaw Orthopedics (an Introduction)." *The Functional Orthodontist* 18, no. 3 (2001): 24–27.

Pallaro, Patrizia, ed. *Authentic Movement: A Collection of Essays by Mary Starks Whitehouse, Janet Adler and Joan Chodorow.* London: Jessica Kingsley, 1999.

Parnia, Sam and Young, Josh. *Erasing death: The Science that is Rewriting the Boundaries Between Life and Death.* San Francisco: HarperOne, 2014.

Partanen, Eino, Teija Kujala, Risto Näätänen, Auli Liitola, Anke Sambeth, and Minna Huotilainen, "Learning-Induced Neural Plasticity of Speech Processing before Birth," *Biological Sciences* 110, no. 37: 15145–50.

Patel, Pooja R, Tabassum H. Laz, and Abbey B. Berenson. "Patient Characteristics Associated with Pregnancy Ambivalence." *Journal of Women's Health (Larchmt)* 24, no. 1 (January 1, 2015): 37–41.

Pearce, Joseph Chilton. *Evolution's End: Claiming the Potential of Our Intelligence.* New York: HarperCollins, 1992.

Pearce, Joseph Chilton. "Mother-Infant Bonding and the Intelligence of the Heart." Touch the Future, YouTube, June 27, 2011.

Pearsall, Paul P. *The Heart's Code: Tapping the Wisdom and Power of Our Heart Energy: The New Findings About Cellular Memories and Their Role in the Mind/Body/Spirit Connection.* New York: Broadway Books, 1998.

Pearsall, Paul P., Gary E. R. Schwartz, and Linda G. S. Russek. "Changes in Heart Transplant Recipients that Parallel the Personalities of Their Donors." *Journal of Near-Death Studies* 20, no. 3 (March 2002): 191–206.

Peerbolte, Maarten Lietaert. *Prenatal Dynamics: A Psychoanalytical Approachment to the Trauma of Birth, Prenatal Traumata and Conception; a Contribution to Female Psychology and to Extra-sensional Perception.* Leiden: A. W. Sijthhoff's Uitgeversmaatschappij, N. V., 1954.

Pember, Mary Annette. "The Midwives' Resistance: How Native Women are Reclaiming Birth on Their Terms." Rewire News Group (website), January 5, 2018.

Pereira, Contzen. "Quantum Resonance & Consciousness." *Journal of Consciousness Exploration & Research* 6, no. 7 (September 2015): 473–82.

Pinar, Sukran Ertekin and Hilal. "Paternal Depression and Attachment Levels of First-Time Fathers in Turkey." *Perspectives in Psychiatric Care* 58, no. 3 (2022): 1082–88.

Piontelli, Alessandra. *From Fetus to Child: An Observational and Psychoanalytic Study*. New York: Routledge, 1992.

Porges, Stephen W. *Polyvagal Safety: Attachment, Communication, Self-Regulation*. New York: W. W. Norton & Co., 2021.

Porges, Stephen W. "Play as Neural Exercise: Insights from the Polyvagal Theory." *GAINS Living Journal Special Conference Edition: The Power of Play for Mind-Brain Health*. March 2015: 3–8. Mind Gains (website).

Porges, Stephen. *The Polyvagal Theory: Neurophysiological Foundations of Emotions, Attachment, Communication, and Self-Regulation (Norton Series on Interpersonal Neurobiology)*. New York: W. W. Norton, 2011.

Porges, Stephen W. and Furman, Senta A. "The Early Development of the Autonomic Nervous System Provides a Neural Platform for Social Behavior: A Polyvagal Perspective." *Infant Child Development* 20, no. 1 (February 2011): 106–18.

Prechtel, Martin. *The Smell of Rain on Dust: Grief and Praise*. Berkeley, CA: North Atlantic Books, 2015.

Qian, Y., Q. Lu, H. Shao, X. Ying, W. Huang, Y. Hua. "Timing of Umbilical Cord Clamping and Neonatal Jaundice in Singleton Term Pregnancy." *Early Human Development*. (March 2020) 142: 104948.

Rank, Otto. *The Trauma of Birth*. New York: Robert Brunner, 1924/1952.

Reuters. "Babies Feel Pain 'Like Adults', MRI Suggests." *The Guardian* (website), April 21, 2015, Accessed August 29, 2021.

Rhodes, Jeane. M. *Pre- and Perinatal Psychology and Health: A Brief History*. Unpublished manuscript, 1996.

Righard, Lennart and Margaret Alade (writers) and Kittie Frantz (producer). *Delivery Self-Attachment* (video). Sunland, CA: Geddes Productions, 1992.

Rilke, Rainer Maria. *Letters to a Young Poet*, London: Penguin Classics, 2012.

Ring, Nicola A., Nessa M. McHugh, Bethany B. Reed, Rachel Davidson-Welch, Leslie S. Dodd, "Healers and Midwives Accused of Witchcraft (1563–1736)—What Secondary Analysis of the Scottish Survey of Witchcraft Can Contribute to the Teaching of Nursing and Midwifery History," *Nurse Education Today* 133 (2024): 106026.

Ripinsky-Naxon, Michael. *Sexuality, Shamanism, and Transformation*. Berlin: VWB, 1997.

Rozman, Deborah. "Global Coherence." In *Heart Intelligence: Connecting with the Intuitive Guidance of the Heart*, 2016. Kindle.

Rubik, Beverly, David Muehsam, Richard Hammerschlag, and Shamini Jain. "Biofield Science and Healing: History, Terminology, and Concepts." *Global Advances in Health and Medicine* (supplement) (November 4, 2015): 8–14.

Sabom, Michael B. and S. S. Kreutziger. "Physicians Evaluate the Near-Death Experience." In *A Collection of Near-Death Research Readings: Scientific Inquiries into the Experiences of Persons Near Physical Death*, ed. Craig R. Lundahl, 148–59. Chicago: Nelson-Hall, 1982.

Sacker, Amanda, Maria A. Quigley, and Yvonne Kelly. "Breastfeeding and Developmental Delay: Findings from the Millennium Cohort Study." *Pediatrics* 118, no. 3 (September 2006): e682–9.

Sallenbach, William. "Claira: A Case Study in Prenatal Learning." *Journal of Prenatal and Perinatal Psychology and Health*, 9, no. 1 (1994): 33–56.

Sanders, Robert. "Babies in the Womb May See More than We Thought: Light Sensitive Cells in Immature Retina are Networked, Suggesting Bigger Role in Developing Brain." Science Daily (website), November 25, 2019.

Sansone, Antonella. *Cultivating Mindfulness to Raise Children Who Thrive: Why Human Connection from Before Birth Matters*. London and New York: Routledge, 2021.

Sartwelle, Thomas P. and James C. Johnston, James C. "Continuous Electronic Fetal Monitoring during Labor: A Critique and a Reply to Contemporary Proponents." *The Surgery Journal (N Y)* 4, no. 1 (March 7, 2018): e23–e28.

Saxby, Darby, and Jennifer Hahn-Holbrook. "Breast Milk's Unique Composition May Actually Help Babies Tell Day from Night" *Science Alert: The Conversation*. (August 12, 2019). Science Alert (website).

Scarff, Jonathan R. "Postpartum Depression in Men." *Innovations in Clinical Neuroscience* 16, no. 5–6 (May 1, 2019): 11–14.

Schaadt, Gesa, Rachel G. Zsido, Arno Villringer, Hellmuth Obrig, Claudia Männel, and Julia Sacher. "Association of Postpartum Maternal Mood with Infant Speech Perception at 2 and 6.5 Months of Age." *JAMA Network Open* 5, no. 9 (September 21, 2022): e2232672.

Schwartz, David A., Elyzabeth Avvad-Portari, Pavel Babál, et al. "Placental Tissue Destruction and Insufficiency from COVID-19 Causes Stillbirth and Neonatal Death from Hypoxic-Ischemic Injury: A Study of 68 Cases with SARS-CoV-2 Placentitis from 12 Countries." *Archives of Pathology and Laboratory Medicine* 146, no. 6 (February 10, 2022): 660–76.

Scrutti, S. "'Genetic Memory' of Grandma's Malnourishment Affects Health of Grandchildren, but Ends There." Medical Daily (website), July 10, 2014.

Serpeloni, F., K. Radtke, S. G. de Assis, F. Henning, D. Nätt, and T. Elbert. "Grandmaternal Stress During Pregnancy and DNA Methylation of the Third Generation: an Epigenome-Wide Association Study." *Translational Psychiatry* 7, no. 8 (2017): e1202.

Shuffrey, Lauren C., Morgan R. Firestein, Margaret H. Kyle, et al. "Association of Birth During the COVID-19 Pandemic With Neurodevelopmental Status at 6 Months in Infants With and Without In Utero Exposure to Maternal SARS-CoV-2 Infection." *JAMA Pediatrics* 176, no. 6 (2022): e215563.

Siegel, Daniel J. and Mary Hartzell. *Parenting from the Inside Out: How a Deeper Self-Understanding Can Help You Raise Children Who Thrive.* Pontiac, MI: Scribe, 2014.

Siegel, Daniel J. *The Developing Mind: Toward a Neurobiology of Interpersonal Experience.* New York: Guilford Press, 1999.

Sills, Franklyn *Being and Becoming: Psychodynamics, Buddhism, and the Origins of Selfhood.* Berkeley, CA: North Atlantic, 2009.

———*Foundations in Craniosacral Biodynamics: Breath of Life and Fundamental Skills v. 1: The Breath of Life and Fundamental Skills.* Berkeley, CA: North Atlantic, 2011.

———*Foundations in Craniosacral Biodynamics vol. 2: The Sentient Embryo, Tissue Intelligence, and Trauma Resolution,* Berkeley, CA: North Atlantic, 2012.

Singh, Gurchara and G. Archana. "Unraveling the Mystery of Vernix Caseosa." *Indian Journal of Dermatology* 53, no. 2 (2008): 54–60.

Sjoo, Monica and Barbara Mor. *The Great Cosmic Mother: Rediscovering the Religion of the Earth.* San Francisco: New York: Harper & Row, 1987.

Smythe, Kara L., Irene Petersen, and Patricia Schartau. "Prevalence of Perinatal Depression and Anxiety in Both Parents: A Systematic Review and Meta-analysis." *JAMA Network Open* 5, no. 6 (2022): e2218969.

Somé, Malidoma Patrice. *Of Water and the Spirit: Ritual, Magic, and Initiation in the Life of an African Shaman.* London: Penguin Publishing Group, 1995.

Spelt, David, K. "The Conditioning of the Human Fetus in Utero." *The Journal of Experimental Psychology* 48 (1948): 338–46.

Stefon, M. "Wuwei." *Encyclopedia Britannica* (website), September 23, 2013.

Stein, Vicky and Daisy Dobrijevic. "Do Parallel Universes Exist? We Might Live in a Multiverse." Space (website), November 3, 2021.

Stevenson, Ian. *Children Who Remember Past Lives: A Question of Reincarnation, Revised Edition.* Jefferson, NC: McFarland & Co., 2016.

Still, Andrew Taylor. *Philosophy of Osteopathy.* Kirksville, MO: A. T. Still, 1899.

Stone, Katherine. "How Your Own Mother and Childhood Trauma Can Impact Postpartum Depression." Postpartum Progress (website), Accessed November 5, 2022.

Stromsted, Tina. "Authentic Movement: A Dance with the Divine." *Body Movement andDance in Psychotherapy Journal* 4, no. 3 (Summer, 2009), 201–13.

Sutherland, William Garner. *Contributions of Thought: The Collected Writings of William Garner Sutherland, D.O.*, eds., Adah Strand and Anne L. Wales. Fort Worth, TX: Sutherland Cranial Teaching Foundation, 1971/1998.

Terry, Karlton. "Implantation Journey: The Original Human Myth, Part 1." *Journal of Prenatal and Perinatal Psychology and Health* 27, no. 3 (2013): 276–88.

Thai, Linda. "Traumatic Stress and the Nervous System," YouTube Video, 2023.

Thomson, Helen. "Study of Holocaust Survivors Finds Trauma Passed on to Children's Genes." *The Guardian* (website), August 21, 2015.

Thornburg, Kent L., Janne Boone-Heinonen, and Amy M. Valent. "Social Determinants of Placental Health and Future Disease Risks for Babies," *Obstetrics and Gynecology Clinics of North America* 47, no. 1 (March 2020): 1–15.

Tiller, William A., Walter E. Dibble, and Michael J. Kohane. *Conscious Acts of Creation: The Emergence of a New Physics.* Walnut Creek, CA: Pavior, 2001.

Tolkunova, Kristina, Dimirii Usoltsev, Ekaterina Moguchaia, et al. "Transgenerational and Intergenerational Effects of Early Childhood Famine Exposure in the Cohort of Offspring of Leningrad Siege Survivors." *Scientific Reports* 13 (July 11, 2023): 11188.

Turner, Jon R. G., and Troya G. N. Turner. "Chapter 5: Prebirth Education Begins Before Conception." In *Prenatal Psychology 100 Years,* 163–249. Cosmoanelixis (website), 2018.

Van den Berg, Gerard J., and Pia R. Pinger. "Transgenerational Effects of Childhood Conditions on Third Generation Health and Education

Outcomes." *Economics & Human Biology* 23 (December 2016): 103–20.

Van de Carr, Rene. and Marc Lehrer. *While You are Expecting: Creating Your Own Prenatal Classroom.* Atlanta: Humanics Trade, 1997.

van der Kolk, Bessel A. *The Body Keeps the Score: Brain, Mind, and Body in the Healing of Trauma.* New York: Viking, 2014.

Van Leeuwen, P., D. Geue, M. Thiel, and D. H. Grönemeyer. "Influence of Paced Maternal Breathing on Fetal-Maternal Heart Rate Coordination." *PNAS* 106, no. 33 (August 18, 2009) 13661–66.

Verny, Thomas R., *The Embodied Mind: Understanding the Mysteries of Cellular Memory, Consciousness, and Our Bodies,* New York: Pegasus, 2023.

Verny, Thomas R., and John Kelley. *The Secret Life of the Unborn Child.* New York: Delta, 1981.

Villanueva Van Den Hurk, Alicia, Cady Ujvari, Noah Greenspan, Dolores Malaspina, Xavier F. Jimenez, and Julie Walsh-Messinger. "Childhood Trauma Exposure Increases Long COVID Risk." MedRxiv (website), (February 22, 2022).

Villines, Zawn. "Maternal Health in Black, Indigenous, and People of Color (BIPOC)." Medical News Today (website), June 21, 2021.

Vinessett, Ava L., Miurel Price, and Kenneth H. Wilson. "Therapeutic Potential of a Drum and Dance Ceremony Based on the African Ngoma Tradition." *The Journal of Alternative and Complementary Medicine* 21, no. 8 (July 28, 2015): 460–65.

Wade, Jenny. *Changes of Mind: A Holonomic Theory of the Evolution of Consciousness.* Albany, New York: State University of New York Press, 1996.

Walters, Joanna. "Tablets and Smartphones May Affect Social and Emotional Development, Scientists Speculate." *The Guardian* (website), February 2, 2015.

Warren, N. "African Infant Precocity." *Psychological Bulletin* 78, no. 5 (1972), 353–67.

Warrender, Emily. "Is Childbirth More Dangerous for Women in the UK?" May 23, 2022. *Open Access Government* (website).

Webb, Jonice. *Running on Empty: Overcome Your Childhood Emotional Neglect.* Garden City, NY: Morgan James, 2014.

Williams, Morika D. and Duncan X. Lascelles. "Early Neonatal Pain—A Review of Clinical and Experimental Implications on Painful Conditions Later in Life." *Frontiers in Pediatrics* 8 (February 7, 2020): 30.

Wolf, Jacqueline H. "Op Ed: American Women are Having Too Many Caesareans, at Too Much Risk." *LA Times* (website), July 29, 2018.

Yehuda, Rachel and Amy Lehrer. "Intergenerational Transmission of Trauma Effects: Putative Role of Epigenetic Mechanisms." *World Psychiatry* 7, no. 3 (September 7, 2018): 243–57.

Zarse, Emily M., Mallory R. Neff, Rachel Yoder, Leslie Hulvershorn, Joanna E. Chambers, and Andrew R. Chambers, reviewing ed. Udo Schumacher "The Adverse Childhood Experiences Questionnaire: Two Decades of Research on Childhood Trauma as a Primary Cause of Adult Mental Illness, Addiction, and Medical Diseases," *Cogent Medicine* 6, no. 1 (2019).

Zhang, Dandan, Yu Chen, Xinlin Hou, and Yan Jing Wu. "Near-Infrared Spectroscopy Reveals Neural Perception of Vocal Emotions in Human Neonates." *Human Brain Mapping* 40, no. 8 (June 1, 2019): 2434–48.

Index